Literacy with an
Attitude

Literacy with an
Attitude

Educating Working-Class Children in Their Own Self-Interest

Second Edition

Patrick J. Finn

SUNY PRESS

The illustrations in this book were done by
Amy Finn Bernier

Published by
State University of New York Press, Albany

For information, contact State University of New York Press, Albany, NY
www.sunypress.edu

Production by Ryan Morris
Marketing by Fran Keneston

Library of Congress Cataloging-in-Publication Data

Finn, Patrick J.
    Literacy with an attitude: educating working-class children in
their own self-interest / Patrick J. Finn.—2nd ed.
        p. cm.
    Includes bibliographical references (p.) and index.
    ISBN 978-1-4384-2805-5 (hardcover : alk. paper)
    ISBN 978-1-4384-2806-2 (pbk. : alk. paper)
    1. Working class—Education—United States. 2. Literacy—United
States. 3. Language arts—United States. 1. Title.
LC5051.F56 2009
371.826'230973—dc22   2008054155

10 9 8 7 6 5 4 3 2 1

To Mary
I still bless the day I found you.

Contents

PREFACE TO THE SECOND EDITION

The first twelve chapters of this edition are essentially the same as they were in the first edition. In them I introduce these ideas:

- There are levels of literacy. Powerful literacy leads to positions of power and authority. It is the literacy of persons who are conscious of their own power and self-interest. Functional literacy, on the other hand, is the mere ability to meet the reading and writing demands of an average day of an average person. It is a literacy that makes a person productive and dependable but not troublesome.
- In American schools children of the rich get empowering education and powerful literacy; children of the poor and working class (and to a surprising degree the middle class) get domesticating education and functional literacy.
- There subtle mechanisms that make it hard to teach liberating education and powerful literacy to poor and working-class students.
- Nevertheless, we must learn to teach powerful literacy to poor and working-class students as a matter of justice. There are teachers, teachers' organizations, civic organizations, and colleges of teacher education that are showing us the way.

In chapter 13 of this edition I reframe the argument: It is not simply a matter of justice; every citizen has the right to powerful literacy. It is a right equal to civil rights and political rights.

I start with the argument laid down in an essay written by T. H. Marshall.[1]

With the onset of the Industrial Revolution around 1700 there appeared three powerful forces that are associated with modern industrial nations; the free-market economy, our social-class system, and the modern concept of citizenship. Citizenship entails civil, political, and social rights. But modern citizenship is a system of equality, and the free market and social class are systems of inequality. The competition between citizenship rights on the one hand, and social class and the free-market economy on the other has played a central role in the history of Western democracies for three hundred years. Education and literacy play an important role in enabling citizens to demand and protect citizens' rights, particularly social rights, and Marshall believed that education does an admirable job through a process that became known as meritocracy. It is here that I part company with Marshall and join scores of others who have shown meritocracy to be a myth.

The meritocracy myth maintains that we offer the same education and powerful literacy to all students. Those who are smart and work hard take advantage of the offer and enter high-status school programs. They leave school with powerful literacy, enter high-paying professions, and end up with power, money, and status *regardless of the socioeconomic status of their parents*. Those poor and working-class students who prosper in this system become border crossers. On the other hand, students who are not smart or don't work hard are relegated to basic school programs. They leave school with only functional literacy and enter low-status, low-paying occupations. They must be satisfied with less power, lower status, and a more modest standard of living *regardless of the socioeconomic status of their parents*. It's a fair and square competition that every one understands.

In order to explain the fact that the overwhelming number of students who prosper are children of affluent parents and the overwhelming number of students who do not prosper are children of poor and working-class parents, part of the meritocracy myth is the logic of deficit: poor and working-class students remain at the bottom of the heap regardless of the opportunities afforded them because of the laziness, bad behavior, and cultural and intellectual infirmities endemic among poor and working-class people. They are offered powerful literacy and they don't take advantage of the offer. They tend not to prosper, but it's their own damned fault.

An interesting outcome of meritocracy is that erstwhile poor and working-class students who become border crossers join the more affluent classes and, therefore, they present no threat to the status quo. Furthermore, because of their powerlessness, poor and working-class students who are left behind are no threat to the status quo either. The meritocracy myth enables us to protect the status quo and have a clear conscience.

The Old Paradigm for education of poor and working-class students in the United States for the past century has been this: Working-class students can be motivated by the desire for the rewards of becoming middle class, and so they will learn whatever it takes to get there. The Old Paradigm is heavily invested in the concepts of border crossing, meritocracy, and the logic of deficit.

But the Old Paradigm is deeply flawed. If border crossing worked for even a majority of poor and working-class students, the approximately 40 to 50 percent of Americans who now have working-class jobs and incomes would join the 40 percent of Americans who already have middle-class jobs and incomes. The availability of such jobs would have to nearly double, and there would be enormous vacancies in working-class jobs. In addition, border crossers must be willing to become middle class, and many poor and working-class students are indifferent or hostile to middle-class values, interests, and attitudes. It's clear to most working-class youngsters that they will not be joining the middle class, and they know it. They are not motivated by the desire to become middle class because they don't think it will likely happen (which is correct), or the price of giving up their working-class identity is too high.

And even if the majority of poor and working-class students were motivated by the desire for the rewards of becoming middle class the present system is unjust: poor and working-class children generally attend schools different from those of more affluent students, and their schools are inferior in every way. And even when, against all odds, they earn high test scores, they do not find their way into higher education as often as affluent students who earn low test scores.

Social justice educators employ a New Paradigm, which relies on different motivation and works toward a different outcome. They urge students to learn aspects of the discourse of more affluent classes (the discourse of more affluent classrooms) not to replace their own but to acquire powerful literacy, the literacy that will enable the majority of them, who will no doubt continue to leave school at the end of high school or sooner, to become better able to demand and protect their civil, political, and social rights. I call this Freirean motivation, named after the famous Brazilian social justice educator.

Powerful literacy (rather than functional literacy) in the hands of the poor and working class is literacy with an attitude. It's a literacy that challenges the status quo. It's exactly the kind of literacy that the folks feared who outlawed Bible reading for common people three hundred years ago. There is an important difference, however. Three hundred years ago people could only imagine one social setup, the ruling class and the rabble. The fear was that literacy would make the rabble aware of the injustice they suffered, and they would attempt to overthrow the ruling class violently and take its place. After three centuries of experimenting in democracy, we understand that change is possible without violence.

This brings us back to the struggle between citizenship rights on the one hand and the free-market economy and social-class system. There are few people, even on the left, who seriously believe that either the free market or social class can—or even should—be eradicated. It's really about finding a just equilibrium between these opposing forces. The Old Paradigm protects the unjust status quo and is instrumental in denying countless citizens their rights. The New Paradigm can produce men and women who are equipped to challenge the status quo, demand and protect their rights, and bring about a more just balance.

Social justice teachers are playing a central role in this struggle, but they are just part of a movement comparable to the great struggles for justice in the past: abolition, organizing labor, suffrage, and civil rights. Older students, parents, university teacher-education faculty, and multi-issue grassroots organizations are working separately and together to help the poor and working class to help themselves and to engage in the political struggle that is necessary to demand and protect citizens' rights and make democracy work.

In chapters 13 and 14 I reframe the argument for providing powerful literacy to the children of poor and working-class parents from a simple matter of justice to a matter of citizens' rights on a par with civil and political rights, and I describe the struggle between citizenship rights on the one hand and the free-market economy and social-class system on the other. In chapters 15 and 16 I describe the genesis of social justice teachers and attempts to put powerful literacy into the hands of poor and working-class citizens. I introduce the New Paradigm and describe teachers who are making it work. In chapters 17 through 19 I introduce the struggle for universal citizens' rights, particularly social rights, as a movement comparable to the civil rights movement and describe people and organizations that are at the forefront of the movement, and I offer my suggestions for a teacher preparation program that will prepare teachers for the New Paradigm and participation in the movement. In chapter 20 I enumerate important concepts from the book in an order that outlines the central argument of the book.

PREFACE TO THE FIRST EDITION

There have been times in history when the prospect of literacy in the hands of the have-nots has been a source of endless angst among the haves. Less than one hundred years after the invention of the printing press laws were passed in England forbidding anyone under the rank of yeoman to read the Bible. Later, when political pamphleteers appeared, taxes were imposed to make pamphlets too expensive for the poor.

But in America from colonial times universal literacy (except for slaves) has been the aim. Today we see illiteracy among the have-nots as the source of many social ills. One explanation is that we have come so far in our democracy that we have nothing to fear from the have-nots. We worry instead that the low levels of literacy among them make them a liability for the rest of us. The idea is that if we could raise their level of literacy they would join the haves. America would have no poor, just rich, richer, and richest.

An idea that is often associated with this point of view is that our schools offer literacy equally to all comers, but somehow the have-nots refuse to take us up on our offer. They're not smart enough or they're lazy or simply perverse.

That's not my explanation. My explanation of why literacy is not seen as dangerous among the working people and unemployed of the United States is that we have developed two kinds of education. First, there is empowering education, which leads to powerful literacy, the kind of literacy that leads to positions of power and authority. Second, there is domesticating education, which leads to functional literacy, literacy that makes a person productive and dependable, but not troublesome. Over time, political, social, and economic forces have brought us to a place where the working class (and to a surprising degree, the middle class) gets domesticating education and functional literacy, and the rich get empowering education and powerful literacy. We don't worry about a literate working class because the kind of literacy they get doesn't make them dangerous.

A conspiracy? No. The beliefs, attitudes, and behaviors of the poor have contributed as much to the present state of affairs as those of the elite. We all participate in this social system as if it were natural, the way things were meant to be. In the past twenty-five years many scholars have abandoned the fruitless search for heartless conspirators among the Carnegies and Rockefellers and have been trying instead to figure out what happened—what social dynamics and mechanisms have led to the present state of affairs. The following are some of the mechanisms they have uncovered.

- Some minorities feel they have been wronged by mainstream Americans and that "acting white" is a betrayal of their people. They develop what sociologists call "oppositional identity." Oppositional identity appears among working-class whites to some extent as well. Talking and acting like a school teacher and valuing things school teachers value doesn't win you a lot of friends in working-class communities.
- Working-class children with varying degrees of oppositional identity resist school through means reminiscent of the factory shop floor—slowdowns, strikes, sabotage, and occasionally open confrontation. The result is the "pretend-school model." Teachers ask little of students in return for enough cooperation to maintain the appearance of conducting school.
- The discourse (ways of communication and the beliefs, attitudes, values, habits, and behaviors that underlie them—especially attitudes related to authority, conformity, and power) of working class communities is at odds with the discourse of the schools. This makes acquisition of school discourse and powerful literacy difficult for working-class children.

- Progressive methods, empowering education, and powerful literacy tend to go together. Traditional methods, domesticating education, and functional literacy tend to go together. Progressive methods are nearly impossible unless children want school knowledge and cooperate.

Contemporary social scientists believe that if we can understand these mechanisms, we can change them and bring ourselves to a different place, one where there is greater equity and justice. That would require that both the rich and poor get empowering education and powerful literacy.

When rich children get empowering education nothing changes. But when working-class children get empowering education you get literacy with an attitude. It's exactly the kind of literacy that the folks feared who outlawed Bible reading for common people three hundred years ago. There is an important difference, however. Three hundred years ago people could only imagine one social setup, the ruling class and the rabble. The fear was that literacy would make the rabble aware of the injustice they suffered, and they would attempt to overthrow the ruling class violently and take its place—same roles, same rules, only a switch in actors in the roles.

Today we understand that many social setups are possible. Roles and rules can be transformed so that there is greater justice and equity. We understand too, after two centuries of experimenting in democracy, that change is possible without violence. People can become conscious of injustice and inequity, and through disciplined, focused, and strategic action, they can bring about change. Such action both requires and promotes powerful literacy in those who struggle for justice and equity.

The status quo is the status quo because people who have the power to make changes are comfortable with the way things are. It takes energy to make changes, and the energy must come from the people who will benefit from the change. But the working class does not get powerful literacy, and powerful literacy is necessary for the struggle. How can the cycle be broken?

Teachers who see themselves as allies of their working-class students can help their students see that literacy and school knowledge could be a potent weapons in their struggle for a better deal by connecting school knowledge with the reality of working-class students' lives.

Just as "the labor organizer" appeared on the American scene as we changed from an agrarian to an industrial society and helped working people realize, harness, and use their power, "the community organizer" appeared on the scene after World War II as more affluent Americans fled the cities leaving the poorest among us behind. Community organizers can help working-class adults and older working-class students see that literacy and school knowledge could be a potent weapon in their struggle for a better deal, not a bunch of sissy stuff for which they have no use.

It's been done. Paulo Freire, an educator who worked with illiterate adults in the slums of Recife, a city in Brazil, pioneered this approach. He was successful enough to get himself jailed and later exiled by the military junta that overthrew Brazil's democratically elected government. He was welcomed back to Brazil only after years of exile, when a democratically elected government returned to power.

Grass-roots activism around schools is springing up all over the nation. People who have felt powerless are organizing and discovering their collective power. They are coming to realize that liberating education and powerful literacy is essential for their children. But demands for better schooling will not solve the problem alone. Teachers, parents, and older students need to understand the mechanisms that have subverted honest efforts to give working-class children a decent education. They must understand the relationships between society, culture, language, and schooling. They must understand the relationships between progressive methods, liberating education, and powerful literacy on the one hand and traditional methods, domesticating education, and functional literacy on the other.

In the first six chapters I discuss the subtle mechanisms that make liberating education and powerful literacy so difficult— oppositional identity and the inability of working-class schools to respond to the changing attitudes of working-class parents and students as high-paying blue-collar work disappears and parents begin to see education as the only chance for their children's survival. In chapters 7–10 I discuss the conflicts between working-class discourse and school discourse and the complications they cause. In chapters 11–15 I discuss the prospect of developing a pedagogy that makes progressive methods, empowering education, and powerful literacy possible with working-class students. This entails organizing working-class adults and older students around issues that are causing them pain and helping them realize that the struggle for justice and equity requires empowering education and powerful literacy.

Chapter 1

TITLE, AUTHOR, AND HARD-BITTEN SCHOOLTEACHERS

I considered several titles for this book. The first was *Educating Our Children and Handling Theirs*. This was based on the observation that schools have learned how to educate the children of the gentry and how to "handle" children of the working class—those who had been handled in school themselves.[1]

Jonathan Kozol's book entitled *Savage Inequalities*[2] traces the notoriously unequal results of schooling between rich and poor children to segregation (both on the basis of race and family income) and unequal funding. This book is also about savage inequalities, but the sources of inequality I examine are in fact so subtle that the average parent, teacher, student, and taxpayer are not conscious of them at all. I considered calling my book *Subtle Inequalities*, but I immediately realized that the inequalities I address are every bit as savage as Kozol's. It is the mechanisms that underlie them that are subtle, and so I tried a new title *Subtle Mechanisms, Savage Inequalities*.

However, as I discussed the book with others, the more I described the mechanisms, the more insistent they became in wanting to know what can be done about them. From the start, I had an answer: Paulo Freire. Freire was a professor at the University of Recife, a city in northeast Brazil. In the early 1960s he started an adult literacy program for the city's teeming, illiterate poor.

There had been numerous literacy campaigns earlier in Brazil, motivated by the desire to make the poor better workers, better citizens, and better Christians—classic reasons for literacy campaigns among the poor since the invention of the printing press. All of these previous campaigns had failed.

Freire believed that while the benefits of such literacy campaigns were obvious to the people behind them, they were not at all obvious to the illiterate poor. He took a different approach. Before he started to teach reading and writing, he asked his students to reflect on the concept of justice—a radical and dangerous thing to do in a country where a huge divide separated a small number of very rich and a vast number of very poor. He asked his students what they might do to secure justice and suggested that literacy would make them far better able to engage in the struggle they would certainly face if they tried to get a better deal. Then he was ready to talk ABCs, and so were they.

The literacy they acquired would not be literacy to become better citizens, workers, and Christians as the rich defined those roles for them; it would be literacy to engage in the struggle for justice. This was dangerous literacy, and for a while I considered the title *Making Literacy Dangerous Again*, alluding to the fact that after the printing press was invented, literacy among the masses was viewed with fear and trembling among the ruling classes of Europe.

But it also seemed to me that the literacy Freire wanted for the poor of Brazil was literacy *with an attitude*. That sounded to me like a great title for a book.

I was the eighth of nine children—six boys and three girls—in a blue-collar, Irish Catholic family in an Irish Catholic neighborhood on the south side of Chicago. The south side, which is predominantly African American now, was mostly white and mostly ethnic—Irish, Polish, and Italian. My father was Irish. There were also a number of Czechs who referred to themselves as Bohemians. My mother was Bohemian.

My father was a plumber and my five brothers became plumbers. I did not follow the family trade because of a birth injury that left my left arm slightly paralyzed. The family did not quite know what to do with me, and so I was encouraged to stay in high school until I graduated. I was pretty good at school, but after working two years in a minimum-wage, dead-end, white-collar job I think I astonished everyone by going to the local teachers college and becoming a teacher.

One of my first teaching jobs was at the Carol Jason Banks Upper Grade Center[3] in a black neighborhood on Chicago's south side. There were about four hundred eighth graders who were sorted by reading scores from the highest to the lowest and divided into fifteen classes, 8-1s being the highest, 8-15s being the lowest. But they didn't divide them exactly equally. While the 8-1s through the 8-13s started out with around twenty-seven students, the two lowest classes started out with only around fifteen. The theory was that the slowest students would get more attention in smaller classes. The reality was that as the year wore on there were spaces available in the "lower" classes to dump troublesome students from "higher" classes. And so by Christmas there were likely to be more than twenty students in the 8-14s and 8-15s, fifteen of whom were originally assigned because of low reading scores, and an additional five or six who were "sent down" because of discipline problems. You want to talk about a tough teaching assignment?

I taught double periods of language arts and social studies, and so I had only four classes. When I started, I had the 8-7s, 8-8s, 8-9s and 8-10s. Teachers with seniority had the higher classes. The younger teachers who had proven their ability to "handle" them had the lower classes. By the third year I had the four lowest classes, the 8-12s, 8-13s, 8-14s, and 8-15s. I was a huge success.

I was from the working class and I knew how working-class and poor kids related to authority. They expected people in authority to be authoritarian, and I gave them what they expected. It was an exhausting job, but my classroom was nearly always quiet. The children were nearly always working. The assistant principal told me once that he always walked visitors *slowly* past my classroom so that they could see what could be done with students in our school.

But, in fact I was schooling these children, not to take charge of their lives, but to take orders. I taught them to read and write a little better, and I taught them some facts about United

States history, but control was uppermost in my mind. When I discussed discipline problems with other teachers, a frequent topic of discussion in the teachers' lounge, I would talk about my teaching methods as methods of control. I had work assignments on the board when the students entered the classroom, and so there wasn't a moment when they didn't have anything to do. I didn't say to an errant student, "What are you doing?" I said, "Stop that and get to work." No discussion. No openings for an argument.

I made the assignments easy so the least able students could do them. I had "extra credit" assignments for students who finished early, usually not too challenging, but time consuming. I corrected and graded and returned every paper by the next class so the students felt that completing assignments mattered, or put another way, students were punished with a zero if they did not do their assignments. But, of course, that meant assignments had to be easily correctable, fill in the blanks, matching, one- or two-word answers on numbered lines on spelling paper.

Mind you, we had our lighter moments. We wrote news stories that might have appeared on the front page of a Boston paper the day after the Boston Tea Party. We colored maps with crayons, showing which European powers laid claim to which parts of North America in 1789, the year our Constitution was ratified. We wrote Mother's Day poems. We wrote summaries of television shows telling why we liked them—this sort of thing, very rarely, however, because they took too long to grade. But the good times (if you could call them that) would come to a sudden halt if the students got too boisterous, a fact of which they were frequently reminded.

"Good students" were obedient students, students who followed orders. The assignments were so easy that all obedient students got good grades, but I gave plenty of bad grades to students who were not obedient, who did not do their assignments. Obedient students were not kept in from recess, but most days there were one or two disobedient students kept in from recess. Obedient students' parents were not called up to school, but on one or two mornings a week I met a parent of a disobedient student who had been summoned to school at 8:30 A.M. before classes began. Obedient students did not get suspended, but disobedient students were suspended at my request at the rate of about one a semester.

I was very flattered when the assistant principal remarked that he brought visitors past my room "so they could see what could be done with our students," but I look back at it now with chagrin. It would have been more accurate if he had said, "so they could see what could be done *to* our students."

I must say that I did a whole lot more for these children than a number of "flower children" (this was the '60s) who came in with the message of universal love and not much appetite for the hard work that teaching, or even handling, children entails, and who were tossed out nearly literally on their behinds by the students in a matter of weeks.

On the other hand there was a woman who taught across the hall from me. Her name was Mrs. Kennedy. I can't remember her first name. I think we actually addressed one another as "Mrs. Kennedy" and "Mr. Finn." She was a strikingly beautiful black woman, a recent graduate of Fisk University. Her classroom was always orderly, but I never heard her raise her voice. If the students saw me as an easily provoked drill sergeant, they saw her as a den mother, a den mother who didn't put up with much nonsense, but a den mother.

I think Mrs. Kennedy might have been doing a better job of teaching than I, but not a whole lot better. All of us—teachers and students—were locked into a system of rules and roles that none of us understood and that did not allow for much in the way of education. And I do not mean in just the "low classes." For the most part, students in the 8-1s were also getting handled— schooled to take orders, to replace their parents at the bottom of the economic heap. My guess is that things are about the same today at Carol Jason Banks Upper Grade Center and thousands of schools like it throughout the country.

When I was twenty-seven, I married another teacher. At the time we were not entirely aware of it, but she was from a different world, a fiercely middle-class world—her father an accountant, mother a school teacher, one sibling, raised in a middle-class suburb, Methodist, Republican, educated at the University of Iowa (not an urban teachers college as I was), and she taught in the suburbs. Thus began a thirty-five year experiment in cross-cultural communication, which has been stormy at times and approached the shoals on a few occasions, but it has taught both of us that most of what goes on in cross-cultural communication when it doesn't go well (which is often) is subtle, covert, unconscious, and often insidious.

I was pretty tuckered out after eight years of handling poor children. During that time, I had earned a master's degree in English. My talent for things academic and probably the know-how of my middle-class wife led me to other pastures. I quit teaching elementary school and went to work at Scott-Foresman editing literature textbooks for a few years. A little later, I taught English at City College of Chicago (where a majority of the students were working-class) and began to work on a doctorate in education at the University of Chicago. It was here I began to read such people as Basil Bernstein and William Labov, people who dealt explicitly with the impact of class on communication style, language, and school success. For the last twenty-five years I have been on the faculty of the Graduate School of Education at the State University of New York at Buffalo, where I have a handful of students working for their doctor's degrees and a whole lot of students working for their master's degrees.

And so for nearly forty years I have been reading, writing, thinking, debating, and teaching about literacy and language and schooling and how they are related to inequality in our society, and at the same time I have been thinking about and teaching teachers how to teach language arts in the elementary school.

Since I teach at a graduate school, my students are a little older than the average person would imagine. They tend to be getting on toward thirty, with a sizeable number getting on toward forty, because they are changing careers or they took time off to have children. Nearly all of them teach full time. My classes are scheduled at 4:00 or 7:00 P.M., and the students, brave souls, come to me after a full day of teaching.

A small number of them are overtly political and they sometimes disagree with my conclusions—some because they are farther to the right and others because they are farther to the left than I. But most of my students are not overtly political. They put me in mind of myself thirty years ago when I was teaching eighth grade and going to graduate school evenings.

My favorite professor was John Carter. He was a widely recognized scholar on Edgar Allen Poe, and he wrote a best-selling novel, *Full Fathom Five*, in 1965.[4] His father had been a physician, and he was raised in Oak Park, an affluent suburb west of Chicago. He sometimes talked to his classes about who he thought we were, and he would refer to us as "hard-bitten" Chicago school teachers.

We understood what he meant. First of all, he intended no disrespect. In fact, he admired us. Because we were mostly young we taught in the poorest neighborhoods. (Teachers moved to richer neighborhoods with seniority.) We wanted our students to succeed and move ahead, just as many of us had. We believed they could do it if only they would try. We knocked ourselves out every day and experienced little success, and so we blamed our students for not trying. That left us a little bitter.

John Carter found us problematic. He couldn't get through to us. He loved Shakespeare and Keats and Byron and Poe and he wanted us to love them as he did, and he succeeded to a degree. But there was always a practical, down-to-earth element in our makeup that defeated him. If getting a master's degree didn't mean a raise in pay, most of us would not have been there. We took the seminar in Keats rather than Shakespeare because it fit better into our child care responsibilities or our bowling nights. And although we did love literature (we could have gotten our master's degrees in psychology or any number of other fields and gotten the same pay raise) we had practical, down-to-earth reasons for studying it. Knowing literature enabled us to pass certification exams, and we looked forward to the day when we would teach in "better" schools where we might venture reading a Shakespeare sonnet in our classes.

We judged everything that John Carter, or any other professor, taught us by one criterion: How would it work in my classroom? That meant that anything that got a little too aesthetic was out. And we didn't think John Carter, or any other professor, had anything to tell us about what would work in our classrooms. We were out there in the trenches and we took no advice from anyone who wasn't out there with us. I think that's what John Carter meant when he said we were hard bitten.[5]

Many of my students are hard-bitten school teachers. They are practical and down to earth, and they judge everything I say by one criterion: How would this work in my classroom? They are dubious about whether I have anything to tell them about what would work in their classrooms. True, I taught school for eight years, but that was thirty years ago.

And because I teach education rather than English there is an aspect to our relationship that was not present in John Carter's relationship with me and my classmates. If John Carter rhapsodized over "Shall I compare thee to a summer's day," I could go along and smile at his naivete in thinking that "a summer's day" would be greeted by anything but howls on Chicago's south side. But when I suggest to my hard-bitten students that poor children are not being as well educated as they could be, they are not amused. They take it as a personal attack from someone who has been living in an ivory tower for the last thirty years, and they resent it—a lot.

So my getting through to these students is a good deal more complicated than John Carter's getting through to me. Benign amusement is replaced by thinly veiled hostility. Unlike my self-consciously political students who sometimes disagree with me on ideological grounds, these hard-bitten school teachers take differences of opinion with me personally.

My hard-bitten teachers have taught me a lesson that I, like many academics, needed to learn: Don't be so damned superior! Don't look down your nose at people out there teaching real children in real and sometimes dreadful circumstances. Don't question their intelligence, or their commitment, or their motives. I hope I have learned this lesson well enough so that I don't set up barriers between them and me such that they are not able to listen to my story and consider my position.

And so I think I've thought it through, and I hope I've learned to deal with the realities of teaching and not to be too smug while assessing problems and suggesting solutions, because no matter what the solutions are, it's hard-bitten school teachers who will need to implement them.

Chapter 2

A DISTINCTLY UN-AMERICAN IDEA
An Education Appropriate to Their Station

Jean Anyon studied fifth grade classes in five public elementary schools in rich neighborhoods and not-so-rich neighborhoods in northern New Jersey.[1] In one school, designated *executive elite*, family breadwinners were top corporate executives in multinational corporations or Wall Street financial firms. Their incomes were in the top 1 percent in the United States. In a second school, designated *affluent professional*, family breadwinners were doctors, TV and advertising executives, and other highly paid professionals. Incomes were in the top 10 percent for the nation. In a third school, designated *middle class*, breadwinners were a mixture of highly skilled, well-paid blue- and white-collar workers and those with traditional middle-class occupations such as teachers, social workers, accountants, and middle managers. Incomes were better than average for the United States but below the top 10 percent. In a fourth and fifth school designated *working class*, about one-third of the breadwinners were skilled blue-collar workers; about half were unskilled or semiskilled blue-collar workers, and about 15 percent of the heads of households were unemployed.

First Anyon noted similarities among the schools. They were nearly all white. They were all located in northern New Jersey and subject to the same state requirements. They all used the same arithmetic books. They had the same language arts course of study. Two of the schools used the same basal reading series. There were startling differences, however.

In the two working-class schools, most of the teachers were born in the same city as the school but lived in better sections. Most of them were young and had graduated from the local teachers college; many of them were single.

In the working-class schools, knowledge was presented as fragmented facts isolated from wider bodies of meaning and from the lives and experiences of the students. *Work* was following steps in a procedure. There was little decision making or choice. Teachers rarely explained why work was being assigned or how it was connected to other assignments. Work was often evaluated in terms of whether the steps were followed rather than whether it was right or wrong. For example, one teacher led the students through a series of steps to draw a one-inch grid on their paper without telling them what they were making or what it was for. When a girl realized what they were making and said she had a faster way to do it, the teacher answered, "No you don't. You don't even know what I'm making yet. Do it this way or it's wrong."

While the same arithmetic book was used in all five schools, the teacher in one working-class school commented that she skipped pages dealing with mathematical reasoning and inference because they were too hard. The teacher in the second working-class school said, "These pages are for creativity— they're extras." She often skipped them as well.

In one working-class school they used a social studies textbook that was described by its publisher as intended for "low ability students." The teachers guide referred repeatedly to "educationally deficient students"—for whom the book was intended. The book was intended to provide a year's work, but there were only sixteen lessons consisting of a few paragraphs followed by vocabulary drill and exercises to check recall. However, these were not special education classrooms. In the two working-class school classrooms combined, the children's average IQ was above 100 and eight children had IQs above 125.

In the working-class schools, social studies instruction typically consisted of copying teachers' notes, writing answers to textbook questions, and craft projects, such as cutting out and making a stand-up figure of a cowboy roping a steer to represent the Southwest when studying U.S. geography. Compared to the more affluent schools in this study there was less discussion of controversial topics such as labor disputes, civil rights, and women's rights and less attention to the history of these issues.

In language arts, the teacher gave each student a duplicated sheet entitled "All About Me" and directed them to write their answers on the lines following questions such as "Where were you born?" and "What is your favorite animal?" This activity was referred to as "writing an autobiography." Children were presented with rules for where to put commas, but there was never any discussion of how commas made writing easier to understand or of the notion that punctuation called for decisions based on the intended meaning.

In science, children were routinely told to copy the directions for doing an experiment from the book. The teacher then did the experiment in front of the class as the students watched and wrote a list entitled "What We Found" on the board. The students copied it into their notebooks. A test on "What We Found" would follow.

Teachers made every effort to control students' movement. They often kept children after the dismissal bell to finish their work or to punish them for misbehavior. There were no clocks in classrooms. Materials were handed out by the teacher and closely guarded. Students were ordered to remain in their seats unless given specific permission to move. When permitted to leave the room they needed a pass with the time and date.

Teachers made derogatory remarks regarding the students. A principal was reported to have said to a new teacher "Just do your best. If they learn to add and subtract, that's a bonus. If not, don't worry about it." A second grade teacher said the children were "getting dumber every year." Only twice did Anyon hear a teacher say "please" to a student in an unsarcastic tone. She heard "Shut up" frequently.

One fifth grade teacher said the students needed the basics—simple skills. When asked "why?" she responded, "They're lazy. I hate to categorize them, but they're lazy." Another fifth grade teacher who was asked why she had students endlessly copy notes from the blackboard in social studies replied, "Because the children in this school don't know anything about the U.S., so you can't teach them much." Another teacher said, "You can't teach these kids anything. Their parents don't care about them, and they're not interested." Another teacher answered when asked what was important knowledge for her students, "Well, we keep them busy." You have to keep reminding yourself that these children did not have low IQ scores. They were working-class children with average intelligence, some with better than average intelligence.

When Anyon asked these fifth grade students, "What do you think of when I say the word *knowledge*?" not a single child used the word *think*. Only one mentioned the word *mind*. When asked if they can make knowledge only one said yes.

In each category of school, Anyon observed what she called a "dominant theme." In the working-class schools the dominant theme was *resistance*. Students vandalized school property and resisted the teachers' efforts to teach. Boys fell out of chairs; students brought bugs into the classroom and released them; children lost books or forgot them; students interrupted the teacher. They showed no enthusiasm for projects into which the teacher put extra effort. They refused to answer questions and were apparently pleased when the teacher became upset. There was less resistance to easy work, and so assignments were rarely demanding.

According to Anyon these children were developing a relationship to the economy, authority, and work that is appropriate preparation for wage labor—labor that is mechanical and routine. Their capacity for creativity and planning was ignored or denied. Their response was very much like that of adults in their community to work that is mechanical and routine and that denies their capacity for creativity and planning. They engaged in relentless "slowdowns," subtle sabotage, and other modes of indirect resistance similar to that carried out by disgruntled workers in factories, sales floors, and offices.

In the middle-class school, about one-third of the teachers grew up in the neighborhood of the school. Most graduated from the local state teachers college, and many of them lived in the neighborhood of the school. Some were married to other teachers, accountants, police officers, nurses, and managers of local businesses.

Teachers in the middle-class school seemed to believe that their job was to teach the knowledge found in textbooks or dictated by curriculum experts. They valued this more than knowledge taught by experience. For example, when a child said that the plural of *mouse* is not *mouses* because "it wouldn't sound right," the teacher said that was the wrong reason. The right reason was that *mouse* is an irregular noun, *as it says in the book.*

A social studies textbook intended for use in sixth grade was used in the fifth grade classroom in the middle-class school. According to the publisher, the purpose of the book was to introduce fundamental concepts. There were "understandings" from anthropology, economics, history, geography, or political science listed in the teacher's guide for each chapter.

Social studies classes involved reading the text, listening to the teacher's explanations, answering the teacher's questions, and occasionally doing reports. There was rarely sustained inquiry into a topic. The teacher rarely used a feature of the text entitled "Using the Main Idea" (applying main ideas to current events and personal situations), because she said she had enough to do to get them to understand the generalizations.

Knowledge in the middle-class school was "more conceptual" than in the working-class school. It was less a matter of isolated facts and more a matter of gaining information and understanding from socially approved sources. Knowledge here was like that in the working-class school, however, in that it was not connected with the lives and experiences of the students.

In the middle-class school, *work* was getting the right answer. Answers were words, sentences, numbers, facts, and dates. You could not make them up. They were found in books or by listening to the teacher. You wrote them neatly on paper in the right order. If you got enough right answers, you got a good grade.

You got the right answer by following directions, but the directions allowed for some choice, some figuring, some decision making, and the teacher explained the purpose of assignments and why the directions would lead to the right answer. For example, students were permitted to do steps "in their heads" rather than write them down. They were allowed to do division problems the long or short way. When reviewing homework they had to say *how* they did the problem as well as give their answer. Social studies consisted of reading passages and answering comprehension questions: who, what, when, where, and sometimes why. However, questions that might have led to controversial topics were avoided because parents might complain.

Work rarely called for creativity. There was little serious attention to how students might develop or express their own ideas. In a social studies project, the students were directed to find information on assigned topics and put it "in your own words." Many of the children's products had imaginative covers and illustrations, which were largely ignored by the teacher who graded on information, neatness, and the student's success in paraphrasing the sources used. Lessons that explicitly called for creativity and self-expression were "enrichment" and "for fun." They did not count toward grades.

The teachers in the middle-class school varied from strict to somewhat easygoing, but for all of them, decisions were made on the basis of rules and regulations that were known to the students. Teachers always honored class dismissal bells. There was little excitement in the school work, and assignments did not seem to take into account the student's interests or feelings, but the children seemed to believe that there were rewards: good grades lead to college and a good job. Remember, these were fifth graders.

When children in the middle-class school were asked what knowledge is, seventeen of twenty used words like *learn, remember, facts, study, smartness, intelligent, know, school, study*, and *brains*. When asked if they could make knowledge, nine said no and eleven said yes. When asked how, they said they'd look it up or listen and do what they're told or they'd go to the library.

The dominant theme in the middle-class school was *possibility*. There was widespread anxiety about tests and grades but there was a pervasive belief that hard work would pay off. These students viewed knowledge as a valuable possession that can be traded for good grades, a good college education, and a good job. There was more excited patriotism around holidays here than in any other school. There were frequent auditorium assemblies with a patriotic flavor. The feeling was that America is full of promise and these children were going to cash in on it.

Anyon observed that in the middle-class school the children were developing a relationship to the economy, authority, and work that is appropriate for white-collar working-class and middle-class jobs: paper work, technical work, sales, and social services in the private and public sectors. Such work does not call for creativity.

Such workers are not rewarded for critical analysis. They are rewarded for knowing the answers, for knowing where to find answers, for knowing which form, regulation, technique, or procedure is correct. While this kind of work does not reward creativity or self-expression, it usually pays enough to enable workers to find opportunities for creativity and self-expression outside the workplace.

In the affluent professional school the teachers came from elsewhere in the state. They all came from middle- or upper-class backgrounds. Most were women married to high-status professionals or executives.

Creativity and personal development were important goals for students at the affluent professional school. Teachers wanted students to think for themselves and to make sense of their own experience. Discovery and experience were important. In arithmetic, for example, students measured perimeters in the classroom and created questions for other students to answer. They collected data in surveys and did experiments with cubes and scales. They made a film on the metric system. In science, students experimented *in their own way* to discover the properties of aluminum, copper, and glass (which heats fastest, for example), and it didn't matter whether they got the right answer. What mattered was that they discussed their ideas. When students asked, "How should I do this?" teachers answered, "You decide," or, "What makes sense to you?"

There were, however, wrong answers. In arithmetic, six plus two was still eight and only eight. In science, the answer had to be consistent with observations. Students were required to have their observations and answers "verified" by other students before handing in assignments.

The social studies textbook emphasized "higher concepts" such as "the roles of savings, capital, trade, education, skilled labor, skilled managers, and cultural factors (religious beliefs, attitudes toward change) in the process of economic development," and the understanding that "the controlling ideas of

Western culture come largely from two preceding cultures: The Judaic and Greco-Roman."

Students read and outlined the text and used it as a guide for "inquiry activities" such as baking clay cuneiform replicas, writing stories and plays and creating murals showing the division of labor in ancient societies. Several students had seen the Tutankhamen exhibit in New York—one had seen it in Paris.

They devoted a lot of time to current events because, according to the teacher, "they're so opinionated anyway, and they love it." Children often wrote editorials and brought in clippings on such topics as labor strife, inflation, and nuclear power. The teacher, however, said she had to be very careful of expressing her own opinion. "One year I had the superintendent's son, the mayor's son, and the daughter of the president of the board of education in my room—all at one time. I *really* had to watch what I said."

Knowledge in the affluent professional school was viewed as being open to discovery. It was used to make sense and thus it had personal value. School knowledge was presented as having relevance to life's problems. Unlike the situation in the working-class and middle-class schools, social strife was acknowledged and discussed.

In the affluent professional school, work was creative activity carried out independently. It involved individual thought and expression, expansion and illustration of ideas, and choice of appropriate methods and materials. Products were often stories, essays, or representations of ideas in murals, craft projects, and graphs. Students' projects were to show originality and individuality, but they had to fit with reality—that is, a creative mural could be marked down if it misrepresented the facts or concepts it was supposed to represent.

One assignment was for students to find the average number of chocolate chips in three chocolate chip cookies. The teacher announced gravely, "I'll give you three cookies, and you'll have to eat your way through, I'm afraid." When work was underway, she circulated giving help, praise, and reminders about getting too noisy. The children worked sitting or standing at their desks or at a bench in the back of the room or sitting on the floor.

In their study of ancient civilizations, they made a film on Egypt. One student wrote the script, the class acted it out, and one of the parents edited it. They read and wrote stories depicting ancient times. They did projects chosen from a list, all of which involved graphic representations such as murals. They wrote and exchanged letters with the other fifth grade in "hieroglyphics." The list goes on.

They discussed current events daily and were encouraged to expand on what they said and to be specific. The teacher's questions were designed to help them make connections between events in the news and what they were learning in school.

In language arts, they did not use textbooks because the principal thought textbooks hampered creativity. Each child interviewed a first grader and wrote a rebus story[2] just for that child. They wrote editorials about matters before the school board and radio plays that were sometimes acted over the school intercom. Lessons on punctuation stressed the relationship between meaning and punctuation.

Products of work were highly prized. The affluent professional school was the only school where Anyon was not allowed to take children's work away from the school. If possible, she could duplicate it and take the copy, but if it could not be copied, she could not have it.

Control involved constant negotiation. Teachers rarely gave direct orders unless the children were too noisy. Instead, teachers commented on the probable consequences of student behavior and asked students to decide accordingly. One of the few rules regulating children's movement was that not more than three children could be out of the room at one time. They could go to the school library at any time to get a book. They merely signed their name on the chalkboard and left the room when they needed to. There were no passes.

They sometimes negotiated what work was to be done. For example, children sometimes asked for more time before moving on to the next subject, and the teacher sometimes acquiesced. There is a remarkable footnote to this discussion. The teacher commented that she was "more structured" that year than usual because of the large number of children in the class who were considered discipline problems.

In the affluent professional school, work was not repetitious and mechanical, as it was in the working-class school; it was not knowing the correct answers, as it was in the middle-class school; it was being able to manipulate what Anyon termed *symbolic capital*.

The children in the affluent professional school had the least trouble answering the question "What is knowledge." Many of them used the word *think* and several alluded to personal activity having to do with ideas. ("Figuring stuff out." "You think up ideas and then find things wrong with those ideas.") When asked, "Can you make knowledge?" sixteen said yes; only four said no.

In the affluent professional school the dominant theme was *individualism* with a minor theme of *humanitarianism*. Emphasis in the classroom was on thinking for oneself, creativity, and discovery in science and arithmetic. But there was also a pervasive climate of mutual help and concern for one another and for humanity. The principal ended morning announcements with "Do something nice for someone today." Social class and class conflict were discussed in social studies, with a liberal spin. Eight of twenty students interviewed expressed antagonism toward "the rich," who they said were greedy, spoiled, and snobby. This is interesting in light of the fact that these students' family incomes were in the top 10 percent for the nation.

Children in this school were developing a relationship to the economy, authority, and work that is appropriate for artists, intellectuals, legal and scientific experts, and other professionals whose work is creative, intrinsically satisfying for most people, and rewarded with social power and high salaries. Although in the workplace they do not have complete control over which ideas they develop and express, affluent professionals are relatively autonomous. Their relationship to people who decide which ideas will be developed (the executive elite whom I'll get to in the next paragraph) involves substantial negotiation.

In the executive elite school, as in the affluent professional school, the teachers were women married to high-status professionals and business executives, but in the executive elite school the teachers regarded their students as having higher social status than themselves.

Knowledge in the executive elite school was academic, intellectual, and rigorous. More was taught and more difficult concepts were taught. Reasoning and problem solving were important.

The rationality and logic of mathematics were held up as the model for correct and ethical thinking.

Social studies knowledge was more sophisticated, complex, and analytic than in the other schools. Questions such as good and bad effects of imperialism and the reasons for conflict between social classes were discussed. However, there was little questioning of the status quo. The present distribution of wealth and power was presented as natural and timeless—going back to the ancient Greeks.

Children were required to plan lessons and teach them to the class. Among other things, they were evaluated on how well they kept control of the class. The teacher said to one child who lost control of his classmates, "When you're up there, you have authority, and you have to use it. I'll back you up."

training

While strict attention was demanded during lessons, there was little attempt to regulate the children's movement at other times. They were allowed into the classrooms when they arrived at school; they did not have to wait for the bell, as in every other school in Anyon's study.

Students were permitted to take materials from closets and even from the teacher's desk when they needed them. They were in charge of the school office at lunch time. They did not need permission or a pass to leave the room. Because of the amount of work demanded, however, they rarely left the room.

The children were sometimes flippant, boisterous, and occasionally rude. However, they were usually brought into line by reminding them of their responsibility to achieve. "It's up to you." Teachers were polite to students. There was no sarcasm, no nasty remarks, and few direct orders.

When asked, "Can you make knowledge?" half the children in the executive elite school said yes; half said no. Compared with the affluent professional school children, these children took a more passive view toward the creation of knowledge. For many of them knowledge comes from tradition. It's "out there" and you are expected to learn it.

The dominant theme in the executive elite school was *excellence*—preparation for being the best, for top-quality performance. There was no narcissistic coddling here, but insistence upon self-discipline instead. The pace was brisker than in any other school and children were often told that they alone were responsible for keeping up.

In the executive elite school the children were developing a relationship to the economy, authority, and work that is different from all the other schools. They learned grammatical, mathematical, and other vocabularies by which systems are described. They were taught to use these vocabularies to analyze and control situations. The point of school work was to achieve, to excel, to prepare for life at the top.

The working-class children were learning to follow directions and do mechanical, low-paying work, but at the same time they were learning to resist authority in ways sanctioned by their community. The middle-class children were learning to follow orders and do the mental work that keeps society producing and running smoothly. They were learning that if they cooperated they would have the rewards that well-paid, middle-class work makes possible outside the workplace. The affluent professional children were learning to create products and art, "symbolic capital," and at the same time they were learning to find rewards in work itself and to negotiate from a powerful position with those (the executive elite) who make the final decisions on how real capital is allocated. The executive elite children? They were learning to be masters of the universe.

Anyon's study supports the findings of earlier observers[3] that in American schools children of managers and owners are rewarded for initiative and assertiveness, while children of the working-class are rewarded for docility and obedience and punished for initiative and assertiveness. Remember the teacher who said, "Do it this way or it's wrong."

This couldn't be more obvious when you compare Anyon's "gentry" schools—her executive elite and affluent professional schools—with her working-class schools. The surprising thing is where Anyon's middle-class school fits into this picture. Like the children in working-class schools, children in the middle-class school were schooled to take orders. They were taught that knowledge in textbooks was more valuable than their own experience. They were taught through traditional, directive methods to look up knowledge, not to create it. They were not taught to manipulate or direct systems, nor was there any effort to connect school knowledge with their daily lives.

On the other hand, Anyon's middle-class school was like her gentry schools in that students saw the knowledge that teachers had to offer as valuable—albeit for the future, for entrance into good colleges, and for procuring highly paid work. And since they valued the teachers' knowledge, they cooperated with the teachers to get it. The theme here was not *resistance*, as it was in the working-class school; it was *possibility*.

Twenty years after Anyon's study Robert Reich,[4] Clinton's first secretary of labor, analyzed America's workforce in the '90s. While Anyon classified Americans in terms of their incomes and the kind of work they do, Reich's analysis added a new criterion on which to classify workers: with whom do they compete for jobs—only other Americans, or with workers in other countries?

Reich identified the top 20 percent as "symbolic analysts." These are the problem solvers and creators of ideas and symbols. They are engineers, bankers, lawyers, writers, designers, and the fastest-growing category—consultants. Theirs is an international job market. The work done by an engineer in Chicago today might go to an engineer in Tokyo or Bonn tomorrow. The same is true of bankers, lawyers, writers, designers, and consultants. Americans educated in our best schools (those Anyon described as executive elite and affluent professional) perform very well in this international competition, and they command enormous salaries.

Reich classifies what I shall refer to as the working class (the bottom 55 percent of American workers) in two ways. He refers to "in-person service workers" and "routine production service workers." In-person service workers are in retail sales, hospital and health care, food services and security. Since these services are delivered to the consumer "in-person," these jobs cannot be easily exported. In-person service work is often characterized as nurturing work or women's work. It has always been and continues to be poorly paid. In-person service jobs make up a little more than half of the working-class jobs in America today.

Slightly less than half of the working class in America today are in "routine production service work." These are the foot soldiers of American industry—assembly line workers in the older "heavy" industries and in the newer electronics industries. These jobs are eminently exportable. While work in newer industries is cleaner and easier, shops are not unionized and the pay is remarkably lower. The number of well-paid jobs in older industries is declining while the number of poorly paid jobs in newer industries is increasing.

What's left is the approximately 20 percent whom I shall refer to as the middle class. Reich refers them to as government workers. These are the teachers, local and federal government employees, and, surprisingly, physicians paid through Medicaid and Medicare.

In the past twenty years numbers have grown at the top and bottom. The number in the middle has declined. Those at the top have gotten a whole lot richer. Those in the middle are in about the same place economically, and those at the bottom have gotten a whole lot poorer. Reich observed that among the fastest-growing occupations in America is that of security guard. Small wonder.

The question is, do the children of the elite and the middle class and the working class still attend schools like those Anyon described. The answer is, you bet! If there were later studies that did not support her findings or that showed a trend in a different direction, I would never have cited her in the first place. But the recent literature supports her conclusions.

In the early '90s, the faculty at California State University at Dominguez Hills (near Los Angeles) described schools attended by children who are disenfranchised because of social class, poverty, or cultural background in much the same way Anyon described the working-class schools in her study a decade earlier.[5] A colleague of mine regularly sends her students out to schools and asks them to compare what they observe to what Anyon observed. They invariably report that matters remain the same. In *Savage Inequalities*[6] Jonathan Kozol reports on schools in upscale communities like Winnetka, Illinois, Cherry Hill, New Jersey, and Rye, New York, and schools in impoverished communities like East St. Louis, Illinois, Camden, New Jersey, and parts of Washington, D.C., Chicago, and New York. City. Nothing's changed, unless, perhaps, it's gotten worse.

In February 1998 I asked one of my classes to write papers comparing Anyon's findings to their own personal experiences. The following are excerpts from two of their papers.

I am from Amherst, New Hampshire. Amherst is one of the most affluent places to live in New Hampshire. About five years ago a high school was built entirely for Amherst families. Amherst originally was sharing a high school with a neighboring middle class town that was not as wealthy. Many parents and families in Amherst wanted a better education for their children, so as a result, a brand new high school was built. The high school was a major development in the town of Amherst, and people from other towns were moving to Amherst, just so their children could go to the high school. I would consider Amherst High School to fit into the affluent professional category. The methods of teaching almost duplicated the strategies taught at the affluent professional school in Anyon's study.

I did not attend the high school, because I went to a private school, but many of my close friends did and my younger sister does now. I was told the students were given extreme privileges and were taught knowledge in creative ways, rather than straight from a textbook. For example, students had their own smoking section, they called their teachers by their first name, there were no honor level classes, and a lot of material taught (from science to English) was done through projects involving the kids to the greatest extent. The students were also able to get away with a lot, because they questioned everything that was assigned to them. Parents were relentless in their persistence to have their kids receive the best education possible.

However, the town Amherst broke away from was left with mostly middle class students, because all the Amherst kids left. As a result, the high school resorted to more traditional styles of educating, which meant teaching straight from a textbook and not giving any choices or freedom to the students. Meanwhile, the Amherst students were receiving progressive styles of teaching and were being educated on how to become superior professionals.[7]

[At first] Anyon's conclusions seemed wildly radical and oversimplified to me. I was not willing to admit that limits so tangible and so obvious existed in classrooms in the United States. After all, America is supposedly the "land of opportunity" where you can achieve whatever career goals to which you aspire. This class culture distinction sounded as severe as the caste system in India. However, the more I remembered various teaching situations I have been in, the more clear class culture perpetuation became.

As a student teacher, I had the opportunity to teach in what Anyon would classify an affluent professional school and a working-class school. Although both schools professed progressive principles, the differences in the two schools were very apparent at the time. However, I never considered how the methods used to teach differed until reading Anyon's study. I find the correlations between my real life experiences and the study frightening. Reading about this type of class tracking in schools is one thing. Realizing that you have experienced it is truly another.

My experience in the affluent professional school was idyllic. The classes I worked with had many activities promoting independence and creativity such as Reading and Writing Workshops. Students had control of how to use their time, and all teacher directed lessons were mini-lessons taking no more than ten minutes of class time. These lessons were often based on questions that students had encountered during their individual reading or writing activities. Students could sit anywhere they pleased in the room, as long as they were working on their projects. All books read and all writing genres exhibited by the students were self-chosen. These conditions mirror Anyon's description of the affluent professional school.

Progressive principles were highly prized, and at each staff meeting, the principal began with the statement, "We are here to consider how we can best serve the whole child in each of our students." Staff went out of their way to interact with students individually in and out of class. All the teachers and administration lived in the school district or in adjacent upper class suburbs and most had attended private colleges for their teacher training. It was inspiring. This was how all of my education professors had told me our classes should run. The students flourished. Parents praised the program on Parent's night. They valued their children's creative efforts.

My next assignment contrasted sharply with the first. Before I began in the classroom my sponsor teacher told me that students at the school were not interested in learning, and were often out of control. She showed me lessons, complete with overheads she had designed instructing students on the proper steps to take if they felt they needed to leave the classroom. Everything was outlined in detail. The desks were always in rows. According to my sponsor teacher, the students "couldn't handle" working in groups.

The most effective way to have students take notes, my grade team told me one day, was to give them Xeroxed copies of the teacher's outline notes with some key words missing. This could have been the school Anyon observed in her study. The control and the bitterness directed at students were shocking.

The teachers in the working-class school lived within the community. In the time I was there, I met four teachers from two grade teams of six each who had graduated from this same school. Almost everyone had attended a state school for their teaching certification. While the affluent professional school's teachers were excited and motivated, the most common refrain I heard among the working-class school's teachers was that they planned early retirement.

The dichotomy still amazes me.[8]

And so I ask, "Those who are smartest and work hardest go furthest?" Who's kidding whom? When students begin school in such different systems, the odds are set for them. President Kennedy once said that he hoped that a person's chance to become president was not determined on the day he was baptized (referring to the fact that some said a Catholic could never become president). I'd like to hope that a child's expectations are not determined on the day she or he enters kindergarten, but it would be foolish to entertain such a hope unless there are some drastic changes made.

Chapter 3

HARSH SCHOOLS, BIG BOYS, AND THE PROGRESSIVE SOLUTION

Daniel Resnick[1] tells an interesting story about the history of American schools and how we got to where we are today. His story begins with the history of the catechism. If you didn't go to a parochial school or attend Sunday school, you might not know what a catechism is. It's a book that teaches religious doctrine in a question-answer format. I still remember the first catechism lessons I memorized, I think in first grade.

Who made you?
God made me.
Why did God make you?
God made me to know Him, to love Him, and to serve Him in this life and to be happy with Him forever in the next.[2]

Through memorizing page after page of such questions and answers I was taught those doctrines of the Catholic church that were deemed appropriate for children my age.

Catechisms appeared in the earliest days of Christianity and continued to be produced throughout the middle ages. Even after the Reformation the catechism continued to be a favored way of teaching religious doctrine. Luther's *Little Catechism* was translated into all the major European languages within a generation.

Similar books and methods were used in the first schools in Europe and in colonial America. *The New England Primer* with its hundred plus questions and answers was the most widely used reader in American schools before 1820. It sold more than two million copies in its many editions. Other school books followed suit, such as *A Political Catechism, Intended for Use in Schools in the United States of America*, which was published in 1796.

Early schools did not permit, let alone encourage, children to generate ideas or to argue about the truth or value of what others had written. Teaching from a catechism discourages questioning, interpreting, or reflecting on the significance of what was presented. "Writing" instruction consisted of copying portions of texts written by others—literally, in "copy books." The schools had no interest in recognizing or developing the independent authority of the student's mind, and they placed a great deal of importance on confirming the authority of received texts.

The frame of mind that gave us the catechism is the same frame of mind that gave us the American schools in the Traditional Era—from colonial times until after the Civil War.[3] The dominant aim of traditional education was to develop character and intellect in the young by teaching them long-established knowledge. The curriculum was narrow—reading, penmanship, spelling, arithmetic, plus a little history, English, grammar, and geography. Subjects were divided into small "teachable" parts and taught in rigid order—from easy to hard or according to some logical idea of what must come before what. Each subject was taught in its own time slot. Little attention was paid to common elements or similarities from one subject to the next. Emphasis was on learning facts and rules.

There was no attempt to relate the curriculum to the children's lives. The curriculum was fixed and followed down to the last detail year after year. The same material was given to all pupils, without regard for individual differences. The school day consisted of lectures, drill, memorization, recitation, and examinations. Interaction between pupils was limited to competition. Cooperation in doing lessons was likely to be seen as cheating. The teacher and the textbook were the only source of information. Students not occupied directly with the teacher were expected to keep quiet. Desks faced the teacher and were kept in straight rows. They were often bolted to the floor. Play was permitted only during recess.

If this all sounds pretty familiar, I'm not surprised. Traditional education has never disappeared, but the worst nightmare versions of it found today pale in comparison to the schools of the Traditional Era. These were the days of the school*master*. Before 1830, few women taught school. Women did not become the majority in the teaching profession until 1870.

The concept of educating a person to be a teacher was unheard of during the Traditional Era. People who could read and write set themselves up as schoolmasters. They were sometimes paid by individual parents, but almost from the beginning of the colonial period, some communities provided free schooling to those who wanted it and could take advantage of it. The teacher's continued employment did not depend on whether he had any particular talent for teaching; it depended on whether he could control the students.

Severity was considered a virtue. Teachers used a three-foot ruler and a flexible sapling about five feet in length "with force and frequency" upon both boys and girls, young and old, when they did not know their lessons or broke rules. During an inspection tour of the Boston schools in 1844, board members found that whippings in a "representative" school of four hundred pupils averaged sixty-five a day. They found "severe injuries" sometimes resulted from these beatings and that the offenses were often "very trifling." A famous historian commented that "There was little 'soft pedagogy' in the management of either town or rural schools before the Civil War."[4]

> "Spare the rod and spoil the child" was a Bible text that received the most literal acceptance both in theory and practice. Even the naturally mild-tempered man was an "old-fashioned" disciplinarian when it came to teaching, and the naturally rough and coarse-grained man was as frightful as any ogre in a fairy tale.
>
> In summer, unless the teacher was an uncommonly poor one, or some of the scholars uncommonly wild and mischievous, the days moved along very harmoniously and pleasantly. In winter, when the big boys came in, some of them grown men, who cared vastly more about having a good

time than getting learning, an important requisite of the master was "government." He ruled his little empire, not with a rod of iron, but with a stout three-foot ruler, known as a "ferule," which was quite as effective. The really severe teacher had no hesitation in throwing this ruler at any child he saw misbehaving, and it is to be noted that he threw first and spoke afterward. Very likely he would order the culprit to bring him the ferule he had cast at him (it was a common occurrence to see in schoolroom walls "dents made by ferules hurled at misbehaving pupils' heads with an aim that sometimes proved untrue"), and, when the boy came out on the floor, would further punish him. Punishment by spatting the palm of his hand with a ruler was known as "feruling." The smarting of blows was severe while the punishment lasted, but this was as nothing to a "thrashing." The boy to be thrashed was himself sent for the apple tree twigs with which he was to be whipped. Poor fellow! Whimpering, and blinded by the welling tears, he slowly whittles off one after the other of the rough twigs. This task done, he drags his unwilling feet back to the schoolroom.

"Take off your coat, sir!" says the master.

The school is hushed into terrified silence. The fire crackles in the wide fireplace, the wind whistles at the eaves, the boy's tears flow faster, and he stammers, a plea for mercy. Then the whip hisses through the air, and blows fall thick and fast. The boy dances about the floor, and his shrill screams fill the schoolroom. His mates are frightened and trembling, and the girls are crying. . . . [5]

"Big boys" were often the teacher's nemesis. Two fairly commonplace forms of disruption often cost the teacher his job and caused the school to be closed until another teacher could be found. The first was referred to as "putting out" or "turning out" the teacher. In 1837 more than three hundred schools in Massachusetts were "broken up" by rebellious pupils—and Massachusetts was always a leader in education. The situation was probably worse elsewhere in the country.

Turning out the teacher was described by Horace Greeley, of "Go west, young man" fame.

At the close of the morning session of the first of January, and perhaps on some other day that the big boys chose to consider or make a holiday, the moment the master left the house in quest of his dinner, the little ones were started homeward, the doors and windows suddenly and securely barricaded, and the older pupils, thus fortified against intrusion, proceeded to spend the afternoon in play and hilarity. I have known a master to make a desperate struggle for admission, but the odds were too great. If he appealed to the neighboring fathers, they were apt to advise him to desist, and let matters take their course. I recollect one instance, however, where a youth [the teacher] was shut out who, procuring a piece of board, mounted from a fence to the roof of the schoolhouse and covered the top of the chimney nicely with his board. Ten minutes thereafter, the house was filled with smoke, and its inmates, opening the doors and windows, were glad to make terms with the outsider.[6]

It seems that in the Traditional Period of American education, the schoolmaster needed to earn his wings every day.

Another widely reported problem was assaults upon the teacher. These sometimes resulted when the teacher's thrashing of a student got to such a pitch that the miscreant or others (the older boys again) began to protest. When shouts failed "forcible, if not indeed armed, intervention might be the result."[7] But assaults arose over other matters as well. One benighted soul was reported to have lost his job over a plan to demonstrate his physical prowess that went awry. He challenged several boys to wrestle during recess. "[H]e was downed successively by two or three and soon, as a result, lost control of the school, as they found they could handle him, and so concluded to have their own way."[8] The teacher was fired.

And brutalizing and humiliating students carried with them certain risks. And as we will see, these were not abandoned for purely altruistic reasons.

This was a time when public schools were not expected to include everyone. In 1850 fewer than half the nation's whites between the ages of five and nineteen were in school, and the number of nonwhites in school was negligible. This was before immigration from eastern and southern Europe and the white population was vastly more homogeneous than it is today.

The concept of individual differences was unheard of. If a student failed or dropped out, it was no reflection on the school. The student was thought to be stupid or lazy. In schooling, blaming the victim is not a new concept.

After the Civil War things began to change. Between 1850 and 1900 the population of the United States tripled. Nine percent of the population lived in cities in 1830, 25 percent by 1870, and 50 percent by 1920. With industrialization and urbanization, the extended family of the rural setting gave way to nuclear families living among strangers in an unfamiliar setting. Children who had commonly worked on farms, now worked in factories. But as sentiment against child labor in industry mounted, child labor laws were enacted, and children became unemployable. In Philadelphia in 1870, it was reported that "upward of 20,000 children not attending any school, public, private or parochial, are running the streets in idleness and vagabondism."[9]

Concern over delinquency, workers' fear of competition from cheap child labor, and some genuine regard for the welfare of children prompted a rising demand for compulsory education. Only Massachusetts had compulsory education laws before the Civil War. Vermont was the first state to follow suit, in 1867. By 1919 every state had compulsory education laws. It was now the responsibility of the schools to take in all children and keep them.

Enrollments soared and schools became overcrowded. Playgrounds, which had been all outdoors in the country, were confined, overcrowded areas in cities as the country urbanized. The student body was no longer homogeneous. Students varied in ability, religion, social status, place of birth, and language. Differences among white Americans, who had hailed largely from northwestern Europe before the Civil War, were dwarfed by differences among immigrants from southern and eastern Europe, Asia, Latin America, and the newly freed African Americans after the Civil War. By 1910 the proportion of students with foreign-born parents topped 50 percent in the nation's thirty-seven largest cities.

With compulsory education, control became the central problem of schools. Older children with no means of escape were even more prone to violent resistance toward the traditional teaching and discipline methods of the past. The assumption that a child who was not ready to recite lessons perfectly was simply lazy and deserving of a thrashing or expulsion no longer worked. Differences in what could be reasonably expected from different students became too apparent to ignore. Finding other means of control became essential.

Industrialization offered more promising kinds of employment for educated men than "keeping school." At the same time, with compulsory education, schools were becoming a big ticket item for taxpayers, and women could be paid less than men. By 1870 the majority of teachers were women and by 1920 more than 80 percent of teachers were women. The school staff was becoming more and more female. Simultaneously, or perhaps in response to the impossibility of continuing business as usual, public attitudes toward brutal treatment of children were changing and prohibitions against corporal punishment were written into most school districts' rules. Something had to happen, and it did. "Progressive" ideals were invoked, but ultimately subverted, to calm the troubled waters.

The ideas upon which progressive education is built can be traced to the seventeenth century and the period referred to as the Enlightenment. Until this time the prevailing view was that human beings are inherently sinful. Enlightenment philosophers argued that man is not inherently good or evil; only his environment makes him one or the other, and so if you could make the environment consistently favorable, there would be no limits on the achievements and virtue of which individuals were capable.

Rousseau (1712–1778) applied this idea explicitly to childhood. He believed that children are endowed with potentials that should be nurtured and permitted to grow naturally in a healthy environment. Pestalozzi (1746–1827) and Froebel (1782–1852) took Rousseau's ideas and translated them into practice in elementary schools and in kindergarten. These ideas found their way to the United States as early as 1808, in a book by Joseph Neef, and found an influential champion in Horace Mann (1796–1859).

In an 1843 report to the Massachusetts Board of Education, Mann criticized the schools and called for reforms, including methods based on Rousseau's ideas and discipline based on love. Mann was immediately attacked by ministers who opposed his beliefs about human nature and by teachers who opposed his educational beliefs. The controversy succeeded in drawing widespread attention to Mann's ideas.

In the 1890s Joseph Rice toured schools in thirty-five cities and wrote a series of muckraking articles that attacked methods of teaching that were designed to "immobilize, automize, and dehumanize students." Lawrence Cremin, a distinguished educational historian, credits Rice's articles with starting the progressive movement in the United States.[10] About the same time, John Dewey (1869–1953), probably the best-known proponent of "progressive education," started the Laboratory School at the University of Chicago.

There are two central concepts of progressive education. First, schools should deal with the whole child—his or her personality, social skills and attitudes, and physical well-being—rather than focusing exclusively on his or her ability to master a narrow, traditional curriculum and parrot back answers. Therefore, education should be interesting, exciting, and enjoyable. Second, children are different. They have different experiences, abilities, and interests. Therefore, although the knowledge and skills included in a progressive curriculum might be quite traditional, they are not likely to be taught in a rigid order dictated by some concept of easy-to-hard or the logic of the subject. They are instead taught in an order dictated by the experiences, abilities, and interests of the individual children. Children are given some choice in determining what they will study and even in how they will go about learning.

Because progressive schools deal with the development of the whole child and recognize individual differences in students' experiences, abilities, and interests, traditional school activities such as reading, writing, and reciting are joined by expressive, creative, physical, and social activities. Art, music, crafts, shop, cooking, sewing, dramatics, and physical education all become part of the regular curriculum. Subjects are "integrated" whenever possible. For example, reading, writing, geography, history, and arithmetic lessons might be incorporated into an ongoing project determined by the students, such as studying the origins of ethnic groups represented in the classroom. Children's activities and learnings will vary. Courses of study (in history, for example) are viewed, not as something that must be covered by each child in a fixed and thorough manner, but as guides for facts, concepts, skills, understandings, and attitudes that might be developed as the teacher deems appropriate for the class and for individual students.

The teacher and textbook are no longer the sole sources of knowledge. Pupils go on field trips, utilize the library and audiovisual presentations, interview local citizens, and so on. Memorization and drill are replaced with efforts to lead students to discover general principles. Pupils are permitted to work independently and in small groups, move about the room, and engage in interesting projects, and a variety of methods and materials are used, including plays, murals, models, projects, games, audiovisual equipment, computers, and field trips.

When children do not do their lessons or don't do them correctly, teachers question whether students have the necessary background or previous knowledge, or they question their own methods or consider how they might capture the students' interest before deciding that the students are lazy or stupid. When, at last, punishment appears to be necessary, it is not physical; instead, it usually involves the loss of some sort of privilege and it is accompanied with sympathetic and constructive suggestions for behavioral changes and explanations of why they are necessary. The ideal is not discipline from above, but self-discipline. Willinsky defines "new literacy," a recent form of progressive education, as "those strategies in the teaching of reading and writing which attempt to shift the control of literacy from the teacher to the student."[11]

Teachers strive to be democratic and friendly. The classroom is informal. Desks and chairs are movable and they are frequently rearranged into circles, clusters, or lines depending on the activity. Distinctions between the school and other spheres of the students' life are minimized. Schools attempt to build on home and community activities with which children are already familiar. But, as we shall see, progressives had fairly upscale homes and communities in mind.

Progressive education unintentionally offered the school an escape hatch from the crisis precipitated by compulsory education laws. Invoking principles of progressive education, schools were able to continue teaching the basics of reading, writing, and arithmetic in grades one through six, but there were now *flexible standards*. Less could be expected (and less demanded) of some students based on their "aptitude" or "intelligence." Everyone in the fourth grade class would move on to the fifth even though there might be a wide range of achievement among them. As early as seventh grade the curriculum would be diversified by adding such courses as shop, art, music, cooking, sewing, and auto mechanics.

The adoption of flexible standards and a diversified curriculum dovetailed with the growing testing movement and created a new profession—school counselling. Intelligence and achievement tests were used to assign students to "tracks" or "streams." An elementary school with sixty or seventy students in each grade might divide them into "low," "middle," and "high" classes, often based on their scores on standardized reading achievement tests. High schools developed academic, commercial, and vocational programs, which, despite protestation to the contrary, soon became identified as "high" and "low" tracks in the minds of everyone. Where schools during the Traditional Era selected students by a process of exclusion, schools in the Progressive Era selected students by differentiating them into different tracks or streams.

There are those who argue that the adoption of progressive ideas was the result of convincing philosophical arguments from scholars such as Dewey. There is no doubt some truth to this, but I generally favor the "escape hatch" theory, because after the dust settled we had arrived at the present system, which is pretty well described by Anyon's study of gentry, middle-class, and working-class schools reported in the last chapter.

Anyon's affluent professional school is about as good as it gets in terms of progressive philosophy and methods and her executive elite school had a progressive feel about it in terms of discipline, student autonomy, and teachers' attitudes toward the students. I would describe her middle-class and working-class schools as traditional schools with a "softened pedagogy," ones where lessons are a little less rigid, but not much, and the brutal assaults have all but disappeared.

I would estimate that today about 20 percent of American schools, those attended by the offspring of the gentry, those whom Reich describes as symbolic-analytic workers, could be described as progressive. The remaining 80 percent, those attended by the offspring of the middle and working classes, are best described as traditional schools with a somewhat softened pedagogy. And I would expect the degree of "softening" to be related to the status of the parents—the higher the status, the softer the pedagogy.

But why aren't progressive methods, curriculum, and philosophy used in all schools? There is not a single reason. There are a lot of them. They're subtle and interconnected. I'll discuss them in the next several chapters.

Chapter 4

OPPOSITIONAL IDENTITY
Identifying "Us" as "Not Them"

Y_ou can't talk about the inequality built into the American school system for long before someone starts to tell you about his or her grandfather or great-grandfather or some ancestor who came here at the age of fourteen from Germany or Italy or Ireland with nothing and worked fifteen hour days and, although he died in very modest circumstances, sent his children to college. Of course, the point of the story is, "My ancestors made it through sacrifice and hard work, and anyone else who's willing to get off his dead ass can do the same."

Good point. Why have some groups seemed to prosper in America, while others have not? For example, in Stockton, California, in the 1930s the children of Chinese, Japanese, and Mexican American immigrants all experienced difficulty in school, probably because of their limited ability to speak English. By 1947, however, school failure had disappeared among the Chinese and Japanese but not among the Mexican American population. In fact, by 1947 there were two-and-one-half times more Asian Americans in junior college than one would have predicted based on the percentage of Asian Americans in the general population. In contrast, fewer than 5 percent of Mexican American students in eighth grade were expected to stay in school through junior college. The African American population in Stockton fared only a little better than the Mexican Americans.[1]

A 1983 study showed that Punjabi students did well in California schools despite the fact that, by and large, their parents held low-status, low-paying jobs, had little formal education, low English proficiency, and a culture regarded as backward by many Americans. Nevertheless, the average Punjabi boy did better than the average "American" boy in the same classrooms.

Studies consistently show that Asian Americans do better in school and score higher on standardized tests than African Americans, Mexican Americans, Native Americans, and Puerto Ricans. Latinos from Central and South America and Cuba perform better in school than Latinos from Mexico and Puerto Rico. In Britain, students from East Asia outperform students from the West Indies, despite the fact that English is the native tongue of most West Indians, while it is not the native tongue of most East Asians.

Maoris, who are indigenous to New Zealand, do less well in New Zealand schools than Polynesian immigrants to New Zealand whose language and culture are similar to that of the Maoris. In Japan there is a minority known as Buraku who tend to do poorly in school when compared with the dominant Ippan students. However, in American schools, Buraku and Ippan immigrants do equally well. Children of the Korean minority in Japan do poorly in school. Korean immigrants in the United States do as well as all other Asian immigrants. West Indian students do poorly in Britain, but they do well in the United States.[2]

John Ogbu[3] believes that all these puzzling facts disprove the common-sense theory that the more a minority is like the dominant culture, the better they will do in school. If that were true, why would immigrant Polynesians do better in New Zealand schools than Maoris who are native to New Zealand? Why would Koreans, whose culture and language is more like the Japanese than American, do better in American schools than in Japanese schools? Why do Mexicans and Puerto Ricans do less well in American schools than immigrants from elsewhere in Latin America? Ogbu believes that these puzzling facts can be explained by the history of the relationships between the minority and dominant groups involved. For Ogbu there are minorities, and then there are minorities.

Ogbu distinguishes between *immigrant minorities* and *involuntary minorities*. Immigrant minorities are people who have come to America for improved economic, political, and/or social opportunities. Ogbu identifies recent Chinese and Punjabi immigrants in California as immigrant minorities. Because of language and cultural differences, immigrant minorities initially feel they are discriminated against and their children experience difficulties in school, but they view these conditions as temporary situations that will improve probably over a single generation. Immigrant minorities in the United States compare their situation with that of their countrymen and -women "back home." If in fact they find the struggle in the United States to be more odious than the conditions they left, they have the option of returning home, as many European immigrants did in the late nineteenth and early twentieth century.[4]

Cultural differences exhibited by immigrant minorities existed before they came into contact with the American mainstream culture. For example, before Punjabis immigrated into the United States they spoke Punjabi, were Sikhs, Hindus, or Moslems, had arranged marriages, and males wore turbans. Punjabis continue to exhibit these characteristics more or less after they come into contact with mainstream Americans. Immigrant minorities perceive the mainstream to be different from themselves, not in opposition to themselves.

Immigrant minorities are willing to engage in "accommodation without assimilation." They encourage their children to "play the classroom game"—that is, to adopt the mainstream characteristics necessary for social and academic success in school without necessarily buying into the beliefs or meanings on which these characteristics are based. This is seen simply as expedient, not as a repudiation of their culture. They do it with confidence that they will be accepted or at least tolerated in the mainstream world and they will prosper. They don't mind that their culture is not represented in mainstream schools. They don't expect it to be. They send their children to public schools to learn mainstream ways and they trust that the schools will teach them what they need to know.

On the other hand, *involuntary minorities* are people who became Americans through slavery, conquest, or colonization and who were relegated to an inferior position and denied assimilation.

They continue to experience failure in school for generation after generation. American Indians, African Americans, Mexican Americans, Native Hawaiians, and Puerto Ricans are examples of involuntary minorities in the United States. Maori in New Zealand and Buraku in Japan are examples in other countries.

Involuntary minorities experience discrimination as permanent. They have no "homeland" to return to. For Native Americans, this is their homeland. For African Americans, hundreds of years of slavery cut them off from Africa. They have nowhere to go back to in the sense that an Irish or Japanese immigrant can "go back." Puerto Ricans can only go back to an island dominated by United States mainstream culture. Although some recent Mexican immigrants can, and do, go back, many Mexicans are from southwestern states that were annexed to the United States through conquest. As a result, their relationship with the dominant group began as that of citizens in an occupied country to the occupying power.

Unlike immigrant minorities, involuntary minorities do not have peers "back home" with whom they can favorably compare themselves. When they make comparisons, it is with their ancestors before slavery, before the "discovery" of America by Europeans, before the United States' annexation of the Southwest and Puerto Rico, and they see themselves as worse off by comparison. They also compare themselves to mainstream whites and see themselves as worse off. They see newly arrived immigrant minorities move up generation after generation while they do not. They see themselves as oppressed.

Such situations result in what Ogbu refers to as "oppositional identity." Members of the oppressed group come to regard certain beliefs, skills, tastes, values, attitudes, and behaviors as *not* appropriate for them because they are associated with the dominant culture. Adopting these is seen as surrendering to the enemy. On the other hand, certain beliefs, skills, tastes, values, attitudes, and behaviors are embraced by the minority because they are *not* characteristic of the dominant group. The dominant group, in fact, may find them offensive. In short, if I perceive myself to be a member of an oppressed people, there are things I will reject because I associate them with my oppressors and to do them is to betray my people. In addition, there are things I will make a point of embracing because they are rejected by my oppressors. I embrace them as acts of freedom and defiance.

For example, a researcher named Perry Gilmore[5] went into a predominantly low-income black urban elementary school (very much like the Chicago school where I taught twenty-five years ago) to study a program called "Academics Plus." She was very surprised to learn that teachers, administrators, and parents alike focused on attitudes rather than achievement when discussing students' admission into the program. They identified two behaviors, that would definitely bar admission. One was called "stylized sulking" and the other "doin' steps."

Stylized sulking is a student response in face-to-face clashes with teachers. It is usually nonverbal and highly choreographed. It conveys rebellion, anger, and uncooperativeness. It is sometimes seen as a face-saving device. Stylized sulking differs for boys and girls. A girl will pose with her chin up, closing her eyelids for long periods and casting downward side glances, turning her head markedly sidewards and upwards, chin on her hand, her elbow supported by the desk. Striking or getting into the pose is usually performed with an abrupt movement that will sometimes be marked with a sound, either the elbow striking the desk or a verbal marker like "humpf."

Boys' stylized sulking is usually characterized by head downward, arms crossed at the chest, and legs spread wide. Often they will mark the silence by knocking over a chair or pushing loudly on their desk, assuring that others hear and see the performance. Teachers, both black and white, identified stylized sulking as a black thing.

Doin' steps occurs outside school rather than in the classroom. It involves chorally chanting rhymes punctuated with footsteps and hand claps. It is often full of taboos and sexual innuendo. Gilmore collected the following versions of steps based on what many will remember from childhood as a jump rope chant called "Mississippi." The children sometimes refer to steps as "Kookelater (crooked letter) Dances."

> MI crooked letter, crooked letter, I,
> crooked letter, crooked letter, I,
> hump back, hump back, I
> M for the money

I if ya give it to me
S sock it (to me)
S sock it (to me)
I if I buy it from ya
S sock it
S sock it
I if I take it from ya
P pump it
P pump it
I[6]

Another version was performed by fewer individuals and was viewed as an accomplished recitation by peers. The jeans theme made it a favorite.

He, Deede, yo
Spell Mississippi
Spell Mississippi right now
You take my hands up high
You take my feet down low
I cross my legs with that gigolo
If you don't like that
Throw it in the trash
And then I'm bustin out
With that Jordache
Look in the sky
With that Calvin Klein
I'm gonna lay in the dirt
With that Sergiert [Sergio Valente]
I'm gonna bust a balloon
With that Sassoon
Gonna be ready
With that Teddy
I'm gonna be on the rail
With that Vanderbail
With the is-M is-I
Crooked letter crooked letter I[7]

In doin' steps, each girl takes a turn. Each has her own style. Girls who were very good became captains who organized and instructed others.

However, the teachers, parents and administrators described stepping as "nasty" and as representing defiance and a bad attitude. Like stylized sulking, stepping was seen as a form of *black* expression and it was banned on the playground. A girl who had been a captain the previous year had given up stepping because she wanted to get into the Academic Plus Program.

But, you may ask, if they know that sulking and stepping is going to get them excluded from the Academics Plus program, why do they keep doing it?

First of all, they were aware that whites identified these behaviors as *black* behaviors and found them offensive, and so engaging in them was an act of defiance.

Furthermore, if these students adopted school-sanctioned ways of saving face in a standoff with a teacher or played hopscotch and jump rope like the girls who are acceptable to the teachers, they would not be who they are; they would be someone else—whites. And if they did make these concessions, would that guarantee that they would get into the Academics Plus program? And if they got into the program, would that guarantee that they would be accepted by mainstream society? Generations of blacks who have "acted white" have not been fully accepted into mainstream society, and have found themselves alienated from their own communities as well.

Robert Coles,[8] a child psychiatrist who has spent his life studying children, tells an interesting story in his book *The Spiritual Life of Children*. He had been interviewing Hopi children in a reservation school asking them such questions as whether they prayed, whether God spoke to them, and what they thought about God. He had carried on such interviews with children all over the world with pretty nearly uniform success, but after six months at the Hopi school he was about ready to admit failure and leave. The children answered his questions as briefly as possible and clearly were not interested in cooperating with him.

Finally, a Hopi mother who volunteered at the school said to him,

> The longer you stay here, the worse it will get. . . . [T]hey won't ever want to talk with you about the private events

in their lives in this building. They learn how to read and write here; they learn their arithmetic here, but that's that. You are asking them about thoughts they put aside when they enter this building. The longer you stay here and put them in a position that forces them to appear silent and sullen and stupid, the less they'll be inclined even to answer you. Maybe they think, "This guy isn't catching on!"[9]

After this conversation, Coles interviewed the children in their homes, and although there was no sudden miracle, within a month the children seemed altogether different. They smiled, initiated conversations, pointed out places that mattered to them, introduced Coles to their friends, and on their home turf, when he wasn't asking anything in particular, they shared some of their deepest spiritual thoughts. For these children, for these involuntary minorities, school was not and would never be their home turf.

When we're talking about oppositional identity in my class, I often do the following exercise. I ask my students what they would think of an American Methodist who converted to Shintoism (the national religion of Japan)? I don't get much of a rise out of them. A little weird, perhaps, but what's to think? Now let's imagine it's 1950 and Japan had won World War II and the United States is occupied by the Japanese. What would you think of an American Methodist who converted to Shintoism? Traitor! Or try these. A Palestinian converts to Christianity. Ho hum. To Judaism. Shocking! An American Irish Catholic turns Protestant. So what? A Catholic in Northern Ireland turns Protestant. Turncoat!

Why? Because in the first cases we are talking about people adopting a characteristic of a culture to which they feel more or less equal, a culture that has never oppressed their culture economically, politically, socially, or psychologically. In the second cases, we are talking about adopting a characteristic of an enemy. It makes all the difference.

Of course, religious affiliations associated with different groups are easy to think of, but the concept applies to many beliefs, skills, values, attitudes, and behaviors—such as ways of expressing resistance to people in charge (sulking) and forms of recreation (doin' steps).

For involuntary minorities, the dominant group is not only different, it is the enemy. Because cultural differences between them and the mainstream are oppositional rather than simply different, accommodation is difficult if not impossible. Cultural differences become cultural boundaries. Once a cultural identification is established *in opposition* to another, a border is established that people cross at their peril. "Border crossers,"—working-class students who adopt the values, attitudes, interests, of the middle class and more or less abandon those of their community—are likely to be censured by their own as traitors and they are not likely to be fully accepted by the dominant group.

not always

Characteristics that facilitate school success are, of course, associated with the culture and language of the dominant group. To adopt these is to adopt the culture of the enemy. Furthermore, some beliefs and behaviors that involuntary minorities acquire in their cultures not only fail to prepare them for school, they can in fact be incompatible with the aims of the schools.

For example, Ron and Suzanne Scollon[10] did a study of the Athabaskans, Native Americans who live in Northern Canada and Alaska. Athabaskans have a high degree of respect for individuality. This makes them highly reluctant to interfere in what others know and believe. Therefore, they are not inclined to bring up a topic in conversation unless they are well aware of the point of view of everyone present regarding that topic. If a topic is introduced and you're an Athabaskan and you don't know where everyone present stands on the topic, you remain silent. Furthermore, in Athabaskan society, a person in an inferior position does not display his knowledge in the presence of persons in a superior position. Adults and teachers are expected to display knowledge and abilities; children are expected to watch and learn. As a result, whites see Athabaskan as unsure, aimless, incompetent, and withdrawn, and Athabaskans see whites as braggarts who talk too much.

Now imagine you're a six-year-old Athabaskan in a first grade classroom at "sharing time." Mindy, a white classmate, gets up and tells how she made candles at camp. In both Mindy's and the teacher's culture it is expected that children will display their knowledge for the teacher. They both have an idea of where Mindy's language development is headed—toward mainstream ways of expression that they both view as natural. However, you, an Athabaskan child, have little to say during sharing time. You feel your reluctance to speak is appropriate. You have an idea of where your language development is headed—toward Athabaskan ways of expression that you view as natural. But the teacher views your silence as a deviation from what's natural, and the teacher has all the power here. It is she who decides what's natural. Lucky for Mindy; too bad for you.

Now it's ninth grade. The teacher asks the students to write a persuasive essay: Should clubs dealing with religion be allowed to meet during school hours on school property? Mindy has been chugging along making progress toward the language style of her home, community, and school. She knows that she is expected to "generalize" her audience. It is not her teacher (who, in fact, is the only person who will ever read the essay) but a "general reader." Her arguments should not be addressed to a fairly devout Catholic, which she knows her teacher to be because she attends the same church, but to this general reader about whose beliefs she is to make no assumptions.

But you, an Athabaskan, have been chugging along making progress toward the discourse of your home and community— but not of the school. You are not to address topics unless you know your audience's point of view. How can you write to a general reader—whose point of view is by definition unknown to you? You are not to display knowledge to a person of superior status. Since the general reader may be of equal or superior status, how can you proceed? An Athabaskan cannot write a "good essay" without adopting values and social practices that are in conflict with her or his own.

Mainstream educators, especially those who keep talking about education as *the* answer to all our minority problems, seem to believe that if education were successful, the involuntary minorities would become fully assimilated. Their separate cultures would essentially disappear as, for example, the defining characteristics of Irish Americans at the turn of the century have all but vanished. Aside from the odd St. Patrick's Day Parade and Irish step dancing competition, middle-class descendants of the teeming Irish slums of turn of the century America are hardly distinguishable from other middle-class Americans either in their culture or *in their level of acceptance by other mainstreamers.*

But there's the rub. Involuntary minorities do not believe that they will be accepted even if they surrender their identity. And they have plenty of reason to believe they will not be accepted.

When we discuss Ogbu in my class, I ask my students to think about the students at the Carol Jason Banks Upper Grade Center, where I taught in 1965. The eighth grade students were divided by reading score into fifteen classes. Those in the top group—about twenty-five students—had reading scores at or a little above the eighth grade level. I ask them to think about them and to think about twenty-five eighth graders in the same year with exactly the same reading scores in Winnetka, an upscale suburb north of Chicago. Eighth graders are about fourteen years old. Today these students would be in their middle to late fifties. Where would you expect to find them working and living?

My guess is that the nearly all the students from Winnetka went to college and are today professionals living in suburbs like Winnetka. It's possible, but it would be very surprising to hear, that some of them are in prison or on welfare or met a violent death. My guess is that eighth graders *with comparable reading scores* at Banks Upper Grade Center in 1965 are in a different place. One or two of them might have made it big. In fact Minnie Ripperton, who was gaining fame as a jazz singer until her tragic death from breast cancer in 1979, was in my class the first year I taught school. Probably some of these students are school teachers and police officers today. Some may have careers in the military. I would be saddened, but not surprised, to learn that one or two were on welfare or in prison or had met a violent death. On average, the benefits that our society has to offer would not be shared equally by these two groups of students whose reading achievement was identical when they were in eighth grade forty years ago.

The connection between hard work, good grades, and life success that is so apparent to a student in Winnetka, is not at all apparent to a child in an involuntary minority. Adopting characteristics of mainstream culture costs them, and they have plenty of reason to believe that they will not be accepted into mainstream, white America.

"But," some of my students tell me, "that's all changed."

"Baloney," is my reply. In the O. J. Simpson case we learned that a Los Angeles policeman bragged about pulling over cars with racially mixed couples and finding reasons to give them citations. The media reported that many middle-class Americans were shocked. I wasn't shocked. I don't know of anyone, white or black, middle-class or otherwise, who was shocked. In 1996, Texaco promptly settled a law suit brought by minority employees for racial discrimination in promotions after tape recordings surfaced wherein top executives in the company jocularly referred to employees as "jelly beans" and commented that "all the black jelly beans seem to be glued to the bottom of the bag."[11] By and large, involuntary minorities do not believe they will be fully accepted by the mainstream even if they adopt mainstream culture, and there's plenty of evidence that this belief is fully justified.

In short, immigrant minorities (Hungarians and Asians, for example) see the characteristics of mainstream culture that are necessary for social and academic success in school as things they can adopt in particular circumstances without compromising who they are, and they have reason to believe that this course of action and effort in school will pay off in terms of success and acceptance in the mainstream world. Involuntary minorities (African Americans and Native Americans, for example) see adopting these characteristics as compromising who they are and as a formula for becoming alienated from their own communities, and they have reason to believe it will not pay off in terms either of success or acceptance in the mainstream world.

So sure, many mainstream Americans' grandfathers or great-grandmothers, or whoever, had a rough time and prospered, but they voluntarily entered a system under circumstances that did not set up a border between themselves and the mainstream. Simply expecting involuntary minorities to do the same is not only unfair; it doesn't help us get any closer to a solution.

I had a hard time trying to decide where to put this chapter in the book. I felt it should come early because it deals with the "My grandparents made it; why can't they?" argument which is the end of all discussion for many Americans. But I didn't want to introduce this chapter too early, because it seems to support the idea that poverty and illiteracy are solely the problem of nonwhite minorities. That simply isn't true.

In the late '80s, 12 percent of the white population, 46 percent of the African American population, and 40 percent of the

Hispanic population were living in poverty. That sure looks like it's a nonwhite problem, doesn't it? But because whites outnumbered blacks by about five to one and Hispanics by about seven to one, there were 5.4 million whites, 4.6 million African Americans, and 2.8 million Hispanics living in poverty in the late '80s. Measures also indicated that around one-half of children classified as "educationally disadvantaged" were white. All other races made the remaining 50 percent.[12] The population I'm concerned about includes children of all races. In terms of raw numbers, I'm talking about as many whites as nonwhites.

Chapter 5

THE LADS

While Ogbu relates the concept of oppositional identity to involuntary minorities, a similar mechanism has been described by other authors dealing with working-class white populations who could not be described as either immigrants or minorities.

Paul Willis, an Englishman, wrote a great book[1] that opened with the words

> The difficult thing to explain about how middle class kids get middle class jobs is why others let them. The difficult thing about how working-class kids get working-class jobs is why they let themselves.[2]

Willis rejects the notion that working-class youngsters get working-class jobs because they are less intelligent or generally incapable of doing school work. He observed that high-achieving working-class students in England were very likely to wind up in low-income, low-prestige jobs while *low-achieving* middle-class students are very likely to wind up in higher-income, higher-prestige jobs.[3] How come, he wondered.

He studied twelve 14- and 15-year-old English working-class boys in a working-class school in a working-class town. They referred to themselves and were referred to by others as "the lads." The most basic and obvious characteristic of the lads was their opposition to authority. Willis recorded the following conversation between himself and Joey, one of the lads, on the topic of teachers.

> **Joey:** (. . .) the way we're subject to their every whim like. They want something doing and we have to sort of do it, 'cos, er, er, we're just, we're under them like. We were with a woman teacher in here, and 'cos we all wear rings and one or two of them bangles, like he's got one on, and out of the blue, like, for no special reason, she says, "take all that off."

> **WILLIS:** Really?

> **Joey:** Yeah, we says, "One won't come off," she says, "Take yours off as well." I said, "You'll have to chop my finger off first."

> **WILLIS:** Why did she want you to take your rings off?

> **Joey:** Just a sort of show like. Teachers do this, like, all of a sudden they'll make you do your ties up and things like this. You're subject to their every whim like. If they want something done, if you don't think it's right, and you object against it, you're down to Simmondsy [the principal].

> **WILLIS:** You think of most staff as kind of enemies (. . .)?

> **Joey:** Most of them. It adds a bit of spice to yer life, if you're trying to get him for something he's done to you.[4]

And here are Joey and Spansky, another lad, on the same topic:

> **WILLIS:** Evans [a teacher] said you were all being very rude (. . .) you didn't have the politeness to listen to the speaker. He said God help you when you have kids 'cos they're going to be worse. What did you think of that?

> **Joey:** They wouldn't. They'll be outspoken. They wouldn't be submissive fucking twits. They'll be outspoken, upstanding sort of people.

Spansky: If any of my kids are like this, here, I'll be pleased.[5]

The lads' lives seemed to be directed by a single principle: To defeat the official purpose of the school. When Willis asked them if they had any rules, they answered that their only rule was to break the "other" rules. In class there was a continuous scraping of chairs and sulking at the simplest request. The vaguest sexual double meaning was greeted with loud guffaws and obscene gestures just barely out of the teacher's view. Lads devised ways to get out of class, to attend class and do no work, to attend the wrong class, to roam the corridors, and to sleep—both in and out of class. They were aware that this was done with the connivance of the teachers "'cos they want to get rid of you, like." They sometimes went to class only because they were bored with wandering about.

They frequently violated the school dress code. The purpose of school dress codes is often to deemphasize sexuality, and challenging it had a special significance for the lads because they felt superior to other students in regard to sexual experience. Even the teachers acknowledged their sexual adventures. One younger teacher commented, "He [one of the lads] has had more than me, I can tell you!"

The lads not only smoked and drank, they flaunted it. Nothing pleased them more than to have a teacher see them smoking on school grounds and not report it. They took this as a sign of weakness on the part of the teacher and a victory for themselves. One lad walked up to a young teacher in a pub and said hello to him. The teacher was flabbergasted. He had been trying to pretend he did not recognize the boy, but he was put in a position of having to acknowledge him. The boy understood the situation very well. When the teacher failed to report him, he felt victorious and bragged about the incident.

The ability to "have a laugh" was another defining characteristic of the lads. They laughed to defeat boredom and fear and as a way out of almost anything. One lad reported

(. . .) I don't know why I want to laugh, I dunno why it's so fuckin' important. It just is (. . .) I think it's just a good gift, that's all, because you can get out of any situation. If you can laugh, if you can make yourself laugh, I mean really convincingly, it can get you out of millions of things.[6]

A laugh can deflect the gaze of authority. It can turn submissiveness into cocky defiance, even while complying with the letter of a direct order from a teacher or boss.

Much of the lads' behavior can be seen as preparation for the shop floor. Clothing, drinking, smoking, sex, and cocky defiance all symbolized coming of age for the lads, and coming of age in a way that was reflected in their working-class culture, and counter to school culture.

People employed in factories are in a highly controlled environment. For many, survival depends on being able to take control of the situation. Slowdowns, goldbricking, extended toilet passes, unofficial job swapping, and even sabotage are mirrored in the lads' attempts to take control of classes, substitute their own timetables, and control their own routines and life spaces. The father of one of the lads expressed this clearly:

> Actually the foreman, the gaffer, don't run the place, the men run the place. See, I mean you get one of the chaps says, "Alright, you'm on so and so today." You can't argue with him. The gaffer don't give you the job, they swop each other about, tek it in turns. Ah, but I mean the job's done. If the gaffer had gi'd you the job you would. . . . They tried to do it one morning gi'd a chap a job you know, but he'd been on it, you know, I think he'd been on all week, and they just downed tools (. . .) They're four hard jobs on the track and there's dozens that's . . . you know, a child of five could do it, quite honestly, but everybody has their turn. That's organized by the men.[7]

Another aspect of the lads' mentality that can be traced to shop floor culture is valorization of physical strength and practical know-how and disdain for "useless" abstract or theoretical knowledge. One of the lads' fathers recounted a story about a "chap who was all theory" who was forever sending away for books. One day, one of the books came in a wooden box, and it's still in that box 'cos he can't open it. Now that in't true, is it? But the point is true. That in't true, that didn't happen, but his point is right. He can't get at the book 'cos he don't know how to open the box! Now what's the good of that?[8]

Of course parents' disdain for theory was conveyed to their children and so the culture of the lads was not simply different from the school, it was antithetical to the school. The lads valued practical knowledge and disparaged "theory." They viewed the art, music, and literature—everything that might be considered upper-class culture—with disdain. They valued violence, sexism, and racism as manly traits. This basic antithesis between themselves and the school bred contempt on both sides and the lads' definition of themselves was formed in part by what they were *not*. If this doesn't remind you of Ogbu and oppositional identity and Anyon's working-class school, it should.

The lads describe themselves as being rather tame until the age of twelve—a little older than Anyon's fifth graders. Then they said they just fell in together in activities involving alcohol and minor vandalism. But the faculty believed "the lads" came to be as a result of a combination of character defects among leaders and weakness among the led as the following school reports reveal.

[Joey] proved himself to be a young man of intelligence and ability who could have done well at most subjects, but decided that he did not want to work to develop this talent to the full and allowed not only his standard of work to deteriorate, except for English, but also attendance and behaviour (. . .) too often his qualities of leadership were misplaced and not used on behalf of the school.

[Spansky] in the first three years was a most co-operative and active member of school. He took part in the school council, school play and school choir in this period and represented the school at cricket, football and cross-country events.

Unfortunately, this good start did not last and his whole manner and attitude changed. He did not try to develop his ability in either academic or practical skills (. . .) his early pleasant and cheerful manner deteriorated and he became a most unco-operative member of the school hindered by negative attitudes.

[Eddie's] conduct and behaviour was very inconsistent and on occasions totally unacceptable to the school. A lack of self-discipline was apparent and a tendency to be swayed by group behaviour revealed itself.[9]

However, Willis believed that neither the lads nor their teachers fully understood how the lads came to be. While he concedes that character defects may have played a part (the poor are no less susceptible to character defects than the rich), he believed that both the lads and the school they attended were the products of societal mechanisms that are so subtle that the teachers, students, parents, and families were unaware of them.

According to Willis, when schools operate the way they're supposed to, teachers and students enter into a bargain. Teachers have something valuable—high-status knowledge, that is, abstract, theoretical knowledge, the kind valued by the gentry. Not business arithmetic, but algebra, geometry, and calculus. Not the ability to read and understand contemporary "adolescent literature," but the ability to read, appreciate, and critique *A Tale of Two Cities*. It's a teacher's job to give such high-status knowledge to students. It's their profession. It's what they get paid for.

never thought of it this way.

That being the case, students have something that is valuable to the teachers—cooperation. That's the deal, high-status knowledge for cooperation. Willis refers to this as the "basic teaching paradigm." I'd prefer to refer to it as the "real-school model." It's the model that operated in Anyon's middle-class, affluent professional, and executive elite schools.

In some schools, such as Anyon's affluent professional and executive elite schools, high-status knowledge is valued for itself It is knowledge of one's own culture. In middle-class schools high-status knowledge is valued for what it "buys." It buys grades, diplomas, degrees, qualifications, and licenses. These can be exchanged for good jobs and high pay. So even though high-status knowledge is not seen as having value in and of itself, it is seen as valuable.

When the real-school model is working, it is the possession of high-status knowledge that gives teachers authority. Students grant teachers authority in exchange for knowledge. Under these circumstances, discipline is not a matter of punishing wrongdoing as much as it is a matter of maintaining a contract to which all parties have agreed.

But what happens when the value of high-status knowledge is called into question? What if students resonate with the fable of the man who ordered a book but could not open the box in which it was delivered? And what if, in addition, they see the school's qualifications and diplomas as irrelevant to their lives—present or future? What if they see school knowledge as antithetical to their culture and a threat to their identity, as did Ogbu's involuntary minorities, Scollon's Athabaskans, Coles's Hopi children, the sulkers and steppers, and the lads?

The school's first reaction to such a student body is to get tough, but this can turn quickly into brute force and brute resistance. Since teachers are always outnumbered, this has not been found to be a good solution. Next, schools adopt the students' definition of useful knowledge—practical know-how.

However, as knowledge becomes more practical, school itself becomes less necessary. Once children can read and write at a functional level they can learn practical things better at home, in the neighborhood, or on the job. It is well known that school "shops" are typically a generation behind industry. Kozol[10] reports on schools teaching typing on broken-down electric typewriters years after business has moved to word processing on computers, and he describes schools teaching auto shop without the electronic equipment necessary to find problems in modern automobile engines.

So the compromise is not quite successful. The school stops insisting on offering the high-status knowledge that students find useless or repugnant, but it cannot quite fulfill the promise of offering knowledge the students will find useful. And so the deal changes. Schools have little to offer, and so they ask little in return. They stop asking for real effort on the part of students. In return, the students offer enough cooperation to maintain the appearance of conducting school. Willis refers to this as the "modified teaching paradigm." I'd prefer to refer to it as the "make-believe school model." Under these circumstances, a "good student" is defined as one who has a "good attitude." This is consistent with Anyon and numerous other studies dealing with schools and social class: working-class schools reward students for docility and obedience rather than initiative and assertiveness.[11]

Most students in working-class schools cooperate, more or less. But some students decide not to cooperate. These are the students who are identified as having "a bad attitude" or simply "an attitude." They set up an opposition between themselves and the school that resonates with larger themes of their culture. In the case of the lads, some of these themes were racism, sexism, and contempt for theoretical knowledge.

Willis refers to this process as "differentiation." The students experience this as a positive, liberating development. They are freed from caring what the dominant culture thinks of them and flaunt their identity in an in-your-face manner. The schools experience this as a breakdown. Remember the sulkers and steppers.

Teachers are understandably outraged by the breakdown and see themselves as victims of inexplicable rudeness. Rather than seeing the logic of the lads' rejection of make-believe school, they see the lads as incapable of participating in school. This, coupled with their anger, often results in belittling and sarcastic retaliation. Teachers tend to be facile with words and so their remarks can be very cutting. For example, here are two remarks Willis observed teachers address to their classes.

> The "Midwich Cuckoos" is about children with frightening mental powers—that won't concern us here.[12]
>
> Y has just asked me, "Do you have to do both sections?" The first section is instructions. It's a good job you didn't have to learn to breathe, Y, you wouldn't be here now.[13]

These remarks are interpreted as insults not only to the students themselves, but to their families and communities.

And so the students' subversion escalates, and the teacher's retaliation increases, and neither teachers nor students are conscious of the logic that instigated the entire process. Locally, the lads appear to win. On a society-wide scale they lose. Locally the teachers appear to fail. On a society-wide scale they are successful in doing what is expected of them. They handle the lads with a minimum of violent disruption.

One of the teachers in Willis's study seemed to understand this more consciously than most. He said,

I've never been one who thinks we are really teaching these lads.... I reckon it's careful containment. We give them little bits, you know, let them think they're big tough men getting their own way, but in all the important things they're doing what you want ... you know, don't confront them, let them think it's going their way.[14]

Willis observed that "the most horrific breakdowns" occur when young teachers innocently try to assert the real-school model of high-status knowledge in exchange for cooperation and hard work. "Nothing," Willis says, "brings out the viciousness of certain working-class cultural traits like the plain vulnerability of the mighty fallen. Nothing annoys [administrators] more than being brought in to sort out the wreckage."[15] The most successful teachers are those who make few demands in return for enough cooperation to maintain the appearance of conducting school—the make-believe school model.

Of course the switch to the make-believe school model is done largely by stealth. The steps taken and the real reasons for them are rarely understood—much less stated—by the teachers, parents, and students involved. The official position of the school remains largely the real-school model: high-status knowledge for cooperation. To admit otherwise would be to acknowledge institutionalized inequality—savage inequality.

Of course, if you go into any school you'll find a certain number of students whom teachers dread having in their classes, and I'm talking about rich suburban schools and elite private schools. There is certainly resistance in all schools, but there is an important difference. If the students' larger community values school knowledge either in and of itself or for its credential-producing value, student resistance finds little affirmation in the community among parents and other adults, or even among other students by and large. There can be little serious oppositional identity between the students' community and the school when the students' community controls the schools.

In fact, Willis studied ten resistant boys from "a high-status grammar school" at the same time he was observing the lads. While all the lads left school at sixteen, the legal leaving age, eight of the ten boys from the high-status school remained in school until the equivalent of "graduation." The resistance of these boys did not result in academic self-immolation as it did with the lads. Willis observed that "once a working-class boy begins to differentiate himself from school authority there is a powerful cultural charge behind him to complete the process."[16] On the other hand, when students from the middle and upper classes begin to differentiate, there are powerful community pressures for them to abandon the process.

However, Willis observes that some nonconformist middle-class students struggle to make their opposition "resonant" with the opposition of the lads, and insofar as they succeed, their futures suffer. On the other hand, he says, insofar as working-class boys *reject working-class culture* and become free of its processes and assumptions, their futures are likely to be enhanced from a middle-class point of view. This is a much better model for explaining social mobility than any notion of intelligence or effort.[17]

Like Ogbu's involuntary minorities, Willis's lads adopted an oppositional identity. As a point of honor, they identified certain mainstream characteristics as ones they would never adopt and certain characteristics of their own—ones the mainstream found offensive—that they would never abandon.

But I don't want to detract from the plight of the involuntary minorities by suggesting that working-class whites face identical obstacles. Due to their different histories and different social and economic circumstances, oppositional identity has different outcomes for involuntary minorities and Willis's lads. Oppositional identity tends to leave involuntary minorities in serious poverty, while the lads were heirs apparent to their fathers' secure union jobs. Buying into the "enemy" culture presents different perils to the two groups as well. Since there are no racial or even ethnic differences between the lads and the bosses, the lads might stand a better chance of being accepted by the dominant group should they decide to cross the border, and perhaps there would be less a sense of betrayal of their own group.

This may suggest that working-class schools stand ready to implement the real-school model any time students drop their oppositional identity and decide to cooperate; however, as the next chapters will demonstrate, once the make-believe school model is in place, it takes substantial pressure from outside the school to displace it.

Chapter 6

CHANGING CONDITIONS—ENTRENCHED SCHOOLS

L ois Weis studied a high school in an American community somewhat like the English city where the lads went to school twenty-five years ago. There were many similarities, but there were also important differences—the most important being that in this city, which Weis called "Freeway," the steel mills that had employed Freeway breadwinners for generations in high-paying jobs had closed a decade earlier. Weis called her study _Working Class Without Work._[1]

Weis never witnessed anything like a breakdown of order at Freeway High School. Students occasionally skipped class, but 94 percent of the students were in school every day. In some ways, however, Freeway boys were like the lads. When asked what they did not like about school, resentment toward authority was a major theme. Here we have a typical interview Weis conducted with a Freeway boy.

> **Tom:** I don't like the principals. Most of the teachers are assholes.
>
> **LW:** Why?
>
> **Tom:** They have a controlling power over the kids, or at least they try to. Me, I won't take shit from no one. That's the way I am.

(. . .) Whatever they do, they can't bother me, 'cause when I get my diploma I can say what I want to them.
(. . .) The kids should have some rights. Like, let me say for one example, I know there's smokers in this school. A lot of kids smoke. (. . .) To solve all smoking problems with kids going outside and skipping classes, give the kids at least once a day a place to go to—a room—and have one cigarette or something. Five minutes a day
(. . .) They [school authorities] play head games with kids . . . They think they can push you any which way they want.

LW: If they're pushing you around, why stay for your diploma?

Tom: 'Cause it helps for, like, a job or whatever. It's like a reference for this, this, this. It's like a key that opens many doors.[2]

On the other hand, Freeway boys were different from lads in important ways. First, the lads were confident that jobs like the ones their fathers had would be there for them when they left school. I suspect that Weis would have found many a lad in the Freeway High School twenty years earlier when the mills were open and an able-bodied man with a minimum of education could earn high wages doing dirty, dangerous, and physically demanding work—a "man's" work.

But the mills in Freeway had closed. Fathers found themselves unemployed or in safer, cleaner, physically less demanding jobs at much lower pay. The whole macho aura surrounding work in the mill was gone. The only jobs available that paid a "family" wage (one that enabled a *man* to retain the role of sole breadwinner in his family—a highly valued ideal among Freeway boys) required education beyond high school, and so Freeway boys did not express disdain for school and mental work as the lads had. They *said* they valued education, if only as a credential-purchasing commodity.

LW: What do you plan to do when you graduate?

Steve: Go to college.

LW: For what?

Steve: I haven't decided (. . .) I just wanna go. Can't get a job without going to college. You got to be educated to get a job, a good job; you don't want to live off burgers when you're old.[3]

Bill: My dad is a machinist. He needs one more day in the plant to get his twenty years. He's fighting now to get one more day.
(. . .) [I want to get to college] 'cause I see what happened to him. He's working for like seven/eight dollars an hour. Like [what] he used to get in the plant, compared to that, it's nothing. To get a better chance, you got to go to college.[4]

While 40 percent of the boys expressed an interest in going to college, only 27 percent of the seniors took the SATs, and the average scores for these students would not have gained them entrance to the state university. For most students this would leave open only the community college, which, generally speaking, prepares students for lower-status, lower-paying, white-collar work. Those who did not express an interest in college expressed an interest in *skilled* working-class jobs such as a mechanic, machinist, or tool and die maker. None of them expressed an interest in general, unskilled wage labor of the sort that does not require further training or education after high school. And so even these boys acknowledged the value of a high school diploma.

Girls at Freeway High School also expressed respect for education as a credential-purchasing commodity. In previous studies, working-class girls commonly expressed an "ideology of romance"—the belief that they will marry and have children with a man who will love them and take care of them, and that paid work is only something to do while waiting for Prince Charming. Not so with Freeway maidens. They thought first of establishing themselves in a career or job. Marriage and family were considered second, after a job or career was established. They rarely talked about marriage without mentioning the *probability* of divorce and the prospect of becoming the sole support of themselves and their children.

LW: Do you hope to get married; do you hope to have children?

Liz: After college and everything's settled.

LW: What do you mean by "everything's settled"?

Liz: I know where I'm going to live. I know what I'm going to be doing; my job is secure, the whole thing. Nothing's open. Everything's going to be secure.

Carla: Oh, I'm going to do that later [get married; have children]. I'm going to school to get everything over with. I wouldn't want to get married or have kids before that.

LW: Why not?

Carla: It'd be too hard. I just want to get my schoolwork over with, get my life together, get a job (. . .) I want to be independent. I don't want to be dependent on him [my husband] for money. Then what would I do if I got divorced fifteen years, twenty years, you know how people are and marriages. Twenty years down the line you have kids, the husband has an affair or just you have problems, you get divorced, then where is that going to leave me? I want to get my life in order first, with my career and everything (. . .) Maybe it has something to do with the high divorce rates. Or the stories you hear about men losing their jobs and not having any job skills, and you see poverty and I just don't want that. I want to be financially secure on my own.[5]

But although Freeway students had come to recognize the value of school credentials, they did not associate school credentials with acquiring knowledge. This was apparent in their attitude toward homework, as revealed from the following excerpts from Weis's journal.

[In a social studies class] **One student to another:** "Did you do this [homework]?"

Another student: "No, I missed it."

[Several others are saying they didn't do their homework.]

Second male: "Fuck. I remember in school and then forget at home." [He grabs the paper of another student and copies it.][6]

[In a social studies class] Mr. ——— walks around checking to see whether the worksheet is completed. They all show him the sheet. As I [LW] walked into the class, Charles was copying from someone. He had the two sheets on his desk. Ed shows Mr. ——— and I said, "Who'd you copy from?" He said, "Sam," and pointed across the room.[7]

[In a study hall] Nine A.M. Several students in the back of the room were either discussing homework, exchanging homework, or returning it after copying it. Technically, there is supposed to be no talking in study hall but almost everyone does.[8]

The language of "Passing" dominated Freeway boys' conversation. Most students earned Cs and Ds and appeared to be satisfied. This was more true of boys than girls, which is ironic, since it was the boys who talked most about the importance of education in preparing for a job that earned a family wage.

[In social studies] **Jerome:** [comes in all smiles.] "This is my last day in this class."

Paul: "Did you pass?"

Jerome: "I passed . . . I got a 68. [65 is passing] I passed!" [He is very excited.][9]

[In social studies. Ed gets his test back. He got a 78, a C.] Ed: [Smiling] "I like to see those passing marks."[10]

[In social studies] Teacher passes the test back. Paul turns the paper over fearfully: "I passed!" [with great happiness; he got a 66; 65 is passing].[11]

According to Weis the appearance of order in the classroom "masked complete nonengagement."[12]

Teachers also referred to the benefits of schooling, not in terms of the inherent value of knowledge, but in terms of what a school credential will buy. The following is taken from a social studies teacher's lecture to the class.

> Why does level of education prevent you from getting a job? Okay. If there are a hundred jobs on a page in the want ads, ten percent of these, you need an elementary education; forty percent of these jobs you need a high school education; forty percent you need a college education; ten percent of these jobs you need a college plus [education].
>
> The door system works as follows: If you have an elementary education, you can knock on ten doors. If you have a high school education, you can knock on fifty doors. If you have a college plus, you can knock on one hundred doors. Each time you have a piece of paper, you can knock on more doors. Each time you get more education, you can *try* [emphasis his] for more jobs. If you have college plus, you may not get a job, but your chances are going to be better.
>
> The people who live in the poor parts of town have less education and it is more difficult for them to get jobs.[13]

Some teachers explicitly stated to the students that the school credential was valuable only because the mills had closed. For example, Weis recorded the following incident in a social studies class. Notice the insult the teacher delivers that reflects on the students' fathers as well as themselves. It is reminiscent of the teacher's remarks regarding the "Midwich Cuckoos" in Willis' study.

> [There is] a long explanation of the electoral system; national nominating convention; campaigns; and elections. Mr. Sykes then hands out a work sheet on the topic, "Answer the five questions on the bottom. I'll see if you understand everything. Take about ten minutes. . . . If the steel plant were still open you guys wouldn't have to worry about this. You could crawl into some coil for an eight-hour shift and fall asleep and still get paid for it. That's probably one of the reasons why the plant closed."[14]

In virtually all classes, knowledge was distributed top-down, even to the point of telling students what line to write on and where to put commas. The following were typical of lessons observed by Weis.

Okay. Open up to page 11 [in the textbook] and get your notebooks out. Skip a line and write "Listening Test—suggestions on how to use your time." There are four steps involved with this.

Roman Numeral I in your notes. Write down, "During the first reading." Number 1. "Listen to the topic, usually stated in the first two sentences, and for the supporting details. Pay close attention to the conclusion which often stresses the main ideas." [This is directly from the book.]

Roman Numeral II. "During your reading of the questions," and [write down] just what it has on your page 11 there, "Your primary goal at this time is to become as aware as possible of all the questions so you will know the specific information to listen for." Roman Numeral III, next page, page 12, "During the second reading, the two things you are asked to do at this time are to listen to the passage and to write the answers. Of the two, the listening is the most important. You must keep listening." Underline the last sentence.[15]

Teacher: Take out your notebooks. The Title. "The Reasons for the Growth of Cities." Put that down. It is at the bottom of page 60. "A. Industrial Revolution"

(. . .) Skip a line. Take the next subtitle [from the text]. "B. Problems Facing Cities and Urban Populations." Take the next five subtopics under that. Skip a line between each.

Joe: Just one line between each?

Teacher: Yes.

Sam: Just the five?

[Time passes]

> **Teacher:** The public health department has two main functions: 1) enforcing health codes, and 2) to aid, assist and help those people who do get sick and cannot afford it.
>
> Put down the functions [in your notes] and then put down a "dash"; then put down "money" and a question mark. [16]

There was never any discussion of the question raised by Mr. Simon regarding the state's ability to support public health. It was simply a point in the prepackaged notes suggested by a "dash," the word "money," and a question mark. Students may have had no idea what was meant by this and perhaps no interest in knowing.

This type of classroom routine was well established at Freeway High. Students wrote notes in their notebooks exactly as directed by teachers. They were later tested on the notes and if they passed, they got credits. When they accumulated enough credits they were awarded a diploma that theoretically bought them admission to further job training in the military (a popular choice for both girls and boys), a trade school, or college (which they viewed as trade school).

At no point in this process was there any discussion, much less serious discussion, of the ideas or concepts contained in the original material—the material from which the teacher extracted the notes. When students asked questions they were for the purpose of clarification—not of ideas, but of the form of the notes themselves ("Just one line between each?"). The routine allowed students no ownership of knowledge, nor did it include any opportunities to engage in analysis, synthesis, or evaluation of abstract, theoretical, high-status knowledge as was evident in Anyon's affluent professional and executive elite fifth grade classrooms.

The only challenge to an idea that Weis observed in the entire year of observation was in the following exchange in an English class.

> **Teacher:** Okay, take out your notebooks. In your notes, just skip a line from where you were. Number 1. *High and Outside*. Author is Linda A. Dove, Setting: A town near San Francisco.

He proceeds to give them notes from the entire book, including characters, plot, and so forth, even though they read the book. [The form of "reading" the book was orally in class.]

(. . .) Skip another line and we get into Carl Etchen, Niki's father, who has treated her like an adult from the age of fourteen by including her in his wine tasting and afternoon cocktail hours. He was trying to protect her from the wild party drinking of other teenagers. But he unwittingly *caused* [my emphasis] her alcoholism.

Holly: How did he cause her alcoholism? [with skepticism; indicating that she understood that alcoholism is a disease and that one person cannot cause it to occur in another].

Teacher: I know what you're trying to say. What we're trying to do here is get some notes for the end of the year [state exams]. Maybe I should change the world "cause."

Holly: No, no.

Teacher: No, you're making a good point.[17]

Note that the teacher does not engage the student in a discussion but capitulates and states explicitly that his purpose is not to stimulate thought or discussion but to present material to be memorized for an examination.

The suitability of this routine at Freeway High went almost entirely unchallenged by either students or teachers. One teacher talked about the possibility of a different routine, but in the same breath he told Weis that when he tried it he was called down to the principal's office, not to be encouraged, but to be chastised.

Freeway parents *said* they wanted their children to go to college, but they didn't *do* anything to make it happen, and looked on with equanimity when their children did not make any moves to actually enroll in college. This attitude has been the norm among working-class parents for generations, as attested to in a book on Chicago steel workers.

Steelworkers may complain about the dirt and hours, but they take pride in their work. Sometimes directly, sometimes merely by example, their attitude is passed on. Key Wychocki [an informant in the study] expresses the contradictory emotions of a steelworker family, as he wryly notes that, "I can always remember my grandfather didn't want my father to work in the mill. And my father didn't want me to work in the mill. And I know I don't want my son to work in the mill. But, it was just taken for granted if your father was in the mill, you were in the mill. It was never thought of that you'd go anywhere else. Your father didn't want you to, but when you were of age and ready to go to work, he was the guy that got you the job, for crying out loud."[18]

This is thoroughly consistent with my experience. I talked about going to college all the way through high school and my mother (my father died when I was twelve) more or less acquiesced, but when I graduated from high school without having applied to any colleges and took a low-paying white-collar job there was no comment from anyone. I took a collection of night school courses in marketing and accounting and I suspect that everyone expected that this too would pass, and they would fix me up with a civil service white-collar job (we were not without "clout") when I settled down. But as I said before, I was something of a problem in that because of a birth injury, I could not follow the family trade—plumbing. My brothers, who were every bit as smart as I was, were marched right down to the union hall for an apprentice card the day they left high school. When I actually quit full-time work and part-time school for full-time school and part-time work, I received little encouragement. I always get a laugh out of my students by saying that my mother did not want me to go to college because she was afraid I would become an atheist and a communist, and so I went to college and became an atheist and a communist so as not to disappoint her.

But I think the dynamics of my failing to attend college right out of high school reflected a universal theme among the working class. My mother was proud of who we were and what we stood for, and she feared that if I went to college I would cut myself off and become different, and perhaps even become one of *them*—the social worker who lectured her for giving her children more oatmeal than they needed during the Depression, for example. This is a sadder memory, because once again mother was right—as was Thomas Wolfe who told us we can't go home again. I have not turned this into an anecdote to amuse my students.

But the situation in Freeway was different from all these, because of a huge structural change. The mills had closed. The way Freeway parents talked about their children going to college lost its tone of platitude and cliche and took on a tone of desperation. Their children *had* to go to college. Weis observed that the rejection of school and valorization of "man's" work has been a centerpost of the working-class male's identity for generations, but with the industrial economy crumbling around them, things changed. Working-class males no longer explicitly reject schooling. They even give lip service to the credential-purchasing benefits of education.

There was no hint from Freeway parents about fearing that their children would be turning their backs on a proud community if they went to college. Since the closing of the mill, there was no community to defend. It was gone. It was now a question of individual survival, and schooling was seen as the only way to survive. Although parents desperately wanted their children to go to college, they didn't know what to do about it any more than Chicago steelworker parents or my parents did a generation ago.

Parents blamed teachers and teachers blamed parents. The chief complaint of the parents against the school had to do with the schools' failure to help their children get into college.

Here are some parents' comments on the subject.

- I don't think they give them enough alternatives and tell them what is a good field to go into. They don't do enough testing on them.[19]
- Even for the SATs and stuff they were supposed to have some preparation for it and they didn't.[20]
- They really don't tell them anything. Like what scholarships are available or anything.[21]
- They could have preparation for SATs. I don't think they go into that enough. And probably more guidance.[22]

Teachers, on the other hand, blamed parents for not being involved in their children's education.

- [about parents] Just general negativeness toward education and educators. [To teachers] "You aren't doing

anything for my kid. You aren't doing anything for me."
Then they expect you to accept the burden of educating
their children without them supporting you.[23]

- I don't think [parents] really care 'bout the kids and even
this isn't saying too much for Freeway. A lot of people, I
shouldn't generalize, like when we would have, just an
example, PTA meetings in junior high, there would be
more teachers than there would be parents.[24]

And teachers continued to blame students. One teacher expressed
the following sentiments:

[A]s of tomorrow I'm going to be off for two weeks [at Easter
break]. Then when we come back the kids aren't going to
do any more work because it just shuts off. Before, they did
very little [work]; now they're going to do none, and then
the days are going to keep getting warmer, and warmer and
warmer, and we are going to go through the graduation cer-
emony where a couple of us are going to stand back there
and whistle the theme for the Laurel and Hardy movies as
they are marching up to the stage. Because that's bullshit,
too. And the kids are going to go up there with their paper
caps and gowns; somebody's going to open up his gown as
he gets his diploma and flash the whole audience wearing
a bikini or cotton cock or something like that, you know,
and at the end they're going to throw their little hats up
in the air, somebody is going to get hit in the eye with one
and that's it. That's what they think of education. It's a big
fucking joke.[25]

It's important to notice that the parents were not unhappy
with what their children were taught or how it was taught
to them. They were unhappy that the school did not provide
"preparation" classes where they would cram facts needed for
the SATs in the same "copy notes, memorize facts, and take the
test" fashion used to teach them everything else. However, Freeway High School did not offer the kind of education that would
enable students to get high scores on the SATs and to succeed
in prestigious colleges and universities. The makers of the SATs
do their best to insure that success on the tests is the result

of eleven years of schooling found in affluent professional and executive elite schools where intellectual autonomy, reasoning, mental agility, creativity, and high-status knowledge were taught and expected.

Weis suggests that a significant part of the problem at Freeway was that the teachers were working-class themselves, and were giving their students the only kind of schooling they knew— the kind they had received themselves. Every female teacher in the social studies department had a father, brother, uncle, or husband who had worked at the mills and every male teacher in the social studies department had worked at the mills at some point in his life. Some had been full-time, year-round employees in the mills before they became teachers. Previous work at the mills was viewed favorably by the school board and it was routinely mentioned on teacher employment applications.[26] Seven out of ten of the faculty had graduated from Freeway or from one of the local Catholic high schools. (Freeway is a very heavily Catholic city.) Seven out of ten of them had gone to one of three local colleges for both their bachelor's and master's degrees. A similarity of background between teachers and students is the rule in America rather than the exception. You may recall that this was true in Anyon's study as well.

The continuation of the make-believe school model—little demand for work in return for enough cooperation to maintain the appearance of school—in the face of a positive shift in student attitude and behavior may have been partly due to the fact that the faculty simply did not know what was being asked of them. If they went to schools like Freeway, as many of them had, their own schooling did not prepare them to employ the real-school model. If they were taught progressive philosophy and methods in their college teacher training courses, and they probably were, they would have been socialized into the "hard realities" of teaching in schools such as Freeway in their first years of teaching—by the students as well as the more experienced faculty.

R. Timothy Sieber[27] did a study that sheds light on these possibilities. Sieber came almost by accident upon a situation where

young upper-middle-class families (probably affluent professional) were moving into an Irish, Italian, and Puerto Rican
working-class neighborhood in New York City and renovating
classic nineteenth-century houses that are referred to as "brown-
stones." I will refer to these people as "Brownstoners."[28]

Although most Brownstoners sent their children to private
schools, somewhere under 100 Brownstone children were in the
public school—approximately twenty in each grade 1 through
5. The parents were apparently silk stocking liberals who felt
obliged to send their children to public schools. However, unlike
the parents of the Puerto Rican majority in the school (most
of the Irish and Italians sent their children to the local Catholic school), the Brownstone parents did not send their children
off to school and trust that the school would provide an appropriate education.

When Sieber came upon the situation there were four classrooms for each grade, labelled 1, 2, 3, and 4, ostensibly in order
of the ability of the students. The Brownstone children were all
in the 1 class in each grade. Other children were in 1 classes, but
only on a "space available" basis after the Brownstone children
were included. In these classrooms the progressive philosophy of
education and methods of teaching would remind you of Anyon's
affluent professional school. Classes were organized for part of
each day in what was called an "open" atmosphere. Children
worked in groups and had a measure of autonomy. Some initiative and creativity were allowed. Liberal amounts of time were
given to creative arts: poetry writing, painting, sculpting, crafts,
and creative dramatics. Materials were available in greater
quantity than in other classrooms in the school. They had some
materials that were probably not found in any New York City
Public schools at the time.

Children formally addressed the class regularly, making
reports, reading poetry, explaining their work, and carrying
on debates. In the upper grades children led class recitations,
taught lessons to classmates, and were sometimes permitted to
give their peers seat work assignments. They were expected
to give positive critiques of one another's performances. Control
of verbal behavior and personal demeanor was greatly relaxed.
Children could move about more and in some classes seats were
never assigned. Children were permitted to initiate and carry

on conversations with the teacher and their peers. Such "talking" was not permitted in other classes in the school. It was permitted here because the Brownstone children were considered by the staff to be "naturally more verbal."

Sanctions in Brownstone classes were "normative appeals" (We don't do that here, or, Everyone else is working; why aren't you?) or reasoning, and explicit moral teaching. In other classes discipline was accomplished through threats, taking away treats, supplies, materials, or privileges, and tight control over movement and student interactions. The superior status of Brownstone children was continually publicly affirmed. They occupied nearly all school-wide offices and public roles. They were chosen for academic competitions. Their art work went to district shows and adorned the pages of school publications. They were the lead performers in school plays. They were school monitors, crossing guards, and main office attendants. They sat in the rear of school assemblies—a position, they were told, "of greatest trust." They regularly received awards, prizes, and other forms of recognition during morning announcements, at assemblies, and at graduation.

But, Sieber discovered, none of this happened "naturally." It happened as a result of an energetic and relentless campaign on the part of the Brownstone parents, with considerable resistance from the teachers and some resistance from the other parents. And the battle wasn't over.

The Brownstoners were not natives of New York City. They had migrated there to work as professionals in law, architecture, advertising, finance, and the arts. Soon after the first Brownstoners purchased homes in the neighborhood, they formed a neighborhood improvement association whose activities centered around beautification, architectural restoration, and protection of the quiet residential character of the neighborhood. They soon selected a new name for the neighborhood, which replaced one that had working-class associations, and they had the area declared a Historic Landmark Preservation District.

Although only 20 percent of the Brownstone children attended the public school, the Brownstoners generally agreed that improvement of the public school was a key element in making the neighborhood attractive to further upper-middle-class settlement. The improvement association formed an education committee. First they gained regular access to the school. They organized a tutorial program for slow readers which brought them into the school on a regular basis. They volunteered to work in the school library. They studied school documents and gathered information on school practices and personnel. They invited school staff to late afternoon teas in their homes, pooling china, silver, and linens to impress the staff with their status. They made a concentrated effort to master educational jargon, which they believed the school staff used to exclude and patronize them.

When they arrived at the school there was a PTA, whose members included a handful of Puerto Rican mothers who were employed as para-professionals in the school and which was dominated by the teachers. In a well-orchestrated meeting, the Brownstoners elected their slate of officers and soon afterward redefined the PTA as a Parent Association; teachers were barred from membership. Brownstoners held all the nine positions on the Parent Association executive board except one, which they referred to openly as the "Puerto Rican slot." They claimed to believe that the Puerto Rican mothers were glad they had taken over because they were better at running an organization. The Puerto Ricans, however, said they were made to feel unwelcome at meetings and that when they attended they found that decisions had already been taken by the Brownstoners in secret. Although the Brownstoners blocked several attempts by Puerto Ricans to regain influence, they frequently referred to the Puerto Rican's apathy.

Before the Brownstoners arrived, students were "tracked" into four classrooms at each grade level based on scores on reading achievement tests. The Brownstoners' children tended to be placed in the 1 classes from the first, but as they established themselves they introduced an innovation, with the backing of the principal. Teachers of 1 classes were required to adopt more "open" organization and methods, and all Brownstone children were assigned to these classes because the new format was more in keeping with the progressive child-rearing philosophy of their parents. The Irish and Italians students who attended the school tended to cluster in the 2 classes while the Puerto Rican majority in the school were concentrated in tracks 3 and 4.

Everyone knew that some of the Brownstone children did not belong in the 1 classes on the basis of test scores, so the Parent Association began to downplay the hierarchical nature of the tracking system and emphasized that a "culturally appropriate curriculum," not test scores, was the operating principle for the tracking system. Soon afterward, the Parent Association succeeded in having the school drop the designations 1, 2, 3, and 4 and refer to classes by their grade and room number. The top second grade room was no longer designated 2-1; it became 2-107 (referring to the classroom number). The result of this was that the Brownstoners were guaranteed a place in the top classes and the spaces left available would be filled by the most able of the other children. You can be certain that the equivalent of the sulkers and steppers would not be counted among the "most able" regardless of their test scores.

As in Freeway, the teachers in this working-class school sprang from working-class roots themselves. They had mixed feelings toward the Brownstoners. They saw the children as bright and gifted, but as overprivileged and disrespectful. They saw parents as pushy, overbearing, and interfering. Many teachers whose seniority would have entitled them to teach the top class in a grade passed up the assignment because of parental pressure and interference. Teachers were particularly bothered by complaints about matters that they believed were trivial, among them, the teachers' tone of voice when addressing students.[29]

The teachers at Freeway did not know how to respond to the change in attitude on the part of their students and their parents. The Freeway parents and students probably did not understand what they needed, and they certainly did not know how to make the teachers respond to their newly found needs. On the other hand, the, teachers who were suddenly confronted with the Brownstoners' children didn't know how to respond either, but the Brownstoners understood what they wanted and knew how to bring pressure to bear. They got results. The teachers were not happy and the parents were not entirely satisfied, but the experience does give us insight into one way a school might be transformed from the make-believe model to the real-school model. Parents can insist on it, but that will take some doing when the parents are like those from Freeway rather than the Brownstoners.

But take courage! What's at work here are subtle mechanisms that, once understood, are not entirely overwhelming. Working-class people tend to use language in certain ways and share values, attitudes, behaviors, and beliefs that make make-believe schooling almost a certainty for their children and make it nearly impossible for them to understand or bring about change. They can learn to use language in different ways and adopt values, attitudes, behaviors, and beliefs (those associated with the gentry) that will make the real-school model possible for their children and empower them to bring about change.

But this can only work if working-class people want to adopt different values, attitudes, behaviors, and beliefs, and as we have seen, oppositional identity makes the whole process problematic. Paulo Freire, the author of *Pedagogy of the Oppressed*, whom I mentioned in chapter 1, has suggested an answer to this dilemma: that we educate working-class children like rich children—in their own self-interest.

In the next few chapters I'll discuss ways of using language, on one hand, and values, attitudes, behaviors, and beliefs on the other that promote the make-believe school model and leave working-class people comparatively powerless. In the last few chapters I'll discuss Freire's solution to the problem of educating working-class children in the face of oppositional identity. Read on.

Chapter 7

CLASS, CONTROL, LANGUAGE, AND LITERACY

In 1980 I was on sabbatical in Scotland. I was a visiting scholar at Edinburgh University working on a book on how to teach reading in elementary school. While there, I came across an announcement about a discussion group on the Brazilian educator Paulo Freire at the Workers Education Association of Western Scotland. The Workers Education Association's history goes back to the early-twentieth-century Fabian Society, a pacifist, left-leaning organization (right up my Quaker alley), including such worthies as George Bernard Shaw. It was later associated with the British Labour Party, and continues today as a somewhat independent organization.

I went, anxiously hoping to find a bunch of bricklayers and factory hands reading philosophy. Instead, I found a bunch of teachers and social workers, and, as advertised, they were reading Freire. I joined them.

It was a very important move. First, it introduced me to Freire. Second, I volunteered to address the group on what interested me at the time, the work of Basil Bernstein, an English sociologist who wrote about the British working and middle classes,[1] their language habits, how those habits affected their success in school, and the savage inequalities that resulted. I have come to see Freire as having the answers for dealing with the many subtle mechanisms I discuss in this book, but I won't get to him until a later chapter. My Bernstein talk was about explicit and implicit language and how they are related to values, attitudes, beliefs, and behaviors of two groups—the working class and the middle class. That's what this chapter is about.

When we are with our family and friends we naturally use implicit language. We rely on shared knowledge, feelings, and opinions when speaking to one another. For example, a man looks at a sweater on a chair in his living room and says to his wife, "Did you tell him what I said yesterday?" She answers, "Yes. But he didn't do it." He says, "Don't feel bad. It's not your fault." Although this is a perfectly clear communication for the husband and wife, it leaves many unanswered questions for the outside observer. The two are relying on context (the sweater apparently identifies the person they are talking about), shared information, and shared feelings. This kind of language is engaged in by nearly everyone when dealing with others with whom they are intimate or at least somewhat familiar.

An explicit rendition of the conversation might go as follows.

> **Husband:** Did you tell our son, Richard, who seems to have left his sweater on the chair again, that I said I would turn him out of the house if he did not call my cousin John and accept the job John offered him?

> **Wife:** Yes, I told him, but he didn't do it. I feel somewhat responsible because I've spoiled Richard and now he's totally incompetent and without ambition.

> **Husband:** Don't feel bad. I think he would have been incompetent and without ambition even if you hadn't spoiled him.

Bernstein believed that the British working class habitually use implicit language and the British middle class habitually use explicit language for reasons that can be traced to their cultures. And because the language of the school is typically explicit, the middle class has a great advantage in school and the working class has a great disadvantage.

The cultural characteristics Bernstein examined were attitudes toward conformity, styles of exercising authority, the amount of contact with "outsiders," and responses to pressures from outside the community—that is, how people deal with government, institutions, and agencies.

Where conformity is expected, where sex roles are rigid, where opinions are dictated by group consensus, there is no need to explain one's thoughts, beliefs, or behaviors. Communication is frequently possible by alluding to shared opinions and beliefs rather than by explicitly expressing them. In such groups communication tends to be implicit.

For example, when the TV networks declared the results of the presidential election in 1996 a cheer went up at the Democratic Party election-watch party in Buffalo. Now, a cheer is a good example of implicit communication. The reason it communicated was that everyone in the room knew what it referred to (it was bound to the context) and everyone present was expected to hold the same beliefs and opinions on that topic.

It is possible that some at the party were not wildly enthusiastic about Clinton's victory. They may really have been interested in the election of their brother-in-law to the county legislature and voted for Dole, but where conformity is the dominant theme, only consensus views tend to be expressed, and they go unchallenged. Under these circumstances meanings need only be implied or alluded to rather than stated explicitly. People who habitually engage in groups where conformity is the dominant theme develop the habit of using implicit language and expecting it from others. Conversely, they get little experience with using explicit language.

The news of Clinton's victory at the League of Women Voters, where people recognize that they represent many political positions, might have been greeted by the odd cheer, but not by a collective cheer. And those cheering might expect to be taken on by others whose reaction was somewhat less enthusiastic. Everyone would have to make his or her position clear in such a situation since no one could assume they knew the others' positions precisely. Where a variety of opinions are expected, explicitness is required. People who habitually engage in these kinds of groups get into the habit of using explicit language and expecting it from others.

The style of authority that is characteristic of a community also affects language habits. In an authoritarian setup, authority is invested in *position*—do what your father, the boss, or the teacher tells you because they are your father, the boss, or the teacher. In an authoritarian home or community there is little need for explicit language to control subordinates. On the other hand, in a more collaborative setup, orders are based on reasons and decisions are made more *collaboratively*. While those in authority may not encourage their subordinates to demand reasons, they are willing to discuss reasons for rules and decisions when they are challenged. Therefore, in a collaborative home or community, there is continuous need for explicit language.

Here we have two vignettes involving fathers and their teenage sons, demonstrating authoritarian and democratic styles of authority.

Authoritarian Style

Pop: Be home by 11.

Son: Why can't I be out till 11:30?

Pop: Because I said so.

Collaborative Style

Pop: Be home by 11.

Son: Why can't I be out till 11:30?

Pop: Because the streets are dangerous after 11.

Son: But they're not any more dangerous at 11:30 than at 11:00. Can't I stay out till 11:30?

Pop: No. You need to get up for school in the morning. Make it 11.

Son: But a half hour isn't going to make any difference.

Pop: I said 11, and that's that!

Whether the style of authority is authoritarian or collaborative is a matter of degree. In the first scenario the father had reasons that the boy probably understood: The streets get more dangerous later at night, and the boy has to get up for school in the morning. But this is not said, it's *implied*. In such relationships, much that is understood goes unspoken, remains implicit.

In the second scenario the father does not immediately resort to authoritarian statements. He states a reason explicitly, which gives the boy an opening to state explicitly what's wrong with the father's reason. This leads the father to defend his reasons or state a further reason, which in turn leads the boy to respond. Finally, the father resorts to his authority, but not before several explicit statements are exchanged.

We have no reason to believe that the one father has more concern for his son or that one father has less of a sense of his authority. The difference is in the style of authority. One style encourages the habit of implicit communication while the other style encourages the habit of explicit communication.

A third characteristic of groups that affect habits of communication is isolation. Where individuals rarely have occasion to deal with strangers, they tend to rely on allusion to shared experience for communication; where individuals must communicate with strangers frequently, they learn they cannot rely on shared experience; they cannot be sure of what the other person knows or thinks.

A number of years ago a group of sociologists went into a town in Arkansas after a devastating tornado—people had been killed and millions of dollars in property was destroyed.[2] When they interviewed people, they found that some people said things such as, "Well, it hit the Jones place and killed all of them and then it swung around down the creek and wrecked the church, but no one was in it." People such as the local doctor or the district judge were apt to say, "Well, the tornado first touched down three miles south of town. It hit the house of a family called Jones and killed them all—the parents and four teen-aged children. It then swung east and destroyed the Congregational church."

One version of that story assumes that the listener knows where the Jones place is, who the Joneses were (how many is *all*?), where the creek lies, and what church was down the creek. The second version makes none of these assumptions. The second version is much more explicit than the first.

According to the study, the difference between the people who did these two kinds of reporting of this incident was their relative isolation. People who were rarely in contact with others from outside their town, neighborhood, or place of work simply had no practice with talking to people who did not know where the Jones farm was or who the Joneses were, and so they didn't have practice at using language that did not rely on shared information. They were in the habit of using implicit language, and they expected it from the people with whom they usually talked. Such communities have been referred to as "societies of intimates."[3] The habit of communicating through implicit reference to shared information reinforces feelings of intimacy.

On the other hand, people who were explicit and did not rely on shared knowledge were people whose occupations and position in the town led them into frequent contact with people whom they did not know, people who lived far away, who were from different ethnic, social, and economic backgrounds. They moved in what has been referred to as a "society of strangers."[4] This led to the frequent necessity of using explicit language. They came to use such language habitually and to expect it from others.

The fourth characteristic of homes and communities that affects habits of communication is the prevailing attitude toward power in relation to the broader society. How do people in a community deal with government, institutions, and agencies? Where powerlessness is the dominant theme (You can't fight city hall!) there is little occasion to make plans, express them to others, and convince others to follow them.[5]

My first real dose of political activism came with the effort to nominate Eugene McCarthy as an anti-Vietnam war candidate for president on the Democratic ticket in 1968. My wife and I were invited to attend a meeting in a neighbor's basement where we were to learn how to gather signatures for a petition to put McCarthy delegates to the Democratic convention onto the ballot. I was an elementary school teacher at the time and I had fairly undisturbed working-class attitudes toward conformity, authority, and feelings of power. I had been married for only a few years, and, of course, it was my middle-class wife's idea to get involved with the McCarthy campaign. My response to the war was more along the "You can't fight city hall" lines—which is, of course, implicit and context dependent.

I went to the meeting with a pretty clear picture of what I thought would happen. I expected that an "expert" would get up and tell us what to do and answer a few questions, and we'd

all go home. To my dismay, the meeting lasted for hours. One
of the organizers got the meeting started and said only a few
words about the petitions he was holding, when someone made
a comment about the injustice and immorality of the Vietnam
war. I thought everyone in the room had the same opinion on
this topic; otherwise, why would we be here, and so I was surprised that the topic was even raised. But suddenly everyone
wanted to say *why* she or he thought the war was unjust and
immoral. Some thought it was because our soldiers were dying
for a cause that did not involve the vital interest of the United
States. Others were upset because of the psychological damage
that our soldiers were suffering because they were faced with
killing innocent civilians. Others insisted that the damage was
spiritual as well as psychological. Others were upset about the
Vietnamese being killed. Others thought the war did not pass
St. Augustine's test for a "just war." Others thought all war was
immoral, St. Augustine be damned.

I didn't think it was important that we decide which of these
views was most defensible, or even that they should be mentioned. I wanted the expert to tell me how to get the damned
signatures and go home. I wasn't used to "wasting my time" like
this and I resented it. In the neighborhood where I grew up,
people did not have meetings to oppose anything that the government did. It was commonly believed that there was petty cor-
ruption in the city government, but living in an Irish Catholic
neighborhood we believed we had "clout," (a word that originated
in Chicago), and therefore we got a little more than we deserved,
and so we had nothing to complain about. If we were annoyed
that garbage collection was not as good as it was in Mayor Daley's neighborhood, or that our streets went unrepaired longer
than other neighborhoods, we'd say, "You can't fight city hall," or
"It's not what you know, it's who you know," or "It's all politics."
Now these are colossally implicit statements. There is a world
of presumably shared knowledge and attitudes behind each of
them. They do not invite challenge, discussion, or nuance.

If we did get upset enough about something that "the powers
that be" (another highly implicit phrase) were doing, we didn't
form alliances among ourselves, much less with comparative
strangers. We went to the Democratic precinct captain whom we
thought of as being one of us, but having access to power. He knew

the right people. We didn't have to go into details in expressing our complaint to the precinct captain since we rightly believed that he knew us well enough to understand our concerns. To this day I can picture and I remember the name (Harry Painter) of our precinct captain, but I don't think I ever saw or knew the name of the alderman who represented our ward.

In communities where people feel powerless, they have very little necessity for using explicit language. They get into the habit of using implicit language and they come to expect such language of others. The people I found myself among in 1968 had a different attitude toward power. They thought that what they knew and believed counted, that they could fight city hall, and that they had the political savvy to get what they wanted or at least put up one hell of a fight.

They were accustomed to joining together with comparative strangers (often absolute strangers) to bring pressure to bear on institutions—even the military-industrial complex and the United States government. They were used to dealing with strangers, and so they understood the need to state their positions explicitly, to find common ground, and to plan unified action. They were not used to being dealt with in an authoritarian manner, and so the man who called the meeting could not tell them to pipe down and listen to the expert.

Getting them to *act* together was the hard part. When ten of them met to discuss a problem, there were ten interpretations of the problem and ten plans for solving it. Developing consensus and a plan where each would play a part demanded explicit language and lot of it. In communities where people feel powerful, they get a lot of practice in using explicit language; they get into the habit of using it, and they come to expect it of others.

I have become accustomed to the discussions that I considered a waste of time in 1968, and now I frequently engage in them myself. I have entered a new culture, but it wasn't easy. I still get bored with such discussions and find those who seem to thrive on them a pain in the neck—an implicit, context-dependent bit of analysis to be sure.

Of course, you see where all this is going. If you're poor or working-class, you're likely to feel powerless and be accustomed to a society of intimates where conformity is expected and where parents, teachers, and bosses are authoritarian. As a result you are likely to be accustomed to using implicit language and unaccustomed to using explicit language. You are also unlikely to have much experience with negotiation. If you're expected to give orders or take them without much discussion, if you live among people who think and act like you, and if you're expected to conform, and you feel powerless, there is not much occasion for negotiation.

On the other hand, if you're affluent, you're likely to feel powerful and be accustomed to a society of strangers where nonconformity is expected and where parents, teachers, and bosses are collaborative in their exercise of authority. As a result you are likely to be negotiating all the time and be accustomed to using explicit language because explicit language is the language of negotiation. The more affluent you are the more likely this is to be true.

Of course, rich people don't use explicit language constantly. Although they spend a lot of time in a society of strangers, they also have families and friends among whom they can be as implicit and context dependent as the most working-classed of the working class. The conversation about the son who is incompetent and without ambition might have occurred in the home of the CEO or a floor sweeper at General Motors.

Nor is the working class incapable of using explicit language. There is a story of a woman who was on the first day of a job as a collector at a rural exit on a toll road. A motorist asked how to get to the Friendship Baptist Church, and she told him to turn left at the pond. The person breaking her in overheard this and pointed out that the pond was dry in August, so the motorist would not know when he had come to it. The toll collector laughed and said she just hadn't thought about that; she was accustomed to talking to people who knew where the pond was— wet or dry. Thereafter she referred to a different landmark to identify the road that led to the church, and she became accustomed to the fact that, when giving directions, she could not rely on motorists' knowing what she knew about the community.

When it comes to schooling, the working class suffers because of the dynamics of class and language in two ways. First, their habitual use of implicit, context-dependent language, and their relative lack of comfort in using explicit language puts them at a tremendous disadvantage in terms of acquiring higher levels of literacy that rely on highly explicit language. Second, their style of authority and their attitude of powerlessness in dealing with institutions and agencies explain why they wind up in classrooms like Anyon's working-class classrooms, those in Freeway High, and in the classrooms where the Irish, Italians, and Puerto Ricans remained in the Brownstoner's school. Conversely, class-related attitudes and behaviors regarding authority and power explain why the Brownstoners were able to get a kind of education for their children that leads to admission in upscale colleges, but the Freeway parents were not.

The language of the school, especially the language of school books, is explicit. The explicit language that more affluent children learn at home prepares them for the ever so much more explicit language of the school, particularly the language of books. The implicit language that working-class children become accustomed to at home doesn't. Children's scores over time on standardized reading tests bears this out. At the end of first grade, when reading tests are essentially tests of word recognition, there is a statistically significant but low correlation between children's reading scores and the status of their parents' occupation.

The language of first graders' books is not like regular books; it's not like the language typically associated with school. It is context dependent—usually about pictures on the same page. It's personal—childhood centered. It does not contain information children are not already expected to have. It's about puppies that get lost and trips to the supermarket with mother. It's redundant. It is much more repetitive, in fact, than normal speech.

But by fourth and fifth grades the language of the texts becomes more and more like the language of regular books. It's impersonal. It has information children are not expected to have. It's about topics that are far removed from everyday life—like the history of the Civil War or the process of photosynthesis. It's accurate, precise, and explicit.

By fifth grade the correlations between reading scores and the status of parents' occupations are considerable.[6] Not that all working-class children do poorly or that all rich children do well, but it would be very safe to bet that the average reading score for one hundred randomly selected affluent kids would be considerably higher than the average reading score for one hundred randomly selected working-class students. It's here that more affluent children's familiarity with explicit, context-independent language pays off, and it's here that the working class's habitual use of implicit language becomes a real handicap.

As working-class children progress through school, their reading scores fall farther and farther below their actual grade level. We presume they don't have the basics, and we give them more phonics. They don't need more phonics. They need to be introduced into and made to feel welcome in a community where explicit language makes sense, where it's necessary—a community where nonconformity is tolerated and even encouraged, where authority is exercised collaboratively, and where students do not feel powerless, where they have choices regarding the topics they will study and the materials they will use and where they are given freedom to work with others (preferably from backgrounds different from their own) and to move around the room. Such classrooms make negotiation possible and even necessary.

This describes affluent professional and executive elite classrooms and the kind of classrooms the Brownstoners were trying to get for their children. The style of authority and use of power in such classrooms is similar to that which tends to be found in professions and at the management level of corporations and institutions. The people involved have a pretty clear idea of who gives orders and who takes them, but power, authority, and control appear to be, and often are, diffuse—distributed and rearranged in subtle ways. This is the style of authority and control that you might expect to find in many affluent professional, executive elite, and Brownstoner's homes. Therefore, when progressive, collaborative methods are used with children from professional and managerial homes they have a reasonable chance of working.

But what of students who come from less advantaged communities? Their parents are not professionals or managers. They are hardhats or factory or clerical workers or tradespeople or unemployed. They live in a world where lines of authority are clear and ever-present. Their cooperation is garnered more often by threats of reprisals than by appeals to self-interest. In such an atmosphere cooperation is grudging. Resistance often lies just beneath the surface.

The lads, the Freeway High schoolers, and Bernstein's working class expect insistence on conformity and authoritarian control in school. They are likely to view a progressive, collaborative classroom as one where no one is in charge, and that spells trouble.

"Successful" teachers in working-class schools are often working class themselves, like the teachers at Freeway high school, the teachers in the Brownstoner's school, and myself thirty years ago, who share the students' attitudes toward conformity and authority. Or, like some of the teachers in the lads' school, they are middle class teachers who take their cues from the students and give them what they seem to expect and to which they respond well. Conformity is demanded; the teacher is authoritarian; the children are given little or no choice, no freedom to move, no power. Because the children are all from the same background, there is no possibility that they might learn to communicate with others who are unlike them, but it wouldn't matter if there were children from different backgrounds since they are seldom permitted to work with one another. The classroom replicates the students' homes and communities.

Of course, working-class, middle-class, and gentry children often find themselves in the same schools and classrooms. My wife made an interesting discovery a number of years ago when she videotaped reading classes in a first grade classroom in a small town in western New York where there was a wide spectrum of social classes in the same classroom. When the teacher began the reading lesson with the "top" reading group, numbering about nine, she called the children to the reading circle; she sat down in her chair a few feet from the nearest child and said, "Open your books to page forty-two." She waited and watched as they opened their books and said something like, "Now who can tell me about the picture." And the lesson was under way.

When it was time for the "bottom" reading group, the teacher was suddenly on her feet. As she called this group to the circle, she moved around the room. She tapped children on the shoulder, picked up reading books and handed them to children, and ushered them to the reading circle. There were only six children in this group. The teacher pulled up her chair to where she could *reach* them all and said something like, "Open your books to page nineteen." But while she was saying it, she reached over and turned pages, gently pushed a child into a sitting position, said to another child, "That's good," because the child had her book opened to the right page and was seated properly, and finally the teacher put her finger on a word in a child's book and said, "Begin reading there."

Now this woman was a marvelous teacher. It was a pleasure to watch her. She was conscientious, creative, hard working. Her affection and concern for the children were obvious and genuine. She was quite clearly exhausted at the end of the three reading groups every morning, and most of her energy was spent on the bottom group. But what she was doing was relying almost entirely on explicit language to communicate with the top group. In the bottom group she was communicating to a large extent through manhandling the children and her language became very implicit and context-bound.

It is not unusual for the same teacher to conduct a very progressive, collaborative lesson with the top group and very traditional, directive lesson with the bottom group. Even when the method used in the two groups is ostensibly the same, the teacher's attitude toward conformity, her or his style of authority, and the amount of choice and freedom of movement and collaboration between the students changes dramatically between the top and bottom groups.

We were doing research on children in this class and we knew a lot about them. The children of the doctors and bankers tended to be in one group, while the children of the postal and steel workers were in the other group—and I don't need to tell you which was which. Of course, the segregation was not complete. In situations like this you will find some working-class children in the top group, and some more affluent children in the bottom group. When teachers make "ability" reading groups, they consider standardized test scores, particularly at the beginning of the year. But as the year progresses other factors are considered.

As I said, the top group had nine children and the teacher exercised a collaborative style of management, one that I would associate with more affluent homes. Children who did not respond to this style, those who were disruptive or nonproductive in this group would soon be reassigned. If they were very disruptive, they would probably wind up in the bottom group where there were fewer children and where the teacher's style was much more authoritarian. And so the working-class children tend to gravitate toward the bottom group, regardless of their reading scores, and the more affluent children and border crossers tend to gravitate toward the top group regardless of their reading scores.

This is not the result of racism or class warfare. In fact, these were all white children, and I don't think the teacher had any nefarious motives. She just responded to the language and behavior of the children without, I am sure, a thought of their parents' occupational status. She did what she thought any good teacher would do.

The resulting inequality—empowering education for some and domesticating education for others—is about as savage as any I can think of, but it's much harder to pin down. It is much more difficult to know where to direct your anger. The easy (but I believe incorrect and ultimately self-defeating) answer is to shout conspiracy. But subtle mechanisms deny working-class children access to higher levels of literacy work so well—even when there are competent teachers and reasonable resources—that there is no need for conspiracy. Savage inequalities persist because a lot of well-meaning people are doing the best they can, but they simply do not understand the mechanisms that stack the cards against so many children.

Of course, this is all a little too pat. Affluent people can be very authoritarian and insistent on conformity, and poor people can be very collaborative and tolerant. Rich people can be very intimidated by institutions and agencies and poor people can be ready to take them on at a moment's notice.

So, Okay, it's a little stereotypical, but my students frequently comment on how much it helps explain what they see every day in their classrooms. Some seem to regard it as an epiphany, the old "scales dropping off the eyelids" phenomenon. I thought of it that way thirty-five years ago when I first read Basil Bernstein, and although Bernstein has his detractors, I haven't seen anything that's changed my mind since.

Chapter 8

WHERE LITERACY "EMERGES"

Okay, you're convinced that the cards are stacked in favor of the gentry and against the working class, but there's more. For several decades linguists, psychologists, and educators have been observing infants from birth and noting their earliest communication with others (usually their parents, more usually their mothers), the beginnings of language, and finally their involvement in written language—all of this before school age, and for some children, long before school age. As we will see, this process, which is referred to as "emergent literacy," is ideal preparation for success in school. It's all quite wonderful but, alas, the whole picture is based on observing the child-rearing practices of the middle class and the gentry.

An idealized version of "emergent literacy" looks like this. Only hours after birth, children react differently to spoken language than to other sounds—even rhythmic sounds like music. Infants show more interest in people than in inanimate objects. In the first several weeks of life, children show a preference for looking at human faces and respond differently to familiar and unfamiliar faces. Infants direct their earliest and most elaborate spontaneous behavior toward people.[1]

The emergence of conversation can be traced to the first few weeks of life. From birth the parent is attentive to the gestures, vocalizations, and changes of gaze initiated by the child and responds to them. Molly may fling her hands up near her face, and her mother imitates her and says, "Whoops!" Molly spits up milk, and her mother wipes her mouth saying, "What a little piggy!" The parent looks at the infant and, following the child's gaze, points at, touches, or picks up the objects the child is looking at. This kind of interaction is believed to be the beginning of conversation. In repeated "conversations" revolving around the routines of feeding, changing, and bathing, words are frequently matched with ongoing activities.

The cries, gurgles, coos, and vocalization of newborn infants are undoubtedly instinctual. Although they may have no intentional meaning for the child, parents constantly watch for meaningful signs. When Harry cries, does he need a clean diaper? Does he want to be held? Does he need to be burped? When Sarah coos, is she happy to see Mommy? Does she feel comfortable in her fresh diaper? Does she like being cuddled?

Adults impose meaning on the sounds and behavior of the child and respond with appropriate behavior. Child-initiated behaviors are followed by parental responses in regular and repeated patterns. Soon the child begins to act as if he or she has caught on to the relationship between behaviors he or she initiates and the response of the adult.

Soon children cry *because* they want their diapers changed; they coo and smile *because* they feel warm and dry and safe in their father's arms; they look from their mother's eyes to the toy on the floor *because* they want her to look there too. As early as six weeks, parents begin to interpret the child's facial expressions and changes of gaze as both meaningful and intentional.

Language begins when a particular vocalization takes on a particular meaning (or meanings). When little Sarah begins to say *uh, uh* when she wants to be picked up and *ba* when she wants milk, another monumental event has occurred. She is using speech sounds to communicate meaning. That is language, in a sense, but there is one more hurdle to jump. Children are born into societies that have language. There are conventional words for expressing meanings such as "pick me up" and "give me milk." Children apparently notice that everyone around them has words for certain meanings that are different from their own. When Sarah abandons *uh, uh* in favor of *up* and *ba* in favor of *milk*, she's got language.

Researchers have collected hundreds of hours of audio tape of toddlers with their parents to gain insights into language acquisition. Here are a few examples.

First we have Mark, age twenty-three months, in the kitchen with his mother and younger sister Helen. Mark is looking in a mirror and sees reflections of himself and his mother.

Mark: Mummy. Mummy.

Mother: What?

Mark: There ... there Mark.

Mother: Is that Mark?

Mark: Mummy.

Mother: Mm.

Mark: Mummy.

Mother: Yes that's Mummy.

Mark: Mummy. Mummy.

Mother: Mm.

Mark: There Mummy. Mummy. There ... Mark there.

Mother: Look at Helen. She's going to sleep. (long pause)

(*Mark can see birds in the garden.*)

Mark: Birds Mummy.

Mother: Mm.

Mark: Jubs. (Mark's word for birds)

Mother: What are they doing?

Mark: Jubs bread.

Mother: Oh look. They're eating the berries, aren't they?

Mark: Yeh.

Mother: That's their food. They have berries for dinner.

Mark: Oh.[2]

Mom's utterances are simple in form and restricted to topics arising from the immediate context. She comments on topics Mark introduces. She follows his lead by asking questions, restating what he has said, and adding new information to support and extend the topics he has introduced. This practice is called "leading from behind" or "scaffolding." Notice that when Mom introduces a topic ("Look at Helen."), Mark makes no response and she drops it.

Researchers have questioned parents such as Mark's mother about their intention to teach their children in conversations like this. They reply that their aim is not to teach, but merely to communicate effectively. They speak in simple utterances so their children will understand. They question and rephrase to check on what the child means and to keep the conversation going. However, when they use words that may be new to the child (such as *berries*), they exaggerate them and repeat them.

Two months later Mark and his mother are in the kitchen again and they have noticed a neighbor working next door in his yard.

Mark: Where man gone? Where man gone?

Mother: I don't know. I expect he's gone inside because it's snowing.

Mark: Where man gone?

Mother: In the house.

Mark: Uh?

Mother: Into his house.

Mark: No. No. Gone to shop Mummy.

(*The local shop is close to Mark's house.*)

Mother: Gone where?

Mark: Gone shop.

Mother: To the shop?

Mark: Yeh.

Mother: What's he going to buy?

Mark: Er—biscuits. [cookies]

Mother: Biscuits, mm.

Mark: Uh?

Mother: Mm. What else?

Mark: Er—meat.

Mother: Mm.

Mark: Meat. Er—sweeties. Buy a big bag sweets.

Mother: Buy sweets?

Mark: Yeh. M—er—man—buy. The man buy sweets.[3]

Once again Mom scaffolds or leads from behind. She takes Mark's topic and, realizing he has invented a reason for the man's disappearance, helps him to develop an account of a shopping trip by asking what the man bought. The resulting "story" is a collaborative effort.

Five months later the following conversation took place.

Mark: All right you dry hands.

Mother: I've dried my hands now.

Mark: Put towel in there.

Mother: No, it's not dirty.

Mark: Tis.

Mother: No, it isn't.

Mark: Tis. Mummy play. Play Mummy.

Mother: Well, I will play if you put the top on the basket.

Mark: All right. There. There. Play Mummy. Mummy come on.[4]

In this short exchange Mark regulates his mother's behavior ("you dry hands") and gets her to do something for him ("Mummy play"). These are forms of persuasion. It's interesting that Mark responds appropriately to Mom's conditional sentence ("I will play *if* you put the top down on the basket"), which seems like a pretty tall order for a two-and-one-half-year-old, but he doesn't supply articles (Put **[the]** towel in there), a task that seems so easy. But Mom does not focus on his mistakes and failures. She focuses on the jobs he is attempting to accomplish with language and cooperates by responding in both language and in action to his meaning.

Next, we have Nigel, a two-year-old who had been at the children's petting zoo with his father earlier in the day. While he was petting a goat, it began to eat the lid to a cup Nigel was holding with his other hand. The keeper rushed over and said the goat must not eat the lid—it would not be good for him. That evening Nigel started a conversation with his parents.

Nigel: Try eat lid.

Father: What tried to eat the lid?

Nigel: Try eat lid.

Father: What tried to eat the lid?

Nigel: Goat . . . man said no . . . goat try eat lid.

Then, after a further interval, while being put to bed:

Nigel: Goat try eat lid . . . man said no.

Mother: Why did the man say no?

Nigel: Goat shouldn't eat lid ... (shaking head) good for it.

Mother: The goat shouldn't eat the lid; it's not good for it.

Nigel: Goat try eat lid ... man said no ... goat shouldn't eat lid ... (shaking head) good for it.[5]

Nigel is trying to tell a story, but he is not quite up to it. His parents ask questions and repeat his not-quite complete sentences, and in the end, he gets it together, more or less. His parents count it a great success. They don't feel they need to work on his last version of the story. It's a terrific accomplishment, and when he's ready, with their scaffolding, he'll improve on it. In both Mark's and Nigel's homes the parents try to help the child accomplish his goals and their efforts are collaborative rather than directive.

In homes like these, exposure to books seems to flow naturally from the talk parents engage in with their children. For example, next we have two-and-a-half-year-old Emily on her mother's lap. Mom is holding a book entitled *Rosie's Walk*.

Mother: *Rosie's Walk* by Pat Hutchins.

Emily: Pat Hutchins.

(*Mother reads that a hen named Rosie went walking in the yard.*)

Mother: What's happening?

Emily: What?

Mother: What's the fox doing?

(*Picture shows the fox jumping toward a rake.*)

Emily: He's trying to catch Rosie.

Mother: Do you think he's going to catch her?

Emily: No.

(*Mother turns page.*)

Mother: What happened?

(*Picture shows the fox hit by the rake.*)

Emily: He banged his nose.

(*Mother reads that Rosie walked toward a pond.*)

Emily: Uhmm.

Mother: What will happen next?

(*Picture shows the fox falling in the pond.*)

Emily: He's gonna splash!

(*Mother reads that Rosie walked by a haystack.*)

Emily: Uhmm.

Mother: What happened?

(*Picture shows the fox covered by hay.*)

Emily: He fell in a "stick" of hay.

Mother: And Rosie kept right on walking.[6]

This exchange continues in a like manner as the book describes Rosie's walk past a flour mill, under a fence, and past a beehive. As soon as the book is finished Emily asks for more and chooses another book.

Emily: This one.

Mother: Which one? This one? *Good Night Owl?* [In a formal reading tone] *Good Night Owl* by Pat Hutchins. This one's by Pat Hutchins, too. She wrote *Rosie's Walk.*

Emily: She wrote it by Pat Hutchins![7]

Soon children like Mark, Nigel, and Emily begin to "read" books to their parents. They look at the pictures and the print and take on a distinctive "reading" voice and they intone the story they have learned by having it read to them over and over again, sometimes word for word. They recognize print around them and begin to "read" it. When shown a Crest Toothpaste box by an experimenter, three-year-olds reported that it said "Brush your teeth," "Cavities," and "Its called Aim." Some of them even said "Crest Toothpaste."[8]

They begin to "write" as well. When asked to "sign" their art work, they produce marks in a line, and they produce approximately the same marks each time they are asked to sign. By the time they are in kindergarten they have some pretty sophisticated notions about writing. A five-year-old kindergartner named Ashley[9] "wrote" a "story" that looked something like Figure 8.1.

When her kindergarten teacher, asked her to "read" the story, her intonation and delivery conveyed the idea that the letters at the top of the page are the title and the drawing is the story itself. Ashley "read" the story as follows:

Figure 8.1

The Runaway Elephant

The elephant squirted her and the girl couldn't find the elephant. But she finally found the elephant and they were friends again.

Ashley's concept of "story" includes introducing characters and narrating some action. She has even introduced a problem and a resolution. Her concept of writing a story is to make marks on paper that represent the story she has created. She has shown an understanding of conventions—the title comes first at the top of the page followed by the story itself. For a child who can't write, Ashley shows a remarkable understanding of story form and literary conventions.

This research shows that some children exhibit reading and writing behaviors in the informal setting of home and community long before they start formal school instruction. Such children take to school like a duck takes to water. They thrive with teachers who encourage them along their path of discovery, rather than insisting that they be "introduced" to the sounds of the letters *c*, *a*, and *t* before they are presented with the word *cat*. Even if they have a more traditional teacher they wind up in the top reading group where the teacher is more collaborative and where the children are given more freedom.

Rosy picture, eh? But unfortunately, we all know that not all children have the idealized experience portrayed in the emergent literacy literature. For example, Shirley Brice Heath[10] observed people in two communities[11] in South Carolina. One was a community of professional people in a small city; the second was a community of white textile mill workers who lived nearby. Adults in both communities placed high value on success in school and urged their children to "get ahead" by doing well in school. However, the children in the two communities had very different experiences in school.

Heath refers to the professional small-city folks as Maintowners. They include both African Americans and whites. Their social interactions center, not on their immediate neighborhoods, but on voluntary associations such as the Elk's Club, Masons, YMCA, Junior League, churches, and tennis and swimming clubs across the city and region.

Maintowners are in constant contact with strangers in their occupations. They turn to professionals for advice about everything from marital problems to landscaping. They make phone calls to people they do not know to get information, complain about service, and make demands on officials and politicians.

Maintown children form associations and friendships with the children of their parents' friends and associates. They spend practically no time hanging out in the 'hood. Their out-of-school activities—music and dance lessons, Boy Scouts, Indian Guides, baseball, swimming, tennis, horseback riding—are planned as rigorously as the school day. Because of their numerous out-of-school opportunities, Maintown children acquired an air of accomplishment and entitlement. It was quite clear that Maintown children are at ease in a society of strangers and that they sense that both themselves and their parents are not without power.

Maintown children grow up in an environment awash in reading and writing and reference to print. Adults around them read in many different circumstances. They read alone and in silence for pleasure and for instruction. At other times they read movie ads, game rules, or instructions for putting new purchases together in the company of others and they talk about what they are reading with those who are present. On other occasions they read aloud from newspapers, magazines, or letters from friends and family.

They rely on print rather than a face-to-face network for information and advice. They choose movies on the basis of reviews; they choose tires on the recommendations of consumers' guides.

Both men and women write both friendly letters and business letters. These include ongoing correspondences, summaries of the year's events to be included in Christmas cards, complaints about products or services, and lobbying letters written to politicians officials, and newspapers. These letters are often followed or supplemented with phone calls or meetings. Adults do a great deal of work-related writing at home. Managers draft reports and memos and write letters. Teachers bring home students' assignments and work on them and make lesson plans. Dinner table conversation refers to consulting professionals about writing tasks—a lawyer to write a will and a real estate agent to write a lease.

There are frequent discussions of writing "for the record." Maintowners formalized and spelled out in writing rules for group activities such as block clubs, church clubs, and senior class trips to Washington. Minutes of club meetings, signed petitions, news accounts, and letters are referred to and held up as having more authority than memory of what was said.

There is a great deal of discussion of schedules in Maintown homes. Rides need to be arranged. Dinner has to be fitted into everyone's schedules. A bulletin board by the telephone and date-books carried by the parents are used to record decisions. These written entries have greater authority than anyone's memory of what was said.

Maintown babies come home to their own room outfitted with a crib, playpen, bookshelves, dresser, toy box, and rocker. Parents place great importance on getting the child on a schedule of a morning and afternoon nap, three meals a day, sleeping through the night. They consult baby books to confirm their notions of when these routines should be accomplished as well as when the child should sit, walk, talk, and be toilet trained.

They consider babies conversational partners, not just from birth, but almost from conception. Expectant parents address comments to the baby in the womb. As soon as the baby is born, they talk to it. Older brothers and sisters are encouraged to talk to the baby. No one except the parents and immediate family is expected to fondle the infant. Talk is the preferred means of communication.

From the start, a new baby's physical and verbal environment is oriented toward literacy. Babies are given books. Their rooms are decorated with murals, mobiles, and stuffed animals that represent characters from books.

Questions account for almost half the utterances of mothers addressed to preschool children, and the most frequent of these are "display" questions—ones where the adult has the answer but wants the child to display its knowledge. Most of these questions are repeated again and again and on similar occasions, bed time, book reading time, or a romp with daddy before dinner. By age three, children begin to have experiences that their parents did not share, at play school or Sunday school for example. Children are asked questions about such activities, and they are expected to give truthful answers in straightforward narrative form.

Mothers begin to read to children as young as six months, and from that age, although they cannot yet talk, children give attention to books and acknowledge questions about books. The adult says, "What is that?" The child attends to the picture and makes a sound. The adult says, "That's Pooh Bear. What does Pooh Bear like?" The child attends to the picture and vocalizes and the adult says, "Pooh Bear likes honey."

With the onset of speech, book reading sessions take on the characteristics of the one reported between Emily and her mother reading *Rosie's Walk*. They are similar to other conversations between parent and child, except now the topic is not whatever the child wants it to be; it must refer to the book. At the end of these sessions, adults often ask children about their likes and dislikes and what they think about events depicted in the book, but they do not insist on answers.

Around age three, adults begin to discourage a child's interactive and highly participative role in book reading. Children learn to sit and listen and to hold their questions until the story is over or until the adult signals a break in the reading.

From the time they start to talk, parent-child conversations allude to books. Parents take every opportunity to relate ongoing events to books. When they see a fuzzy black dog on the street the mother asks, "Do you think that's Blackie [a dog in one of the child's books]? Do you think he is looking for a boy [Blackie was looking for a boy to own him in the book]?"

Maintown children learn that talk about books suspends a lot of rules. When they engage in book talk, they can interrupt adults who are conversing; they can say things that are not true, and they can divert attention from otherwise troublesome matters such as a plate of uneaten food.

Books and book-related talk count as entertainment. Waiting in the doctors' office or travelling on a bus, parents read to their children. If a book is not available, they talk about objects as if they were pictures in a book. What is it? What is it like? What features of it make it similar to or different from other objects the child knows about?

Around age three, Maintown children begin to attend Sunday school and nursery school. Here they learn to sit with others and listen until the story reader signals that it is time for questions or discussion. Then they can talk to the teacher or group as long as they stay on the topic and do not interrupt one another. They are permitted to talk to each other as long as they do so briefly, quietly, and on the topic at hand.

Factual questions about the content of the story are often followed by questions such as, "How do you know?", where children are expected to relate what they have learned to specific portions of the text or pictures. For example, the teacher might ask, "Whose bed did Goldilocks fall to sleep in? Can you find that picture?" Finally, children are encouraged to share knowledge that they are reminded of by the story—the mention of a desert reminds a child of his visit to Arizona; a story about a dog triggers pet stories—but they learn to hold such contributions until the end of the lesson.

Reading lessons in school are very similar to bedtime story routines in Maintown. First come factual questions—Who, What, When, Where? Only after these are answered do they proceed to "reason" explanations—Why, Why not, How? And finally they address questions of feeling—Did you like it? Why or why not? How did it make you feel? Thus, Maintown youngsters learn the Maintown way of taking meaning from books and Maintown ways of talking about the meaning taken from print. For Maintowners this seems natural. It's the only way they know, but since nursery school, kindergarten, elementary school, high school, college, graduate school, professions, management, and Western forms of wielding power are based on this model, it's the only way they need to know. In Maintown it is true that the hand that rocks the cradle rules the world.

Maintown seems like a case study for the cultural characteristics that lead to habitual use of explicit language. Authority in the home tends to be collaborative rather than authoritarian. Parents and children live in a society of strangers where little can be assumed about what your communication partners know or what they believe. Parents feel powerful. They rarely accept any situation where they feel put at a disadvantage without attempting to negotiate. Because of this example and because they are given many advantages, their children take on an air of entitlement.

᠗

I've talked earlier about the way a community's language (what is expressed, how it is expressed and to what purpose) is affected by characteristics of the community (accepted behaviors, values, and attitudes toward authority, conformity, and power, for example). Linguists refer to this whole package, the language and all the things that are behind it and underneath it as a discourse[12] and they refer to a community that shares a discourse as a discourse community. I've described several discourse communities in this book: The Athabaskans and Punjabis in Chapter 4, the lads' community in Chapter 5, the Thruway high school student's community in Chapter 6, Bernstein's working-class and middle-class communities in Chapter 7 and Maintown in this chapter.

We all get one discourse "free" at our mother's knee, so to speak. This is our primary discourse, the discourse of face to face oral communication with those close to us in the community where we start life. The primary discourse I acquired in my large, Irish, Catholic, working class, big-city family was somewhat different from the discourse I would have acquired in a large, Italian, Catholic, working class, big city family, and very different from the discourse my wife acquired in her small, generic "American," Protestant, middle class, suburban family.

As we sally forth we acquire secondary discourses, those of the play ground and Sunday school for example. Discourses are sometimes defined or arrived at in contrast or opposition to other discourses. The male chauvinist discourse and the feminist discourse are each defined in many ways in contrast or opposition to the other. The same is true of the discourses of management and labor, doctor and patient, student and teacher, for example.

Categories we are born into such as gender, class, and ethnicity determine to a degree the secondary discourses to which we will be exposed, and our ability to acquire the secondary discourses is determined to some extent by the degree to which it is similar to our primary discourse. But dissimilarity is not the main impediment to acquiring a secondary discourse as we saw in Chapter 4 with the Punjabis who immigrated to California but whose children seem to have little difficulty acquiring the discourse of the school. The real impediment to acquiring a secondary discourse is the degree to which its values and attitudes are in conflict with our primary discourse. This was evident with Ogbu's involuntary minorities and Willis's lads whose primary discourses are in serious conflict with the discourse of the school.

The primary discourse of Maintown, on the other hand, is similar to and congenial with school discourse. It is particularly consistent with the discourse of progressive classrooms as described in the affluent professional and executive elite schools. Therefore it's easy for Maintown children to acquire school discourse (so easy in fact that it seems natural). How can these children fail? Even if they are not particularly bright or energetic, most do all right in school and in the affluent professional and executive elite world for which their classrooms prepare them.

But, alas, the story is different for the children only a short distance away in Roadville.

Chapter 9

WHERE CHILDREN ARE TAUGHT TO SIT STILL AND LISTEN

Only a few miles from Maintown is a working-class community of textile workers, which Heath refers to as *Roadville*.[1] The people of Roadville like their town the way it is. Its rural setting gives them opportunities for hunting and fishing and offers a slow pace of life. They value their solidarity, their sameness. They believe that they are closer to each other and to their churches than people in other parts of the country. They are a community of intimates. One woman commented, "We, uh, mamma used to talk about how we [members of the community] were cut from the same pattern. We all knew what to expect." Another added, "We learned at church and at home too that things were either *right or wrong*; you did things the *right* way and you were *right*. You did wrong or said wrong and *everyone* knew it was wrong. Most everybody accepted that. Those that didn't just didn't fit in at all."[2]

Most Roadville parents regularly attend fundamentalist churches where they are reminded frequently to be strict with their children and to raise them the "right" way. Gender roles are clearly defined. Men support the family. Women stay home with the children, especially when the children are young. Even when women work outside the home, men are defined as the bread winners. Men decide on large expenditures for recreation and maintenance of the house; women decide on appliances and furniture.

Once beyond the age of two, boys and girls are separated for play. Beyond early ABC books and books of basic objects, toys and games are sharply differentiated for boys and girls. With the exception of toys for the very young, such as a post onto which rings of graduated sizes can be placed, educational toys are segregated as well. When they are older, girls help their mothers cook, can, freeze, and take care of younger children; boys help their fathers gardening, doing house repairs, painting, and working on the car, boat, and camper.

Roadvillers respect authority. They say, "Spare the rod and spoil the child," and they mean it. Talking back to parents is severely punished by strapping. They believe old folks know more than young folks, and men know more than women, although women are generally better educated than their husbands and are more likely to attend adult education classes. In Bible study, Roadville adults like to have the pastor, the person with authority, lead the discussion.

Wow.

Stories play an important part in Roadville. Stories are usually told in response to an invitation. "Has Betty burned any biscuits lately?" or "Brought home any possums lately?" are invitations to tell a story, one the speaker has heard but others in the group have not. The focus of a story is a transgression, a deviation from the behavior expected of a "good cook," "good hunter," or "good handyman."

The point of a story is often left unspoken. You don't say, "George is a bit of a know-it-all," although that's the point of the story. Everyone present knows that, and they are all good enough friends to have a laugh on George and yet remain his friends. They will not tell a story behind George's back that they would not tell in his presence.

In telling a story, individuals show they belong to the group. They know and accept the norms that were broken. One story triggers another and each reaffirms the familiarity of everyone in the group with the experiences being recounted. Stories are expressions of conformity and solidarity.

Roadvillers do not rely on print the way Maintowners do. They prefer to look to their own experience or the experience of one of their own for guidance. When Roadville families get a new game, they rarely look at the directions. Usually one of the children has played the game at a friend's house and he or she teaches the game to the family. In assembling toys, fathers often look at the directions, but then proceed by using "common sense." There is no discussion as the toy is assembled, except for an occasional implicit, context-dependent utterance such as "That doesn't look right." Women tend not to try recipes that have not been tried by friends, and when they do they usually make substitutions or change the directions, relying on the friend's experience rather than the printed word.

As in Maintown, babies in Roadville are typically brought home to their own room decorated in a nursery rhyme motif with a bed, changing table, dresser, book shelves, and toy box. During the first three months, a great deal of emphasis is placed on keeping a schedule for eating, napping, changing, bathing, and bedtime.

Mothers assign intentions to their babies' crying—because he's hungry, uncomfortable, or overtired—and talk to them from birth. Young mothers at home alone with their infants often strap them into their infant seat and move them from room to room talking to them as they work. All the parent's friends and relatives are expected to talk to the baby when they meet. Men who do not are forgiven for being ignorant about babies. Only little boys are not expected to talk to a baby belonging to a relative or family friend.

Parents scaffold their children's early attempts at language as we saw with Mark and Nigel, but there is an interesting switch. Unlike Mark's mother, who always scaffolded his meanings and dropped topics as soon as he lost interest, Roadville parents are more likely to stay with a topic long after the child has gone on to something else. Heath records an example of a mother and child who were making Christmas cookies. The child bit the head off a snowman cookie and said "noman all gone." This prompted a sixty-word monologue on the part of the mother despite the fact that the child showed no interest and chattered on about other topics concerning cookies, but not the snowman.

Adults invite children to tell stories to other adults and they carefully monitor them. Stories are to be told in strict chronology and any exaggeration is considered a lie. Important details, *as the adult remembers them*, are to be included.

For example, what follows is a transcription of a dinner conversation involving Sally, a four-year-old, her mother, and a teenage brother. Sally and her mother had been out that day and had a flat tire. Mr. Jones, the gas station man asked Sally to "help" him by counting the lug nuts as he took them off the bolts and put them into the hubcap. Shortly afterward Sally found a wounded cricket and built a fence of small sticks around the cricket and talked to it while Mr. Jones fixed the tire.

> **Mother:** Can you tell your brother what you helped Mr. Jones do today?
>
> **Sally:** We went to get gas, 'n there was this cricket, and he was in a field. I found some sticks to make one.
>
> **Mother:** But wait, wait, why did we go to the gas station?
>
> **Sally:** Mr. Jones helped us!
>
> **Mother:** Yes, but why did Mr. Jones have to help us? Come on, you know what happened.
>
> **Sally:** We couldn't go to the store. The car broke. 'n I found a cricket.
>
> **Mother:** What broke on the car?
>
> **Sally:** The tire broke.
>
> **Mother:** And did you help Mr. Jones fix the tire?
>
> **Sally:** Yes. The cricket was fun, but I had to leave 'im. I took down the fence.
>
> **Mother:** Well, let me tell you what happened to us. . . . [3]

Parents "taking over" in parent-child interactions is a marked departure from the middle-class model we saw with Mark and Nigel. Heath believes it stems from the fact that Roadville parents have a different attitude from middle-class parents regarding communication with their toddlers. Middle-class mothers scaffold to keep the conversation going. Roadville parents are much more conscious of their responsibility to teach the child to "pay attention, listen, and behave."

In Sunday school, children are also told "moral" stories, ones where a child is offered a clear-cut choice between right and wrong and does the right thing. These are followed by pertinent Bible passages. Occasionally children are asked to recount similar choices that they have made, but situational ethics—what if a person had to do a bad thing or something worse would happen—are strictly discouraged. When children start to suggest "what ifs" the teacher tells them to "pay attention to what the story says and don't go wandering off somewhere and making things up."

Play with toys by adults and preschoolers has strong elements of both language interaction and manual manipulation. While playing with rings that fit on a pole parents ask, "Where does this go?" "Does this go on next?" A father playing with a toy work bench might say, "This is a hammer, see, I'm gonna hammer Bobby's shoe. Hammer goes bang, bang." Bobby is then asked, "What's this, Bobby? Where does it go? How does it go [what sound does it make]?" and Bobby is expected to repeat the response exactly as it was taught to him.

Parents later tell the children stories connected with toys such as the work bench. The stories have morals or lessons such as "Don't put screwdrivers into electric sockets," or "Don't pound a hammer while daddy is sleeping." When an infraction occurs the parents asks, "What did I tell you?" and the child is expected to repeat the story and its moral.

By the time children reach age four, emphasis on educational toys and playing with children diminishes. Fathers begin to teach their sons to play ball and generally roughhouse with them. Language is either absent or implicit and context dependent when parents teach their children to do such things as hold a bat, wear a baseball mitt, make Jell-O, or sew an apron. Adults say, "Do it this way. This way! Not like that." "That looks right." "Next time, be more careful." Children say, "Want me to do it like this? Is this right?"

The way things are done at school in, for example, science or shop—listing materials, taking one step at a time, and so on—is not seen as having any relevance to doing tasks at home. Although occasionally an annoyed parent may say, "Can't you read? What are you going to school for?" the domains of home and school are kept separate by both the child and parents by the end of the primary grades.

Most one-year-olds are active participants in book reading. They find letters from their alphabet blocks in their ABC book. They name pictures and parts of pictures. They imitate sounds of characters in books. Although Roadville book-reading episodes are similar to those of Maintown, Roadvillers do not relate book reading to other events in the day. They do not, upon seeing a thing or event in the real world, remind children of similar things or events in a book and launch a conversation on the similarities and differences.

By age three, nearly all the children can pretend to read. They associate print on boxes and packages with the items they contain—Bugles, Animal Crackers, Crest Toothpaste, and so on.

For Roadville children there are three overlapping stages of experience with print before school. First they are introduced to discrete bits and pieces of books—the alphabet, simple shapes, basic colors, and commonly represented items in children's books such as apple, baby, clown, and doll. Parents ask questions and expect the answers they taught the children. If adults decide that a dog in a book is a *dog*, other answers—*a puppy*, *a mutt*, or *Blackie* are counted as wrong. During this stage there is full participation by the child who sometimes poses the questions and pretends to read to the adult.

During the second stage beginning around age three, books with story lines are introduced such as *The Three Bears* and stories with characters from Sesame Street. Parents and Sunday school teachers expect children to sit and listen to a story and not participate either verbally or physically. Bedtime stories become something of a struggle as the stories get longer and the mother's objective includes teaching the child to "learn to listen."

Around age four, the third stage begins. Children are given activity books such as follow the dots and push out and paste shapes and letters. They are taught to print their names and draw straight lines and stay in the lines in their coloring books. The children are constantly reminded that these are things they will need to learn before they go to school.

Also around age four, children begin to go to bed later and without any special routines. Many children are enrolled in church nursery schools. At this point parents comfort themselves that they have taught them "right" and set them down the road for school, which they must now travel alone.

Roadville parents seem to follow the emergent literacy script when their children are infants. Mothers attend to their babies' every sound and gesture and adults speak to infants from birth, but soon after they deviate from the script Mark and Nigel's parents seemed to be following. In conversation they follow the child's lead, but try to keep the child on the topic long after he or she loses interest.

Their book-reading episodes are not like Emily's experience reading *Rosie's Walk*. Parents start with alphabet books rather than stories and focus on teaching letter recognition. They are strongly focused on teaching the child to "pay attention, listen, and behave" from the start. Characters from books are not referred to while engaging in other activities with the children. Older children are taught to concentrate on *who, what, where*, and *when* questions in responding to stories. They are not taught to answer *how* and *why* questions, and they are explicitly discouraged from considering *what-if* questions.

Children's writing-like activities are confined to printing their names, drawing straight lines, and staying within the lines while coloring. A Roadville four-year-old is not likely to "write" a story like Ashley's "The Runaway Elephant."

When Roadville children go to school, they usually do well in grades one through three. They arrive at school knowing their alphabet, colors, and shapes. They sit still and listen and answer *who, what, when, where* questions. They do well in reading workbook exercises that focus on parts of words and specific information from the story. When the teacher asks at the end of a lesson, "What did you like about the story?" few Roadville, children answer. When she asks, "What would you have done if you had been Billy [a character in the story]?" most Roadville children say, "I don't know."

As they proceed through the grades, they continue to handle basic lessons satisfactorily, but they flounder when the lesson calls for independent action or thinking. When asked to make up a story they repeat stories from their reading books. They rarely provide emotional or personal commentary in recounting real *interesting*

events or book stories. They do not compare two items or events and point out similarities and differences.

Most Roadville children find hypothetical questions impossible. For instance, a fourth grade class is studying the culture of Hopi Indians on their reservation. The teacher asks what customs of the Hopi Indians might cause trouble if they moved into the city.

Roadville children answer by listing all the customs of the Hopi Indians *on the reservation*. All the "what ifs" have been drilled out of them.

Thus, by the time they reach fourth grade, the knowledge and habits that served them well in the primary grades begin to fail them. The teacher's talk and much of the material students are required to read become more and more explicit and context independent. The teachers' questions and assignments call for independent thinking and creativity, and the bulk of Roadville students have no way of keeping up.

Consistent with other studies of working-class students,[4] average and even good Roadville students do only the minimum of what is asked of them in school. They never seem to see the point of most of what they are asked to do. They see school as a place where you have to look up definitions all the time and then have a test, but they see no reason for using a word whose definition they learned in conversation or even in a school written essay.

Schools generally fail to help Roadville children see the relevance of school work to their lives. Although Roadville parents talk about the value of school, they often act as if they don't believe it. One woman talks of the importance of a "fitting education" for her three children so they can "do better," but looks on with equanimity as her sixteen-year-old son quits school, goes to work in a garage, and plans to marry his fifteen-year-old girlfriend "soon." In another family one daughter is going steady and everyone expects she will quit school and get married when she turns sixteen, and a son talks of going to college on a baseball scholarship, but admits he hates school. Yet the parents of these children talk about the prospect of their children going to college without any hint that they see a contradiction between their aspirations and their behavior.

By the time Roadville children reach high school they write off school as having nothing to do with what they want in life, and they fear that school success will threaten their social relations with people whose company they value. This is a familiar refrain for working class children. It is a milder version of the oppositional identity Ogbu described in involuntary minorities.

Roadville seems like a case study for the working-class discourse community described by Bernstein. Roadvillers live in a community of intimates where conformity is expected. Parents are authoritarian. Language is implicit and context dependent. The point of stories is implied, not stated. When parents teach children, they *demonstrate* skills and say context-dependent things such as, "Do it like this."

The discourse Roadville children acquire in their homes and communities is dissimilar and in serious conflict with the discourse of the progressive classroom as described in the affluent professional and executive elite schools. This is not simply because of differences in language habits but because of differences in the beliefs, behaviors, values, and attitudes that underlie language habits. What we see here is a clash of discourses. On the other hand, their primary discourse is very similar to the discourse of Anyon's working-class school, Freeway High School, and in the classrooms where the Irish, Italian, and Puerto Rican children remained in the Brownstoners' school.

That explains why people keep saying that traditional directive methods "work" with working-class children. No one seriously thinks these methods *educate* anyone. They keep the lid on, while giving the children a kind of domesticating literacy, which prepares them to take their parents' places in society. It's our old friend economic reproduction, and when you understand it, it just won't do.

Chapter 10

THE LAST STRAW
There's Literacy, and Then There's Literacy

While nineteenth-century anthropologists divided the world's people into primitive and civilized societies, twentieth century anthropologists have divided them into oral and literate societies. Oral societies are described roughly the same way primitive societies had been—as small, homogeneous, regulated by face-to-face encounters rather than impersonal laws, and having a strong sense of solidarity. Literate societies are described roughly the same way as civilized societies had been—as large, diverse, logical, scientific, technological, having a sense of history, regulated by impersonal laws, and sacrificing solidarity somewhat in favor of individualism. It is a short step to conclude that literacy *causes* the characteristics attributed to literate societies.

Havelock[1] gave us a brilliant example of a people who emerged from a "primitive" to a civilized state shortly after the widespread introduction of literacy—the ancient Greeks, no less. Havelock argued that during Homer's time the Greeks fit the description of a primitive society. They passed down their values and knowledge through spoken epic poetry, which, in the absence of writing, was limited by human memory. To facilitate memory, the epics were recited in a heavy metrical rhythm. Characters, actions, and events were stereotypical. The teller and the audience identified closely with the story to the extent that they "came under the spell" of the poem. Under such conditions, new ideas or challenges to existing knowledge and beliefs were difficult, if not impossible.

But then, around the time of Plato, literacy in an alphabetic script became widespread. What was written could be seen as a text, an object to be examined. It's hard to "look back" at what you're listening to, especially if you are caught up in the rhythm of an epic poem, but you can look back at a written text. It's commonplace for students who first begin to write fairly lengthy papers to be surprised to find that what they wrote on page twelve is inconsistent with what they wrote on page two. With experience, writers are no longer surprised; they expect this to happen. Writing permits us to reflect on our knowledge and beliefs, notice inconsistencies, and work them out.

Writing also permits us to lay texts side by side and compare them. This enables us to find inconsistencies in knowledge and beliefs that might go undetected in an oral culture. And with writing there is also less tolerance for inaccuracy because writing permits us to check facts and sources and rewrite before "sending" the message in ways that speech does not permit.

Because writing can be moved away from the writer, the writer is apt to be unfamiliar with his or her audience. A writer cannot gauge the distant reader's knowledge, beliefs, and opinions with the accuracy that is often possible in speech. Therefore, with writing, facts are more likely to be stated explicitly; descriptions and explanations are apt to be more precise, and arguments are more apt to be reasoned in greater detail. Is it any wonder, Havelock asks, that philosophy, science, and history burgeoned in Greece following the introduction of widespread literacy?

Others, engaging in similar reasoning, concluded that societies become large, diverse, logical, scientific, technological, become regulated by impersonal laws, acquire a sense of history, and sacrifice solidarity in favor of individualism once literacy becomes widespread in a society. It's a short step from believing that, just as literacy causes the transformation of a primitive society into a "civilized" one, literacy causes a similar transformation of individuals within a society.

There are well-known correlations between various kinds of trouble and low levels of literacy. Juvenile delinquents, criminals, people on welfare, high school dropouts, the chronically unemployed, teenage parents, and people having minimum wage jobs tend to have low levels of literacy. This painfully obvious observation leads many to believe that illiteracy causes social ills and literacy cures them.

The War on Poverty during the Johnson administration was essentially a literacy program. The idea was that if children of the unemployed, the underemployed, and those employed at minimum wage jobs learned to read,[2] they would, like Plato's Greeks, discover inconsistencies in their thinking and begin to engage in higher levels of thought. They would begin to produce texts that are explicit, nonredundant, accurate, and logical. As a result, they would learn to deal with and become part of powerful institutions such as schools, big government, corporations, and professions that are built on and require this kind of literacy. They would, in short, get jobs or get better jobs and poverty would disappear.

But what happened when we taught the children of the poor to read and write but found that they did not become explicit, concise, accurate, and logical in their talk and writing and they did not understand texts that had these qualities? We thought, "We haven't made them literate enough." And we kept drilling phonics and spelling and grammar lessons into seventh and eighth graders and high school boys and girls thinking, if we just get them literate *enough*, the rest will happen.

The trouble was, and is, that basic literacy does not lead automatically to higher forms of thinking, either in societies or in individuals. Widespread literacy has occurred in numerous societies where a golden age comparable to that of Greece did not follow. One of the most remarkable and successful literacy campaigns in history took place shortly after the Reformation in Sweden under the auspices of the government and Lutheran church. Many places experiencing intensely pious religious fervor—Scotland, New England, and Protestant areas in France, Germany, and Switzerland—reached "near universal literacy" by 1800. None of the litany of "higher cognitive functions," "modernization," or "progress" happened in these places. It was literacy

Basic literacy doesn't lead to ↑

for domestication and that's what they got—domestication—not a riot of intellectual inquiry and progress.

Of course we don't need to go into the past to find examples of literacy that has not triggered an interest in science, logic, and so on. We need only to look at Anyon's working-class fifth graders, the lads, the Freeway high schoolers, the Irish, Italian, and Puerto Rican children in the Brownstoners' school, and the people from Roadville. They were all literate, but none of them were in the early stages of a process that would inevitably lead to the Ivy League.

There's literacy, and then there's literacy. The children from all of Anyon's schools (the working-class, middle-class, affluent professionals, and executive elite) were literate, but this fact obscures more than it reveals. The children from Anyon's schools demonstrated different *levels* of literacy.[3] The lowest level is simply the ability to "sound out" words and turn sentences that are typical of informal face-to-face conversation into writing. It is referred to as the "performative level." Quite obviously, fifth graders in all four schools were literate at the performative level.

The next level is the "functional level." It is the ability to meet the reading and writing demands of an average day of an average person. Reading *USA Today*, filling out a job application, understanding directions for using a household gadget, and writing a note to leave on the kitchen table for your spouse are some examples of functional literacy. The children in Anyon's working-class school were learning functional literacy. Work for them was following step-by-step directions. When asked, "What do you think of when I say the word *knowledge*?" no one used the word *think*; only one child used the word *mind*.

The third level is the "informational level." This is the ability to read and absorb the kind of knowledge that is associated with the school and to write examinations and reports based on such knowledge. The children in Anyon's middle-class school seemed to be working toward informational literacy. Work for them was getting the right answers; it rarely involved creativity. Knowledge for them was remembering facts. When asked, "Can you make knowledge?" they answered that they would look it up.

The fourth level is "powerful literacy." Powerful literacy involves creativity and reason—the ability to evaluate, analyze, and synthesize while reading and listening and to persuade and

powerful literacy needs political a sensibility

negotiate through writing and speaking. It is literacy used to understand and control what's going on around you. It is the literacy of persons who are conscious of their own power and self interest. It's the literacy of negotiation.

James Gee[4] traces the powerful literacy of the present to seventeenth century England, where literacy combined with political, economic, and cultural forces to produce an *invention* that was to be developed over the next hundred years. This invention is one we were all introduced to in school—the essay.

The British essayists, Sir Francis Bacon and that crowd, devised ways to exploit writing for the purpose of formulating original knowledge. Essayists took an assertion (what we all learned in school as the "thesis" or "topic sentence") and examined it, ferreted out the assumptions upon which it was based, and stated them as explicitly as possible. Explicit, explicit, explicit. When the essayist was through, unstated and frequently unconscious assumptions and implications had been made explicit; inconsistent assumptions and implications had been confronted and resolved. New knowledge was therefore created.

The essay is public rather than private. It is not addressed to any individual and the identity of the author is unimportant. The focus is on the content. It is accurate. Writers and editors check facts and reformulate statements after reflecting on their accuracy, precision, and consistency. It is intended for a large audience with whom the author is not intimately acquainted. Facts are stated explicitly; descriptions and explanations are detailed, and arguments are spelled out precisely. It is revised and edited to eliminate redundancy.[5]

The essay became a powerful tool in the hands of an already powerful class. Institutions associated with the most highly developed physical, natural, and social sciences, government, politics, economics, literature, art, and language in the West were developed using powerful literacy and these institutions continue to depend on it in their day-to-day operations and development.

The children in Anyon's affluent professional and executive elite schools were learning forms of powerful literacy. The affluent professional school stressed using literacy to *create* while the executive elite school emphasized using literacy to *understand and control*.

I often ask my students, most of them school teachers, to write their definitions of literacy and to share them in small groups. They nearly always write a definition like the following: Literacy is the ability to read a paragraph and understand the meaning the author intended. It is also the ability to write one's ideas so that another person can understand them.

Then I introduce the concept of levels of literacy—performative, functional, informational, and powerful literacy, and I ask them to decide where their definitions fall. They nearly always classify their definitions as informational, and sometimes even powerful. When I tell them that I don't agree, that I would classify their definitions as functional at best, they argue their definition implies informational and powerful literacy because these levels are based on the ability to understand the meaning an author intends and to write ideas so others can understand. They see schooling as allowing children to progress naturally from the lower forms of literacy to the higher.

This is what Gee refers to as "the autonomous model of literacy"—that is the belief that if you teach students to read as well as, say, the average fourth grader, all of the knowledge, wisdom, and culture in print is available to them, and they will just naturally pursue them in the style of Abe Lincoln. If they don't it is because there is something unnatural about them. Of course, it's not so. If powerful literacy is not the typical literacy of your discourse community, and if you are not taught powerful literacy, you're not likely to acquire it.

Nothing happens automatically when a person learns to read and write at a performative or functional level, certainly not powerful literacy. It is especially unlikely that anything will happen when performative and functional literacy are taught for domestication as it was in Protestant Europe or New England in the seventeenth-century or in Anyon's working-class or middle-class schools, for that matter.

Children of the gentry learn to read and write in classrooms whose discourse mirrors that of their own communities. They continue to make progress toward powerful literacy, which is, of course, the literacy of their homes and community. The children of the working class learn to read and write in classrooms whose discourse mirrors that of their own communities, but they do not make progress toward informational and powerful literacy. Their progress ends with functional or perhaps informational literacy, which is, of course, the literacy of their homes and community.

Do we instill in working-class children the understanding that the purpose of literacy is to create new knowledge that is relevant to their lives? Do we teach them procedures and invite them to create their own procedures or make our procedures more congenial to themselves or more useful to themselves? No. We say, "Do it my way or it's wrong." We say, "What we're trying to do here is get some notes for the end of the year [state] exams."

Do we run classrooms in such a way that working-class children will learn the attitudes and behaviors of powerful people regarding authority, conformity, isolation, and power, which in turn make the use of explicit language sensible and necessary? No. Instead we replicate the attitudes and behaviors of powerless people regarding these matters in our classrooms.

Both the Brownstoners and the Freeway parents wanted the kind of literacy for their children that would get them into the better four-year colleges—powerful literacy. The Brownstone parents understood the connection between progressive classrooms and acquiring higher levels of literacy, and they had moderate success. The Freeway parents did not understand the connection between higher levels of literacy and progressive classrooms, and they had no success.

We are mystified when working-class children learn to read and write but do not progress to informational and powerful literacy, and so we try to teach them the basics of reading and writing *better*—back to basics again and again in the vain hope that if we make them literate *enough* they will do what's natural and become logical, scientific, technological, explicit, and on and on.

The older they get the harder we try to give them the basics and the more frustrated we become. We blame them for being so lacking in intelligence that they cannot do what's natural or so perverse that they will not do what's natural. By this time, their oppositional identity is making itself felt, school's over, and the war is on.

Giving children more and more drills in phonics and basic skills never has and never will lead to powerful forms of literacy.

In fact, directive, domesticating teaching styles such as those we observed at Freeway, which invariably accompany the skills and drills "solution," replicate the authoritarian, conformist, powerless societies of intimates that make implicit, context-dependent language and communication inevitable and explicit, context-independent language unnecessary. When forms of powerful literacy and the ability to operate as powerful persons in powerful institutions are seen as the ultimate objective of the schools, the teaching methods we saw in Anyon's working-class schools and at Freeway High School are not the solution. They only exacerbate the problem.

Chapter 11

LITERACY WITH AN ATTITUDE

T he history of American schools between the Civil War and World War I shows that public education of the poor in this country was motivated by the recognition that democracy requires a literate electorate on the one hand and by rapidly growing cities and child labor laws that resulted in hordes of unemployed youths on the other hand. But the beginnings of government involvement in the education of the poor in England appear to have been motivated by fear of an unruly working class that was becoming literate in ways that the ruling class found dangerous. There are important lessons to be learned from this history.

In the middle ages, the few books that existed were in Latin rather than in the languages of the people. Popular literacy was simply nonexistent. But with the invention of the printing press around 1450, printing shops spread throughout Europe, and books in modern language began to appear. The availability of such books gave rise to considerable self-taught literacy. Less than one hundred years after the invention of the printing press a law was passed in England forbidding all women and men under the rank of yeoman from reading the Bible.

By 1600, one of ten agricultural laborers (the lowest on the economic scale) in England could read. Those who could read were "exposed to a steady hail of printed pamphlets of news, political and religious propaganda, astrological prediction and advice, songs, sensation, sex and fantasy."[1] "This literacy was a political and social force . . . , a constant bit player in revolution."[2]

In a single year, 1642, there were some two thousand different pamphlets published in England. In an effort to control the flow of information and opinion, laws were passed requiring that books and papers be licensed. In 1712, taxes were imposed to make pamphlets too expensive for the poor. Soon, groups began to chip in to buy single copies and read them together. Owners of taverns where this activity went on were sometimes threatened with arrest on charges of sedition.[3]

This type of popular literacy reached its height at the end of the eighteenth century, 1790 to 1810. This is the period E. P. Thompson describes in his classic *The Making of the English Working Class*.[4] There was enormous social upheaval in Europe and America. The Industrial Revolution was well under way in Britain. The American colonies had rebelled against British rule and had ratified a Constitution and Bill of Rights guaranteeing freedom of speech, freedom of the press, freedom of religion, freedom of assembly, and the right to bear arms. In France the monarchy was overthrown, Louis XVI and Marie Antoinette were beheaded, the aristocracy was decimated in public executions, and there was mob rule referred to as "The Terror" from June 1793 to July 1794.

In 1791, Thomas Paine's *Rights of Man* was published asserting the rights of all Englishmen. It was "republican, democratic, and fiercely anti-aristocratic."[5] During a civil disturbance in 1792, a local worthy, General Lambton, was accosted by a mob with these words: "Have you read this little work of Tom Paine's? No? Then read it—we like it much. You have a great estate, General; we shall soon divide it amongst us."[6]

In 1793, when a portion of *Rights of Man* was published in pamphlet form, 200,000 copies sold in one year—one for every fifty people in England, a nation of ten million. Paine's book was not the initial cause of the unrest, but it gave fuel to a revolutionary spirit already awake in England. One manifestation of this spirit was the "corresponding" societies that sprang up all over England.

The most famous of these societies was the London Corresponding Society, which was formed in 1792 when nine "well-meaning, sober and industrious men" met in London to discuss politics and reform. They formed themselves into a society and collected dues to buy paper for the purpose of corresponding with other like-minded groups. For admission, members were asked to agree that "the welfare of these kingdoms require that every adult person, in possession of his reason, and not incapacitated by crimes, should have a vote for a member of Parliament."

Society membership was unlimited, that is, no one was to be excluded. This was a radical step because it overturned the centuries-old identification of involvement in politics (political rights) with property rights. It opened the door for self-activating and self-organizing processes among the common people. By 1795, The London Corresponding Society is believed to have had five thousand active dues-paying members and another five thousand enrolled but not fully active.[7]

Similar societies appeared throughout England. Many of their prominent members were skilled artisans, shopkeepers, and physicians. There is no doubt, however, that those on the very lowest level of the economic ladder were represented. A government spy reported of the membership in London:

> There are some of decent tradesmanlike appearance, who possess strong, but unimproved faculties, and tho' bold, yet cautious. The delegates of this description are but few. There are others of an apparent lower order—no doubt journeymen, who though they seem to possess no abilities and say nothing, yet they appear resolute . . . and regularly vote for every motion which carries with it a degree of boldness. The last description . . . and which is the most numerous, consist of the very lowest order of society—few are even decent in appearance, some of them are filthy and ragged, and others such wretched looking blackguards that it requires some mastery over that innate pride, which every well-educated man must necessarily possess, even to sit down in their company . . . These appear very violent & seem ready to adopt every thing tending [to] Confusion & Anarchy.[8]

The reason these were called "corresponding societies" was of course that they corresponded with one another. After debating a question or reading and discussing a tract they would summarize their findings in writing and send them off to other societies and letters from other societies would also be read and discussed. A government agent wrote that in Sheffield, 2,500 of the "lowest mechanics" were enrolled in a "Constitutional Society" where

> they read the most violent publications, and comment on them, as well as on their correspondence not only with the dependent Societies in the towns and villages of the vicinity, but with those ... in other parts of the kingdom.[9]

The purpose of the societies was eloquently stated by a witness giving testimony at a trial (for treason, of course) of Thomas Hardy, one of the London leaders:

> To enlighten the people, to show the people the reason, the ground of all their sufferings; when a man works hard for thirteen or fourteen hours of the day, the week through, and is not able to maintain his family; that is what I understood of it; to show the people the ground of this; why they were not able.[10]

And, of course, the societies came to the conclusion that "the ground of this; why they were not able" was *not* that it was the will of God, or the natural order of things, but the result of the way society was organized. They further concluded that this organization of society continued with the cooperation of working men and that it could be changed if working men no longer cooperated.[11] This kind of talk led to charges of high treason—the penalty for which was to be hanged by the neck, cut down while still alive, disembowelled, beheaded, and quartered. The gentry was not amused by this kind of talk among "persons of the lowest order."

Meetings were described by some members as being very sociably egalitarian, and orderly.

> The usual mode of proceeding at these weekly meetings was this. The chairman (each man was chairman in rotation) read from some book ... and the persons present were invited to make remarks thereon, as many as chose

did so, but without rising. Then another portion was read
and a second invitation given. Then the remainder was
read and a third invitation was given when they who had
not before spoken were expected to say something. Then
there was a general discussion. [12]

Government spies, on the other hand, paint a somewhat row-
dier picture.

Almost everybody speaks, and there is always a very great
noise, till the delegate gets up. People grow very outra-
geous and won't wait, then the delegate gets up and tries
to soften them.[13]

In poorer neighborhoods, meetings were held in taverns with
"songs, in which the clergy were a standing subject of abuse,"
where there were "pipes and tobacco," and where "the tables
strewed with penny, two-penny, and three-penny publications."

The Corresponding Societies encouraged people from different walks of life to come together in a "society of strangers," to
question authority and exercise power. Their whole point was
for members to reflect on society and their place in it, to learn
what others were thinking, to discuss it, evaluate it, come to
conclusions, formulate new ideas and opinions, and exchange
those conclusions, opinions, and ideas with others in the form of
correspondence. If this doesn't remind you of powerful literacy,
it should.

The literacy of the Corresponding Societies was literacy *with
an attitude*—not the self-defeating attitude of the lads or the
sulkers and steppers, but the attitude of critical agents who
recognized the potential power of literacy combined with civic
courage.

The reaction of the British government was panic and repres-
sion. Leaders of the London Corresponding Society were tried
for treason in 1792, but acquitted by their juries. *The Rights of
Man* was banned as seditious libel in 1793 and Paine was driven
into exile. Leaders of Corresponding Societies in Scotland were
tried and transported to penal colonies. Public meetings were
outlawed. Corresponding Societies were no longer welcomed by
tavern keepers who feared being charged with sedition, and the

societies began to disband. In 1799, Corresponding Societies were outlawed and strict controls were imposed on the printing trade.

At the same time, other measures were taken to *use* literacy to counter the dangerous ideas of the literate masses. Pamphlets attacking Paine's ideas, and more often his character, were widely distributed. Other tracts appeared condemning the violence and ideals of the French Revolution. Among the pamphleteers was Hannah More, a Quaker who characterized British supporters of the French Revolution as "the friends of insurrections, infidelity and vice."[14] She also organized Sunday schools where poor children were taught to read.

When criticized by those who saw literacy among the poor as a threat, More replied "My object is not to make them fanatics, but to train up the lower classes in habits of industry and piety."[15] She and many of her cohorts saw schooling, not as a threat to political stability, but as a new means of regulation and discipline, a new way to shape the habits and character of the people.[16]

In 1806, Patrick Colquhoun, wrote in his book, *New and Appropriate Systems of Education for the Labouring People*:

> The prosperity of every state depends on the good habits, and the religious and moral instruction of the labouring people. By shielding the minds of youth against the vices that are most likely to beset them, much is gained to society in the prevention of crimes, and in lessening the demand for punishment. . . . It is not, however, proposed by this institution, that the children of the poor should be educated in a manner to elevate their minds above the rank they are destined to fill in society, or that an expense should be incurred beyond the lowest rate ever paid for instruction. Utopian schemes for an extensive diffusion of knowledge would be injurious and absurd.[17]

Colquhoun had a full agenda. He argued for an organized police force, amassed lurid statistics to demonstrate the threat posed by the laboring classes, and is one of the first to comment on a correlation between criminal behavior and illiteracy. He favored a monitorial system of schooling where older children taught younger ones, and where the brightest among the eldest were appointed "monitors" who reported to a headmaster. One of the chief attractions of this system was that it was cheap. One teacher could oversee the training of scores of children. It also imposed a regime of constant surveillance, inspection, and regulation.

Colquhoun, More, and others like them had the insight that would carry the day. Literacy is only dangerous among the working class when it is used to further working-class interests, as it had been used in the Corresponding Societies. However, schooling could be used by the upper class to get control of the children of the poor; they could turn working-class literacy into a tool to protect the status quo. Literacy could domesticate the poor rather than rile them up.

Although public support for church schools in Great Britain between the years 1780 and 1850 was undoubtedly motivated by philanthropy to some degree, it also served the purpose of steering the poor away from radical ideas. At the same time it was becoming clear that a work force with functional literacy was advantageous, if not essential, for continued industrialization and that only the state had the resources to school large numbers of children.

The Corresponding Societies of the 1790s where working men learned to read and write were replaced fifty years later by state-supported schools for children. By the 1830s, working class literature saw a marked shift away from the educational and political toward sensational periodicals and fiction. This was the beginning of the commercial entertainment and information industry.[18]

Since 1800, violence or the threat of violence has never really disappeared in the struggle against ideas that threaten political and economic privilege, but as tactics, violence and threats of violence have been replaced by domesticating education, which has become the bedrock of class relations. Nearly two centuries later Paulo Freire observed that education is never neutral. It either liberates or domesticates. The Corresponding Societies represented education for liberation. Soon after 1800, when the first feeble attempts at state-supported education for the poor appeared in Great Britain, it was education for domestication.

People using literacy to Δ the system.

Domesticating rhetoric, etc.

Chapter 12

NOT QUITE MAKING LITERACY DANGEROUS AGAIN

Progressive classrooms have something in common with the Corresponding Societies of England in the 1790s. This leads some observers to wonder whether we are in for some interesting times. First, let's have a look at a couple of these classrooms.

Marla McCurdy[1] gathers her first graders around her and asks them how they would spell some words. Soon she has the sentence "The dog chased the cat" written on the board in the following way:

a dg sd a ct

After writing a few such sentences as a class project, McCurdy suggests to the children that in the future, when they are writing, they should try to write their own words without asking her how to spell them. She reminds them to put a space or dash between words and to write from left to right.

At first she is a little discouraged, but soon finds that if she gets to the children as soon as they finish, many of them can read back what they have written. For example, a nonreader writes something such as what you see in Figure 12.1 and reads back to her, "This is my imaginary friend, Bgooga." The writing of other children is more easily understood, as in Figure 12.2.[2]

Figure 12.1

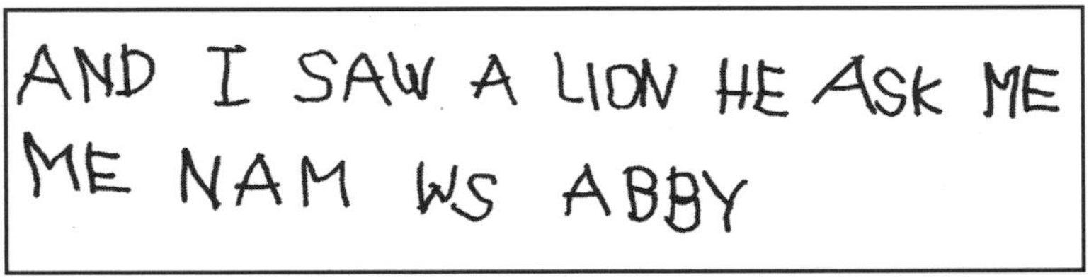

AND I SAW A LION HE ASK ME
ME NAM WS ABBY

Figure 12.2

By the end of the year, McCurdy's writing program incorporates the following features:

Children are expected to write every day. Blank books made from lined paper and with construction-paper covers are always available in the storybook corner. Children's works in progress also are kept there.

McCurdy talks individually with the children on a regular basis. She helps them decide what to write about. She listens as they read their books to her. She reads their books as they listen and then asks them questions. For the "story," *When I go home, I play with my dog.* she might ask, "What kind of dog is it? What color? What games do you play? How old is the dog? How is the dog special?" Sometimes, as a result of these conferences, the children add to their stories or revise them. Sometimes they do not. Their choice.

When children are satisfied that their stories are finished, McCurdy or an aide types them, using conventional spelling, punctuation, and capitalization. Covers are made and books are created that are added to the classroom library of children's works. Children often read works in progress aloud to other students, and they borrow ideas from one another. They read one another's published books from the library and show a great deal of interest in them.

Nancie Atwell[3] is a middle school teacher. She teaches writing in a workshop format. She begins each workshop with a short lesson introducing writing techniques as students in the class appear to need them. These lessons are kept short because they are not the most important part of the workshop. The most important and effective teaching happens during Atwell's personal responses to students writing—conversations in which students begin to discover what they really want to say.

After the short lesson Atwell calls on each student and asks what he or she will be working on that day and where the student is in the process. Students respond with, "A story, I'm writing the first draft," "Editing a poem," "Working on the letter I started yesterday."

Once every student has committed himself or herself and begins working, Atwell takes a primary grade chair and carries it to the side of the desk of a child where she sits down and asks, "How is it going?" This signals the beginning of a brief teacher-student conference. During these conferences Atwell responds to the students' writing. She listens, tells what she hears, summarizes, paraphrases, restates, asks questions about things she does not understand or would like to know more about, and asks what the writer might do next. She makes suggestions, but she does not write them down or indicate that they are more than suggestions. This underscores a central tenant of Atwell's method: ownership. The students have control over their writing. The teacher does not.

The four corners of the room are designated conference areas. When students need a response to something they have written or to an idea, they are free to ask one or two other students to join them in a conference area where they consult in quiet voices.

Seven or eight minutes before the end of each workshop, "group share" begins. Students sit together in a circle on the floor, and one or two read a paper or part of a paper. Atwell models productive ways of listening and responding, and the group discusses useful and not very useful responses.

When a student is satisfied that his or her paper is finished it says what he or she wants to say, the way he or she wants to say it, the piece is submitted to Atwell for final editing. She makes any editorial changes necessary to bring the piece up to minimal standards. She records the skills that the student seems to have mastered plus one or two skills that need attention. The next day, Atwell has an editing conference with the student, where she teaches the one or two skills she has identified from the paper as needing work and makes note of what she has taught. She continues to work on those skills in future editing conferences with the student.

Sharing in conferences and during group share is the easiest and most frequently used form of publishing. A few of the other publication opportunities Atwell recommends to her students are photocopying papers to share with family and friends; posting writing on bulletin boards; submitting writing to contests, school newspapers, local newspapers, and magazines; tape-recording radio plays; and videotaping commercials.

Atwell also teaches reading in a workshop format. Students choose their own reading material from the library, bookstores, or home. Each student has a notebook called a "dialog journal." Students are required to write one letter a week to Atwell or to another student in their journals. In these letters students tell why they chose a particular book and what they liked or did not like and why. The person addressed responds to these letters in the student's journal, and the journals are returned. Through reading and responding to the students' journals, Atwell learns where students need guidance and exposure to new ideas. She teaches short lessons at the beginning of each reading workshop that grow out of what she learns from students' literature logs.

John Willinsky refers to the methods used in McCurdy's and Atwell's classrooms and the assumptions that underlie them as "New Literacy," which he defines as "strategies in the teaching of reading and writing which attempt to shift the control of literacy from the teacher to the student."[4]

New Literacy has some important similarities with the Corresponding Societies. The "steady hail" of pamphlets to which members of the Corresponding Societies had access is reflected in the wide range of reading materials introduced into New Literacy classrooms. In McCurdy's first grade, children read their stories to each other and borrow ideas from one another, and McCurdy reads their stories to them. In Atwell's reading workshop, the students bring books of their choice. Students' writings on topics of their choice become reading material for other students as well.

In New Literacy classrooms, as in the Corresponding Societies, the line between oral and written communication is indistinct. Writing is not on the model of the solitary writer and the anonymous audience. Talking is encouraged. Students frequently read what they have written as a form of publication. They discuss what they have read. But in terms of empowering students, the most important characteristic that New Literacy shares with the Corresponding Societies is that expression is emphasized over correctness. In the Corresponding Societies, ideas were not rejected if they were not expressed in standard received English. In the New Literacy classroom, children's ideas are not rejected if they are not expressed in standard English or written "correctly."

The Bgooga story is certainly an example of accepting expression in a most unconventional style rather than insisting on conventionality first. McCurdy's habit of typing the children's stories using conventional spelling, punctuation, and capitalization is a real sticking point with many traditional teachers who see this as a form of cheating. But McCurdy sees it as a way of accepting the child's expression rather than waiting for the child to master the conventions—to achieve correctness. And, of course, as a result, in McCurdy's class everyone publishes.

In Atwell's class, where students are older, students share ideas and help one another with their stories and essays. Atwell brings the students' writing up to acceptable standards in terms of mechanics and conventions in the proofreading or editing phase, and everyone publishes. Of course, in both classes the teachers' responsibility to teach standard English usage and conventions of writing is taken seriously, but expression and publication are not put off until the students have mastered the canons of correctness.

In the traditional, teacher-directed classroom the paper that gets "published" is first of all correct by the standards of school literacy, and it is assumed standards have been met largely through the individual student's knowledge of conventions and her or his solitary efforts. Group editing and teacher editing are seen as "cheating" and dishonest. Students whose knowledge of conventions fails to produce writing that meets the standards of schooled literacy are effectively silenced. Whether they have anything to say in their writing is not an issue. In a traditional classroom, a principal, if unconscious, function of teachers is gatekeeping—prohibiting expression on the part of students until they have conformed to school standards of "correctness."

Gatekeeping has an immediate and lasting effect on children. Donald Graves[5] and others asked primary grade students to tell him what you have to do when you write. Children who are identified by their teachers as "good writers" (ones who pass muster and produce conventional "stories" written legibly and correctly) say that you must tell a good story, make it exciting, give details, and so on. Children who are identified by their teachers as poor writers (those who do not pass muster) answer that you must make your letters right, spell correctly, know where to put commas, and so on. Even college students describe writing in a similar fashion. Good writers talk about quality of expression; poor writers talk about mechanics and conventions—that is, "correctness."[6]

The gatekeeping function of the school starts early. The following transcript records two first grade children making contributions during "sharing time."[7] Mindy is from a middle-class community. Deena is not.

Mindy: When I was in day camp we made these candles.

Teacher: You made them?

Mindy: And, uh, I tried it with different colors with both of them, but one just came out. This one came out blue and I don't know what this color is.

Teacher: That's neat-o. Tell the kids how you do it from the very start. Pretend we don't know a thing about candles. Okay. What did you do first? What did you use? Flour?

Mindy: Um. Here's some hot wax, some real hot wax that you just take a string, and tie a knot in it, and dip the string in the wax.

Teacher: What makes it have a shape?

Mindy: Uh. You just shape it.

Teacher: Oh. You shape it with your hand. Mmm.

Mindy: But you have ... first you have to stick it into the wax and then water, and then keep doing that until it gets to the size you want it.

Teacher: Okay! Who knows what the string is for?[8]

Mindy has in effect "published" with the enthusiastic support of her teacher.

Same teacher, different child:

Deena: I went to the beach Sunday and to McDonalds and to the park and I got this for my birthday. My mother bought it for me and I had two dollars for my birthday and I put it in here and I went to where my friend named Gigi—I went over to my grandmother's house with her and she was on my back and we was walking around by my house and, um, she was heavy. She was in sixth or seventh grade ...

Teacher: Okay. I'm going to stop you. I want to talk about things that are very important. That's important to you, but tell us things that are sort of different. Can you do that? And tell us what beach you went to.[9]

Deena was cut off by a well-meaning teacher who had a pretty clear idea of what successful "sharing" is like. It's like Mindy's. It's not like Deena's. A year and a half later, a researcher asked Deena what she thought of sharing time in first grade. Deena replied "Sharing time got on my nerves. She was always interrupting me, saying, 'That's not important enough,' and I hadn't hardly started talking!"[10]

Gatekeeping appears in reading instruction as well. James Collins[11] cites three examples of teachers interrupting students' oral reading when their word recognition and understanding of the text is flawless. In one example, the child correctly reads "What did the little duck see?" but the teacher interrupts to insist that the child pronounce the *t* in *what* distinctly. Collins points out that most speakers of English would *not* pronounce the *t* in what distinctly (if at all) when followed by the *d* in *did*. The problem is that the teacher has identified this child as one who speaks a dialect where the final sounds are "dropped," and so she is unwittingly overprecise. Another teacher interrupts a child to insist that he pronounce *I'll* as she did rather than "Ah'll" as he did. In another case, a teacher interrupts a child who reads "'. . . for goodness sake why?' axed Olive." The teacher says, "Asked." The child rereads the phrase, stressing the word *asked* but still pronouncing it "axed."

Children whose dialect and pronunciation are similar to the teacher's are given the opportunity in oral reading to exhibit their word recognition ability and their comprehension and feel affirmed. But when insistence on correctness before expression is the *modus operandi* of the school, and it is typically the *modus operandi* of the school, children whose word recognition skills and comprehension are equally as good, but whose dialect and pronunciation differ from the teacher's are not permitted to exhibit their accomplishments.[12]

Gatekeeping continues in many forms throughout students' school careers. Researchers in a junior high school in an East Harlem Puerto Rican community observed the following lesson in a United States History and Civics class.[13] The teacher, whom the researchers referred to as Ms. S, was teaching a lesson supplied by the New York City Board of Education on vandalism. Each student had a copy of a text that defined vandalism and discussed its negative outcomes. There were pictures and questions for discussion accompanied by a fill-in-the-blanks test. If Ms. S had followed the lesson as it was designed she would have tied the discussion to the test, thereby focusing and controlling the flow of ideas. However, Ms. S was a very competent teacher who was well in tune with the economic and political realities of her students lives and was committed to "empowering" them. She rephrased and repeated questions and topics and called on students to answer and contribute.

Things were going quite well in this question-answer format. She was soliciting more and more student opinions on wider and wider topics until a student suggested that he might commit an act of vandalism if his friends asked him to and she asked, "Would you break the law for a friend? What do you owe them?" All hell broke loose. The students became very animated leaning out of their desks, waving their hands for recognition. One shouted out "I'd help my friend cheat on a test," and another shouted, "I don't owe them anything. Like I didn't ask my mother to bring me into this world. It depends on the situation." This last rather puzzling contribution came from a student named Ellie.

The researchers report goes on as follows.

> At this point, the discussion gets very animated and proceeds much faster. Several students are talking at once. The teacher is trying to call on those with hands raised, and for a while she tries to summarize, and mediate between, points made by different students. For example, she says more than once, "Wait a minute, wait a minute! There's not as much difference between what Ellie is saying and the rest of you as you think," following this (when the students allow her) with an explanation and summary of points different students have offered. But more and more students shout out short responses to Ellie, who sticks to her original point (which may not be well understood by everyone, but it is an open question of how much the precise argument mattered to each of the students). Students confer with each other in loud overtones, giving each other their own viewpoints. They give the impression that they are too eager to say something to wait to be called on. Some bang hands or books on desks when someone else makes a particularly funny joke or a salient or controversial point. They sometimes mimic disgust with someone's expressed view, sometimes support it with a nod and a "right on!"
>
> The students are clearly excited about the argument and are very eager to participate. But this is no longer a performance *for* the teacher, but a real exchange of views between the students. Ms. S finally stops attempting to intervene (it is difficult to get the floor in all the uproar), and lets the students compete freely for turns at talk, which results in a lot of simultaneous turn-taking and use of both verbal and nonverbal strategies for getting a chance to be heard by others. When the bell signals the end of the period, the students continue to argue, shout, and laugh as they file

out of the room, still focused on the issue of what one owes one's friends.[14]

The teacher's observations about this incident are what mine would have been 25 years ago. She felt it was all right to "let them go" like that once in a while, but not too often. She used to do it more often when she started teaching but she worried that they were not learning enough "skills" when she did, and that too much of this was "touchy-feely," When the researcher asked if she could not make a connection between this excitement and these skills, she explained that she would give them a writing assignment the next day on the question, "What responsibility does the President have?"

I haven't the slightest idea what Ms. S thought the connection was between the assignment and the ideas expressed in the free-for-all. One thing was certain. Their expression during the discussion was not "received" as valid. Discussion was rare in Ms. S's classroom, and when it happened it was considered touchy-feely, not the real stuff of the classroom. Consider how the same lesson might have played itself out in Anyon's executive elite school, but here the discussion would have conformed to school discourse, and the gateway to expression would have been open. In East Harlem, the discussion did not conform to school discourse, and the gate was slammed shut.

In another case, a sixth grade class in Boston had been to see the circus. The following day the teacher told them that their assignment was to write two or three paragraphs about their favorite act at the circus. Elliot, a boy in the class, produced the following text:

The Pink Panther Act

I liked the Pink Panther Act very much. Because he is my favorite character. I've seen him on T. V. cartoons and movies. Where he is not on. But there a man named Inspector Clooseau. Who is trying to catch the Pink Panther. The movies are in color as a cartoon. When he's in the circus the best act is when hes on a three wheeler and two men are chasing him on motor cycles. And they are chasing him all around the areana. I really liked the circus a lot. It was amazing.[15]

When Elliot brought his draft to the teacher, she was very puzzled by the line "I've seen him on T.V. cartoons and the movies. Where he is not on." Elliot tried to explain (not very clearly) that Pink Panther Movies open with a cartoon of Inspector Clouseau chasing the Pink Panther, but the movies themselves were not about the Pink Panther; they are about Inspector Clouseau. The Pink Panther is not in the movies; he's only in the opening credits. The teacher still could not understand and became exasperated, when a researcher who was observing the class intervened and explained what Elliot was trying to say.

The teacher decided that all the business about the movies was irrelevant—it wasn't about the circus act—and she directed Elliot to leave it out. She made some further suggestions, and Elliot's third and final draft read.

The Pink Panther Act

On October 19, 1984, our classroom went to see the Barnum and Bailey Circus. It was lots of fun. I liked the Pink Panther Act very much, he was my favorite character. The best part I think is when the Pink Panther is on a three wheeler and two men are chasing him on dirt bikes. They are chasing him all around the arena. I've seen the Pink Panther on T.V. cartoons, and in the movies. I really liked the Circus a lot. It was amazing.[16]

When the researcher interviewed Elliot, she discovered that Elliot had seen all the Pink Panther movies and watched Pink Panther cartoons on Saturday mornings. The Pink Panther was in fact Elliot's "favorite character." When asked whether he liked his piece better with or without the reference to Inspector Clouseau, he responded:

The teacher knows best. Miss Stone said for me to take it out 'cause it wasn't, it was like changing the subject. She's the teacher and I have to listen to her. But I think it would have made the story more interesting.[17]

Although the paragraph is vastly improved in terms of correctness, what Elliot wanted to say got edited out. That's gatekeeping.

Gatekeeping effectively silences many people for life. English teachers like myself often would rather not say what they do for a living in a group of strangers, particularly among working-class strangers. If you do, you can be certain that a number of them, the more confident ones, will make lighthearted but apologetic references to their "English" despite the fact that in most cases there is nothing remarkable about their English—either good or bad. Working-class people's experience of English teachers is that they are not interested in what people have to say; they are interested in judging the correctness of the way they say it.

But what if that were to change? What if the teacher's role as gatekeeper were severely curtailed? What if New Literacy became widespread and expression were put first—before correctness? Might we have at the turn of the twenty-first century in America what they had at the turn of the nineteenth-century in England—a lot of have-nots who have found their voice and who begin to use democratic processes the way they are designed to be used, while becoming more and more literate in the process?

That's not likely, for several reasons. First, there is nothing inherent in New Literacy that leads to challenging the status quo.[18] There are classrooms on the cutting edge of New Literacy where students never write anything other than fictional narratives and "reports" of the most bland nature. You can scour the several books and articles on the topic by Nancie Atwell, for example, and not find a hint that she sees challenges to the status quo as a desirable, likely, or even possible outcome of her approach.

Second, New Literacy tends to demand more resources, more teachers, and harder work than traditional methods, especially in working-class classrooms where some degree of oppositional identity has been established. Contrast the resources and effort necessary on the part of the teacher in a class like Atwell's to those things in a classroom at Freeway, where the chief "method" is having students copy notes from the blackboard to be memorized for a test.

So, although there is a growing movement toward collaborative approaches in education, these approaches still are found in only a minority of American schools. They appear in executive elite and affluent professional schools and in "gifted" programs in middle-class schools. They are rare in "average" classes in middle-class schools and they are nearly nonexistent in working-class schools, where traditional methods are nearly universal even in the "top" classes.[19] I would be very surprised, for example, if the Academics Plus program that the sulkers and steppers were excluded from did not employ very traditional methods.

In most cases, progressive methods such as New Literacy will not be employed unless parents demand it. Anyon reported that the methods employed in her middle-class school were very much like those in her working-class schools. It has been my experience that most middle-class students and parents are willing to endure traditional methods because it gives them what they want—preparation for well-paid middle-class work. This may change as middle-class, as well as blue-collar jobs, disappear. Middle-class parents may come to want a better education for their children, but it is an open question whether they will know what to demand any more than blue-collar parents in Freeway did.

What happens when New Literacy is introduced into the classrooms of gentry children? Nothing. The Brownstoners were after something like New Literacy classrooms. To the extent they succeeded, and even if they had succeeded more, these classrooms were not to become hotbeds of political unrest like the Corresponding Societies. They were to become, rather, bulwarks of the status quo.

That is not to say that progressive education never appears in working-class schools. Shirley Brice Heath acted as a consultant to schools in the area where she did her study. She asked teachers who were familiar with her findings to observe in their classrooms and school communities as she had done in Maintown and Roadville. Previous to this experience, teachers seemed to think that children from communities like Roadville were trying to engage in school discourse and failing. Under Heath's tutelage the teachers began to realize that these children were engaging in the discourse of their own communities. They were not trying to learn or engage in any other discourse. The teachers began to realize that they had been *expecting* school discourse; they were not teaching it. Through Heath's work the teachers began to learn some of the precise differences between working-class and school discourse, and they began to think about how they could teach school discourse since it is necessary for school success.

In one school, teachers in grades one through five began to have their students dictate stories into tape recorders. The teacher typed these stories and made copies for the entire class. Each story was discussed by the entire class and among smaller groups of students and revised and rewritten by the author. Even in first grade, all the children's stories began to take on the characteristics of conventional Maintown stories. They became more explicit as others asked questions and writers became aware that there were details that people from other communities could not know. By the sixth grade, children were comparing tape recorded oral versions, written transcripts, and revised written versions, and they were discovering ways of communicating meaning in writing with punctuation, choice of words, sequencing events, building complex sentences, and supporting ideas with facts. In teaching history, the sixth grade teacher used the children's accounts of events in their lives as starting points for writing fictional accounts of events from the point of view of characters in history.

One teacher seized on the opportunity presented when a blind student joined her class in mid-year. She asked students to take the boy on tours of the classroom and the school and tape record their talk as they toured. At the end of each tour the students spoke a summary of their tour into the recorder. Later, the entire class listened to the tapes, paying special attention to the questions the blind boy asked. They then wrote descriptions of parts of the school based on the tapes, starting with a general description of the area, followed by details and concluding comments. These activities went on for several weeks and concluded with students writing reports on topics they chose, starting with generalizations followed by supporting details and conclusions.

In another class, students brought in documents their parents were faced with every day such as traffic tickets, housing regulations, warranties, directions for appliances, and income tax forms. They tried to make sense of these documents in small groups and wrote lists of questions as they arose. Finally they rewrote the documents in more easily understood language.

In one fifth grade classroom of nearly all boys, the teacher started an eight-week science unit on growing vegetables by having Heath talk about her work as an anthropologist and show a film of a Latin American village where she had worked. She suggested that the class study the food of their own community and how it was grown as if they were anthropologists. They decided they would try to discover the farming techniques of the "best farmers" for growing "the most common foods." They would present their findings in writing, photographs, charts, and diagrams in a book that the students in fifth grade next year would use for a textbook.

They discussed the idea of "reliability of sources" and decided that they would need to find at least two sources—one spoken and one written—for each fact they discovered. They decided they needed to define "best farmers" and "most common vegetables." They decided that farmers who were mentioned for special accomplishments in the gardening columns of the local newspapers, such as growing a one-hundred-pound watermelon, were the best farmers. They examined cookbooks published by local churches with recipes for preparing local produce to determine the most common vegetables.

They interviewed the best farmers to get their life stories and to get answers to specific questions. They listened to the tapes over and over until they could write a brief summary of each life story. The teacher typed the summary and placed it in the book along with a photograph of the farmer. They gathered "folk concepts" and explained them with scientific reasons found in science books and commercially prepared booklets for farmers. For example, it was a folk concept that seed store potatoes are better for planting than potatoes bought for the table. The scientific reason is that seed store potatoes are treated with pesticides, and therefore produce healthier plants.

Under the guidance of the teacher these students learned to take the implicit, context-dependent knowledge of home and community and translate it into explicit, context-independent categories and abstractions valued in schools. For example, they all knew greens are eaten more than any other vegetable in their community. Through their investigation, they began to wonder *why*? They discovered that it's because there is only one growing season for other vegetables while there are two growing seasons for greens, and some greens grow wild all year round. The important thing is that the children thought of this question and answered it for themselves. It was not dictated to them in the following way

> Write *why, question mark*. And then on the next line write *two growing seasons, dash, wild greens grow all year.*

—as it might have been at Freeway High School.

By the end of eight weeks, these students were using words like *source, check out* (verify), *summarize,* and *translate*. They had not only inquired, compiled, sorted, and refined information; they understood these processes. Although many of them were from communities where questions were usually answered indirectly with a story, they had been forced to formulate specific questions to get at specific bits of information or definitions, and they began to understand why "story" answers are problematic for science. They laughed together about the fact that they could not get "old Mr. Feld" to answer a direct question. They remarked as the unit test drew near that they would be asked direct questions and would have to give detailed answers—no stories.

These fifth grade students had learned to engage in school discourse. They were able to translate personalized, context-dependent, orally expressed knowledge into the depersonalized, context-independent, primarily written knowledge of the classroom, and they understood some of the values, attitudes, behaviors, beliefs, ways of learning, and ways of expressing what one knows that make up school discourse.

In this class of twenty-three students, twelve scored in the 90s, eight in the 80s, three in the 70s on the standardized unit test accompanying the science text book. None failed. None of these children had ever passed one of these tests before.

In another school, during the first weeks of school a second grade teacher asked community members, parents, lunch room workers, the school custodian, and the principal to come into her class and talk to the students about the way they talked, what they read and wrote, and why. They brought in samples of what they read and wrote as well.

Before these visits, the teacher prepared the students to become "language detectives." For each guest they answered the questions: What sounds did I hear when she/he spoke? What did she/he say about how she/he speaks? What did she/he read? What did she/he write?

Based on these talks, the children talked about formal and informal speech of local visitors as compared with television newscasters. They talked about words they heard in casual local speech that they did, not hear on network news, such as *ain't* and *yonder*. Throughout this study the students were doing their regular phonics and reading skills lessons as usual, and they talked about sounds they learned in their phonics lessons that they did not hear in local casual speech, such as the *-ng* and *-s* endings on many words. The teacher had a tenth grade art student come in and draw stick figure cartoons of different people reading and writing in different settings. Soon the second graders were creating such cartoons of their own. By the end of the year these second graders were able to notice that the principal talked one way when reading morning announcements on the loud speaker and another way when he was kidding around with the older children in the hall, and they could say what the differences were and the reasons for them.

These stories would be interesting and even heartening if they were told about affluent professional or executive elite schools, but they would not be amazing. Teaching such as this is more or less expected in such schools. What makes these stories amazing is that they happened in working-class schools.

Ten years later, however, the lessons that had worked so well with Heath's input had disappeared from these schools. Some of the teachers had left. Those that remained spoke of the period when these methods were being used as the high point of their careers. But things change. The teachers pointed to "a lack of faith in schools," resulting in increased bureaucratic interference and more testing dictated from the state capital and Washington. The most outspoken of them said that teachers had become "lackeys in a system over which we have no control."[20]

They also reported that Heath's presence in the schools had been responsible for a great deal of what they did. They viewed her as both an insider and an outsider. As a former teacher who acted as an aide and co-teacher in the classroom, she was a "member of the club." Yet she was an outsider who had useful knowledge, but had no power within the school. She made suggestions and helped implement them; she didn't give orders and

blame teachers when things didn't work out. She was collaborative, not directive.

If you're not a teacher you probably do not realize what hard
work I've described on these last few pages. Isolated occurrences
of this kind of teaching appear quite regularly in working-class
schools, usually as the result of the know-how and energy of a
single teacher or principal. These bright spots tend to remain
isolated and to soon disappear. To sustain them, teachers need
support of one another, administrators, parents, the community,
and the nation, and they don't get it. There is no powerful con-
stituency insisting on such schooling for working-class (and, to
some extent middle-class)[21] children, as there is for affluent professional and executive elite children. The Brownstoners knew
what they wanted and they knew how to make it happen. The
Freeway parents didn't. Until a powerful coalition is built of
working-class parents, teachers in working-class schools, *and
their allies* we will not mobilize resources or give teachers the
support they need to make such schooling work across the board.
It's going to take organization and muscle to afford powerful literacy to all our children. We're talking politics here, friends, with
a capital *P*.

What would happen if working-class students had political
motives for acquiring literacy? What would happen if the schools
encouraged working-class students to view education as the
means to furthering a working-class agenda and create a truly
democratic society?

The answer proposed by some is that we would get classrooms
populated by working-class children that would really resem-
ble the Corresponding Societies. These classrooms would look
like New Literacy classrooms, but with an attitude. That might
make literacy dangerous again.

Chapter 13

SCHOOLS AND A SQUARE DEAL FOR WORKING PEOPLE

In 1873 Alfred Marshall (1842–1924), one of the most influential British economists of his time, gave a speech to the Cambridge Reform Club entitled "The Future of the Working Class,"[1] where he addressed the question of whether there were limits on the amount of improvement working people could expect in their lives. He came to the conclusion that we cannot all be equally rich and powerful, but we can all be gentlemen (sorry, ladies). He observed that skilled artisans were learning to value education and leisure more than the "mere increase of wages and material comforts" and that "[they are] steadily developing independence and manly respect for themselves and, therefore, a courteous respect for others; they are steadily accepting the private and public duties of citizens; [they are] steadily increasing their grasp of the truth that they are men, and not producing machines. They are steadily becoming gentlemen."[2] Marshall talked about working men assuming the duties of gentlemen. The privileges of gentlemen would undoubtedly be reserved for "real" gentlemen.

Alfred Marshall believed that the sorry physical, moral, and intellectual state of working men was due to their long hours of heavy, deadening, and soul-destroying labor that "put civilization beyond their grasp,"[3] but he believed that this kind of work would eventually be eliminated through mechanization, and, like artisans, humbler workers would learn to value education and leisure more than mere increases in wages and material comforts.

Alfred Marshall believed that the state needed to compel only one thing of individuals. It needed to compel children to go to primary school, because the uneducated cannot appreciate, and therefore freely choose, "the good things that distinguish the life of a gentleman from that of the working classes." "[The state] is bound to compel them and to help them make the first steps upwards; and it is bound to help them, if they will, to make many steps upwards."[4] Free choice would take over as soon as the capacity to choose had been created through compulsory schooling. Alfred Marshall obviously believed in the autonomous model of literacy—if you teach people to read as well as, say, the average fourth grader, all of the knowledge, wisdom, and culture in print is available to them, and they will just naturally pursue it in the style of Abe Lincoln. Generations of teachers will tell you that it's just not so.

In 1950 T. H. Marshall (another Englishman, but no relation to Albert Marshall) revisited Alfred Marshall's topic in a series of addresses, later to be published as an essay entitled "Citizenship and Social Class."[5] In the seventy-five years since Alfred Marshall's speech it had become clear that all Englishmen had not become gentlemen, and T. H. Marshall proposed that the status we all ought to aspire to is not the hierarchical, class-laden status of gentleman but the egalitarian status of *citizen*. Citizenship is "a status bestowed on those who are full members of the community." The urge toward citizenship is "an urge towards a fuller measure of equality."[6]

T. H. Marshall believed that citizenship was made up of three kinds of rights—civil rights, political rights, and social rights— that were won first by the upper classes beginning about 1700 and "passed down" to the less fortunate. The right to justice has a special status in that it underlies all three categories of citizenship rights.

- Civil rights are necessary for individual freedom—freedom of movement, speech, thought, and religion; the right to own property and to conclude contracts. Civil rights were won in the courts between 1700 and 1800.

- Political rights are the rights to participate fully in the political process—to vote and hold office, to assemble, demonstrate, form political parties, and petition. Political rights were won in the legislatures between 1800 and 1900.

- Social rights (economic and cultural rights) are the rights to economic security (a decent standard of food, housing, clothing, health care, childcare, education) and to live the life of a cultivated human being according to the prevailing standards of the society. Social rights have an additional and extremely important role in that without social rights, people are not able to fully exercise their civil and political rights. Poor, uneducated people are hardly in a position to assert their right to own property or to run for office, for example.

The concept of social rights would have sounded very strange to America's founders, but with Roosevelt's New Deal in America and a Labour Government in Great Britain, they were on the agenda on both sides of the Atlantic by the middle of the twentieth century. Marshall believed social rights were being won in the public schools beginning around 1900 and the process would be complete by 2000.

According to Marshall (henceforth all instances of *Marshall* will refer to T. H. Marshall), the modern concept of citizenship appeared around 1700 with the onset of the Industrial Revolution. Two other powerful forces appeared at the same time: the free-market economy, and the social-class system of modern, industrial nations. Modern citizenship is a system of equality predicated on justice. The free market and social class are systems of inequality that can function perfectly well without justice. The competition between citizenship on the one hand, and social class and the free-market economy on the other has played a central role in the history of Western democracies for three hundred years.

The social-class system is inconsistent with all three categories of citizenship rights.

- *Civil rights*. In the past, persons with lower social status have been denied freedom of speech and movement ("whites only"), and their right to own property has been limited.
- *Political rights*. In the past, a person needed to own property to vote and custom often determined who could engage in political activity. Legal barriers to political activity based on class are gone, but there is still a strong correlation between political activity, wealth, and class status.
- *Social rights*. Different levels of access to the national culture continues to result from differences in levels of education.

Curiously, the free-market economy does not conflict with civil rights. In a free-market economy every individual is theoretically engaged in an unfettered struggle for economic gain, and so civil rights, particularly the right to own property and to enter into contracts, are necessary to a free-market economy. But the free-market economy comes into conflict with political rights when democratically elected governments attempt to regulate the workings of the free market—for example, when environmental protections are enacted into law that affect trade and manufacturing.

The free-market economy comes into its most serious conflict with social rights, particularly economic rights. Social rights dictate, for example, that full-time workers deserve a living wage, that a minimum standard of health care should be available to everyone, and that the government should provide jobs or unemployment insurance in periods of high unemployment. But the free market demands that wages, access to health care, and rates of employment be determined by market forces. When legislatures pass minimum wage laws, they enhance social rights, and they limit the freedom of the market. On the other hand, when legislatures cut unemployment benefits, they unleash free-market forces that curtail social rights. Milton Friedman, the ultraconservative University of Chicago economist, believed that the only education the government owes citizens consists of basic job-related skills; any education beyond this should be made available only to those able and willing to pay the market price for it. And so, by Friedman's lights, most government-supported education infringes on the free market.[7]

Marshall, a champion of citizenship and especially social rights, didn't believe that the free market or social class systems could be abolished or that in fact they should be abolished. He did believe that they should be moderated or controlled. He believed that between 1850 and 1900 the concept of citizenship had gained momentum, and it inspired efforts to moderate the unequal distribution of wealth that is inherent in social class and a free-market economy and that infringe on workers' enjoyment of civil and political rights. He believed that when this process was completed through education, there would be an equal quality of life shared by all citizens. "The skyscraper [referring to the class structure of the very rich and the very poor] will have been converted into a bungalow surmounted by an architecturally insignificant turret."[8] The schools were to be, therefore, the final venue of the three-hundred-year struggle for full citizenship for everyone.

According to Marshall's thinking, schools provide children the knowledge and skills necessary to make a decent living as adults. A decent living provides adults and their families with a decent standard of housing, clothing, food, and health care. Schools also provide children with the knowledge and skills that give them access to the common culture of the nation through the study of the liberal arts and sciences—history, art, music, literature, mathematics, and science. Of course knowledge of liberal arts and sciences often contributes to a person's economic salability as well.

But Marshall recognized that children do not appear to have equal capacities, nor are they all equally willing to put forth the effort required for this kind of learning, and so schools cannot provide equal income and equal access to the national culture for every citizen. His plan was to let all students compete for high-status educational programs on the basis of examinations. He believed that students who are smart and work hard would earn high scores on examinations, get places in high-status school programs, enter high-status, high-paying professions, and end up with more money and status than the average citizen *regardless of the socioeconomic status of their parents.*

On the other hand, those who are not smart or don't work hard earn low scores on examinations, are assigned to low-status school programs, enter low-status, low-paying occupations, and must be satisfied with less status and a more modest standard of living *regardless of the socioeconomic status of their parents.* This setup came to be called "meritocracy," a term that was coined in the 1958 novel *The Rise of the Meritocracy*, by Michael Young, who ridiculed the idea.[9]

Some version of meritocracy has always been part of the American psyche. It became fully entrenched about the same time that Marshall wrote, due to the rise of the testing movement and the growing importance of scores on tests like the SAT in making college admission decisions. These aptitude or achievement tests were originally intended to give bright students of modest origins more access to elite colleges like Harvard and Stanford, rather than confine it to the hereditary elite (bright and not so bright), as had been the case for generations.[10]

 I believe Marshall was wrong about meritocracy in four ways:

1. Poor and working-class children are not as well prepared for elementary school as middle-class, affluent professional, and executive elite children, and so poor and working-class children's test scores are related to the socioeconomic status of their parents from the start.
2. Poor and working-class children attend different schools from middle-class, affluent professional, and executive elite children, and poor and working-class schools are inferior.
3. Poor and working-class children who earn high test scores against all odds do not have the same access to higher education, especially high-status higher education, as more affluent students.
4. On the other hand, middle-class, affluent professional, and executive elite children who are not very bright or lazy or both still find their way into higher education (often high-status higher education).

Poor and working-class children do not have the same preparation for elementary school as middle-class, affluent professional, and executive elite children. Generations of scholars have found that the economic status of families is the most powerful factor in predicting children's school success. For example, in the

1960s the U.S. government funded a huge project that came to be known as The First Grade Reading Studies to determine once and for all which method of teaching beginning reading was most successful.[11] After years of study in carefully controlled experiments involving numerous teachers and children, the results were that no one method appeared to be decisively superior. The two variables that did make a difference were teachers (some got better results—or worse results—no matter what method they used) and the socioeconomic status of children in the classrooms (working-class children were on average less successful than more affluent children no matter what the method.).

There was hardly a pause in the fierce debate over which *method* would solve the problem of children with low reading scores. That debate continues today unabated, but there has never been a serious discussion in mainstream educational policy circles of ameliorating poverty, regardless of the fact that poverty has been shown again and again to be a primary cause of school failure.

In 2002 Lee and Burkham found that by age five, the average cognitive scores of children with the highest socioeconomic status were 60 percent higher than the scores of children with the lowest socioeconomic status and that poor children have more health and behavioral difficulties than affluent children, which of course negatively impact school performance.[12] These authors acknowledged that class intersects with race and ethnicity in educational outcomes, but they found that social class alone accounts for almost all differences in cognitive measures—more than race, ethnicity, or whether the child comes from a one-parent or two-parent home.

Rothstein found that when it comes to teasing out the factors that contribute to school success in terms of scores on standardized tests, social class accounts for most of the differences between white and black students; that is, low-income students tend to score low and high-income students tend to score high no matter what their race and no matter what the test.[13] Class trumps race in nearly every statistic that Rothstein cites to describe the racial achievement gap.

In addition to cognitive measures, the self-defeating (as far as schooling goes) tendencies fostered by oppositional identity among working-class students and the conflicts between working-class discourse and school discourse have adverse effects on the school achievement of working-class students. By and large, working-class homes and communities simply do not prepare children for progressive schooling or high-stakes tests, while the culture of rich children's homes, communities, and schools do.

Poor and working-class children attend different schools from middle-class, affluent professional, and executive elite children, and poor and working-class schools are inferior. In most states, school districts that educate the largest number of poor students get about $1,000 less funding per student than districts that educate the fewest poor students. These differences per child translate into enormous differences per school. In New York, for example, the state with the largest discrepancy ($2,150 per child), a school of four hundred students in a rich district would receive $860,000 more per year than a school of four hundred students in a poor district.[14]

In a 2000 California lawsuit, plaintiffs seeking equitable funding for schools charged that schools attended by poor and working-class children were "schools that shock the conscience." The plaintiffs charged that these schools lacked "trained teachers, necessary educational supplies, classrooms, even seats in classrooms, and facilities that meet basic health and safety standards." The state did not attempt to refute these claims. It fought the suit on other grounds. When Arnold Schwarzenegger was elected governor, he ordered the state to settle, essentially because he agreed with the plaintiffs.[15]

Lee and Burkham found, "However school quality is defined— in terms of higher student achievement, more school resources, more qualified teachers, more positive teacher attitudes, better neighborhood or school conditions, private vs. public schools— the least advantaged U.S. children begin their formal schooling in consistently lower quality schools. This reinforces the inequalities that develop even before children reach school age."[16]

Furthermore, as the Brownstoner's story and Anyon's and Weis's studies demonstrate, poor and working-class children attend schools where content consists almost entirely of isolated facts learned through memorization and where they are rewarded for being docile and obedient. Recall that in Anyon's working-class school even students with above-average IQ test scores were using a social studies text designed for "low-ability students," and the teacher was skipping certain pages in the arithmetic text because they were too hard. Students in such schools might be given the opportunity to become border crossers, but they are not given much that will enhance their social rights if they don't choose to or are unable to become border crossers.

On the other hand, the richer the children are, the more likely they are to attend schools where content consists of problem solving, analysis, and criticism (the kind of knowledge and skills associated with powerful literacy), where they are rewarded for being inquisitive and assertive (attributes associated with powerful discourse), and wher   e there is continuous reflection on the social class structure of society with a spin—that it is right and natural that their families are powerful and need to maintain power. All of this contributes to maintaining and enhancing the social rights of already advantaged students.

Poor and working-class children who earn high test scores against all odds do not have the same access to higher education, especially high-status higher education, as more affluent students. A certain number of working-class students do exceptionally well in school and on tests like the SAT, but their chances of entering college programs that lead to high-status professions remain remote, and in fact they are becoming increasingly more remote. In 2003, one out of five poor students (bottom one-quarter in family income) who had outstanding SAT scores (top one-quarter) did not even enroll in college.[17] A generation ago Pell grants for high achievers from poor families covered 84 percent of in-state university costs; in 2003, Pell grants covered 42 percent of in-state university costs. Even with grants and staggering loans, the average poor student fell $3,800 short of covering a year's college costs. And so, more and more low-income high achievers are barred from college. Those who do attend are likely to attend a lower-status institution, and many of them must work during the school year, contributing to lower grades, a high dropout rate, and less promising futures for those few who graduate.

On the other hand, middle-class, affluent professional, and executive elite children who are not very bright or lazy or both still find their way into higher education (often high-status higher education). George W. Bush was born the child of Barbara Bush, a publishing heiress, and George H. W. Bush, son of a senator who was later to become our forty-first President. Although George W. Bush is alleged to have had a very modest SAT score, he was admitted to Yale, where, he brags, he was a "C" student. He winks at his own youthful hell-raising, which included driving under the influence. There is plenty of evidence that George is not all that bright and that he did not work very hard in school. Nevertheless, he has a BA from Yale and an MBA from Harvard.[18]

In 2003, 35 percent of students from families with income of $25,000 attended college, while 80 percent of those from families with income of more than $75,000 did. Even among top achievers, "only 78 percent from low-income families [with high test scores] . . . attend college—about the same as the 77 percent of rich kids who rank at the bottom academically." So if you had a very low score and you were rich, you had as much chance of going to college as a student who had a very high score but was poor.[19] And yet I believe most Americans, including most teachers, never question the validity of the meritocracy myth for a second: It's a fair contest and poor and working-class students who fail to prosper do so because of intellectual, cultural, and moral deficits. Oakes and Rogers call this the logic of deficit. Meritocracy doesn't work as a philosophical concept without the logic of deficit.

Ruby Payne has sold over a million copies of her book, *A Framework for Understanding Poverty*.[20] Her workshops and materials are referenced on Web sites of education agencies in thirty-eight states, several Canadian Provinces, and places in England, Ireland, and Australia. Teachers in such diverse places as Orange County, California, Native American tribal schools, and Buffalo, New York, have been required to attend her programs.[21] The *New York Times Sunday Magazine* ran a laudatory cover story on Ruby Payne in 2007.[22]

Payne divides the population into three parts: people in poverty, the middle class, and the upper class. She observes that people in poverty make up about 12 percent of the population; however, she states that students whose family incomes are above the poverty level may still exhibit behaviors, attitudes, and beliefs that she associates with poverty because even when household income is above the poverty level, "patterns of thought, social interaction, cognitive strategies, etc. [associated with poverty], remain,"[23] and so her book appears to be about more than 12 percent of the population. My experience with teachers who have taken her workshops is that they think she is referring to most families in the inner city and first-ring blue-collar suburbs.

Payne introduces us to people in poverty in seven scenarios describing "case studies with which I have become acquainted," and she adds," [I] have deliberately omitted most of the physical, sexual, and emotional abuse that can be present."[24] For example, Vangie is a twenty-four-year-old black mother of four children. The first was born when she was thirteen. Her sister wants to stay with her because her boyfriend has beaten her again, but the last time she stayed, her twelve-year-old handicapped son would not leave Vangie's five-year-old daughter alone. The reader is left to imagine what "would not leave her alone" means. Vangie's nine-year-old boy was "cut [stabbed?] badly at school," and she owes the hospital two hundred dollars for treating him. Her boyfriend is in jail for assault.

Naomi is a twenty-seven-year-old Hispanic mother of five who does not speak English. Her husband of eleven years is a minimum-wage concrete worker. Her parents live nearby and help out with money when they can. She goes to Mass every Sunday and often sees her parents and her brothers' and sisters' families. Her car is broken down, her baby is sick, and her husband has been off work for two weeks because of rain. Most of Payne's scenarios and "case studies" elsewhere in the book are as sordid as Vangie's. The few "deserving poor" she describes, like Naomi, are married women who go to church and are victimized by those around them.

Payne observes that poor children come from cultures where storytelling is important, but stories are not related in a chronological, linear fashion as is typical of school discourse.[25] She asserts that "if an individual depends upon a random, episodic story structure for memory patterns, lives in an unpredictable environment, and has not developed the ability to plan, then . . . he/she cannot predict . . . cannot identify cause and effect . . . cannot identify consequence . . . cannot control impulsivity . . . [and] has an inclination toward criminal behavior."[26]

On the other hand, Payne says nothing about actual research that shows that poor urban families are determined to raise healthy children, provide loving environments, care for their children's safety and well-being, have structured home environments, tend to believe in their own abilities, and value their children's independence and competence.[27] She says nothing about research describing the "funds of knowledge" that are found in poor and working-class homes and communities.[28] She doesn't mention the abundant literature regarding using progressive methods with poor and working-class students, nor does she mention Freire or his many followers.[29]

She repeatedly reports crises precipitated by sickness, but she does not suggest that lack of universal health care might contribute to the problems of the poor. She refers to crises brought on by broken-down cars, but nowhere does she suggest that the decision to put public money into expressways out to the suburbs rather than public transportation throughout urban areas might contribute to the problems of the poor. She repeatedly refers to female-headed households and provides charts showing that at all levels of educational attainment women's wages are 30 to 50 percent lower than men's wages,[30] but she does not suggest that government policy and enforcement regarding minimum wage and equal pay for equal work contributes to the problems of the poor. She observes that the rate of child poverty is two to three times higher in the United States than in most Western Industrialized nations, that between 1975 and 1994 the child poverty rate increased in the United States by 39 percent, and that those in extreme poverty doubled from six to twelve percent, but she does not suggest that government policy in the United States (as compared to other Western nations) has anything to do with the problems of the poor. She does not suggest that low-income students' problems in school can be attributed to inadequate funding of poor schools, discrimination within schools, and to careful resource management by the rich and powerful that favors children from their own class backgrounds.

Bomer and others have rightly observed that Payne's program is popular with school administrators and teachers chiefly because she appeals to generally held beliefs among teachers and in society at large.[31] That explains how it is possible that the meritocracy myth persists.[32]

Chapter 14

CITIZENS' RIGHTS VS. SOCIAL CLASS
AND A FREE-MARKET ECONOMY
Acknowledging Conflict and Seeking Equity

It is astonishing that Marshall saw so clearly that if the working class were to win social rights and full citizenship, the powerful institutions of class and the free-market economy would necessarily have to give up ground, and yet he proposed meritocracy as the solution. Meritocracy demands no concessions from the free-market economy. There would be the same rules and the same roles, only different people might fill the roles. Meritocracy does not challenge social class; it simply gives affluent classes cover. They can blame the poor and working class for their apparent failure and congratulate themselves for their victory in a "fair contest."

Marshall did not factor the role of struggle into his analysis. He believed that civil and political rights had been won by the upper classes and "passed down," and that the urge toward equality—that is, to social rights—would continue in its inevitable, noncontentious way. This was a serious flaw in his analysis. To paraphrase Frederick Douglass,[1] power concedes nothing without demand. It never did and it never will. Discover what people will submit to, and you have discovered how much injustice is imposed upon them and will continue to be imposed upon them until they resist.

When the schools support the status quo (which is nearly always), they are neither controversial nor contentious, and so they seem to be apolitical. But if citizens are to win social rights through the schools, the schools must challenge the prerogatives of social class and the workings of the free market, and the process will be both political and contentious, and the political nature of the schools will become apparent.

Marshall's rosy outlook might be explained by two facts. First, he was upper middle class himself and may have looked more benignly on the class system than those less fortunate. Secondly, in 1950 he had reason to believe that the goal of full citizenship and universal social rights had been nearly accomplished in Great Britain and would be fully accomplished by the end of the twentieth century. A Labour government had established extensive public housing and the National Health Service, and it had plans to make the public schools of such high quality that practically no one would think of sending their children to private schools.

Roosevelt's New Deal and legislation favorable to labor were taking the United States in the same direction. These were successful attempts to enhance full citizenship and social rights of the poor and working class by securing concessions from the forces of social class and the free-market economy. These concessions were taken back by Conservative governments in Great Britain beginning with Margaret Thatcher at about the same time citizens' rights came under attack in the United States (where social rights had never advanced as far as in Great Britain) beginning with the Reagan administration.

Marshall's scheme, which became known as meritocracy, is seriously flawed by a naïve, simplistic understanding of the role schools play in the balance between social class and the free-market economy on the one hand and citizenship rights on the other. Meritocracy does not extend social rights to the poor and working class. It's another border-crossing scheme.

Most educational reform consists of what Oakes and Rogers call technical, interior educational reforms.[2] These are, for example, new ways of grouping students for instruction, high-stakes testing, zero-tolerance discipline policies, or changes in principals, teachers, curriculum, and methods of teaching. Unemployment, low wages, lack of public transportation to available jobs, hiring discrimination, wage discrimination based on gender, and poor health care create conditions in poor and working-class families that affect children's ability to achieve, and no interior educational reform can affect these factors.

But studies reviewed by Anyon show that when low-income parents get better jobs and increased family supports, their children are more successful in school.[3] In a 2001 review of the data from five programs that provided income supplements to poverty-wage workers, the Manpower Development Research Association showed that family income supplements as low as $4,000 per year improved children's school achievement, as measured by test scores and teachers' ratings, by 10 to 15 percent, and small improvements in children's school achievement can translate into larger differences later.[4] One of the programs reviewed, The New Hope Program, targeted parents living in two inner-city areas of Milwaukee. Participants had to be over eighteen with an income below 150 percent of the poverty level and able to work at least thirty hours a week. Nearly 90 percent of the participants were single mothers, and 80 percent of participants were receiving public assistance. Participants got earnings supplements, subsidized health insurance, subsidized child care, and help in getting jobs. The program's annual cost per family was $5,300.[5]

After two years and again at five years, New Hope families were compared to a group of families who were in similar circumstances but were not in the program. The academic performance of children in the program was better, particularly in reading and literacy. The effect was slightly better for boys than girls. Adolescents reported more engagement with schools and higher expectations of finishing college. New Hope's results are consistent with other programs that have improved children's outcomes by providing wage supplements and subsidized child care for their families.[6]

Anyon also reports evidence that simply increasing children's economic well-being reduces negative behavior, which is likely to translate into better behavior and performance in school. In 2003, a longitudinal study of 1,420 children ages nine to thirteen was completed in rural North Carolina. A quarter of the children were from a Cherokee reservation. Psychological tests were given each year of the study. At the start of the study about 68 percent of the children were living below the poverty line. On average poor children exhibited more vandalism, stealing, and bullying than children who were better off economically. About half way through the study a casino on the reservation began distributing profits to the Cherokee families. By about the sixth year of the study these dividends reached $6,000 per person. Negative behaviors for children in these families who were no longer poor dropped by 40 percent, down to a level equal to those children in the study who had never been poor.[7]

If poverty is the culprit, what's the solution? Up until recently the solution has been a belief in our old friend border crossing. But border crossers leave the poor and working class one by one, and the poor and working class are left untouched—without improvements in their social rights *or* school performance. What if we asked, "How can schools improve the social and economic well-being of poor and working-class families as a whole so that schools that serve them will not be hamstrung by the negative effects of too little money in the homes of their students?" This is not about the logically impossible task of making everyone middle class. It's about improving the lot (the citizen's rights, particularly the social rights) of the working class as a whole by working through the political process for such things as universal health care, decent minimum wages, adequate unemployment insurance, good public transportation, and adequate child care.

Policy and law at the local, state, and especially federal level can enhance social rights (usually by limiting the free play of the free market and social class), or they can limit social rights (usually by allowing the free play of the free market and social class and infringing on social rights), and only political struggle can change government policy. Improved family and community resources of poor and working-class students can improve their school success. Improved school success can make poor and working-class students better advocates of sound government policy when they are adolescents and adults. There are, of course, limits to this process imposed by the pushback from those who benefit from the status quo. This is how our democracy works.

Rights are not passed down. They are claimed and protected through political struggle by those who would be denied.

The meritocracy formula—education determines income, and income determines access to higher standards of housing, medical care, and so on—works for border crossers. That is why it is so dear to the hearts of most Americans. But it misses the fact that education accounts for only about a third of the differences in income levels of adult workers when factors such as gender, ethnicity, access to health care, and unionization are considered.[8]

- Gender affects earning potential. Women high school graduates make less than male high school dropouts. Women with master's degrees earn less than men with bachelor's degrees alone. A 1991 study found that in traditionally women's occupations, except nursing and teaching (e.g., child care, hairdressers, and receptionists), job requirements were increasing while wages were falling.[9] There are no effective laws to guarantee equal pay for comparable work. Those on the books are rendered ineffective by government's policies of turning a blind eye or underfunding agencies charged with enforcing the laws. Lafer found that effective laws to give women equitable pay would enable 40 percent of poor working women to leave public assistance.[10]
- Race and ethnic discrimination affect earning potential as well. Minority workers at every level of education make less than whites with comparable education. Over time black and Latino entry-level workers have increased their skills, both in absolute terms and as compared to whites, but at the same time their wages have fallen relative to whites.[11]
- Access to health care has a profound effect on economic well-being. Parents should not be forced to decide whether to pay the rent or buy their child's asthma medication. Either decision is likely to adversely affect the child's school performance. The United States is the only developed nation without some form of universal health care.
- Labor unions have been the most reliable and effective organizations through which the poor and working class have asserted their rights and improved their social and economic position in comparison with the middle and upper classes. In 2000 wages of union workers were 28.4 percent higher than

wages of unorganized workers, and because union workers often win medical insurance and pension plans, the total package for union workers was as much as 50 percent higher.[12] The differential is most pronounced in service occupations, the fastest growing sector of the economy, and it is more pronounced for women than men. Union women earned 30 percent higher wages than nonunion women workers doing the same work; union men earned 19 percent higher wages than nonunion men doing the same work. For whites the union versus nonunion differential was 27 percent; for black workers it was 37 percent; for Hispanic workers it was 55 percent.[13]

Since the federal government turned so blatantly pro business beginning with the Reagan administration, laws protecting union workers and union organizing have been repealed, and federal policy has allowed businesses to fire or penalize workers for attempting to form unions. In 1978 25 percent of the U.S. workforce was unionized. In 2000 that figure was down to 14 percent.[14] As late as 2006 U.S. corporations and the U.S. Chamber of Commerce were attempting to prevent China, the only nation in the world where Wal-Mart employees are unionized, from passing pass laws favorable to unions, and Republican senators without exception voted to keep a bill from being voted on that would make union organizing easier and more effective here in the U. S.[15]

A four-year college degree makes a dramatic difference in a worker's income. In 1999, income for a college graduate was on average 74 percent higher than for a high school graduate.[16] However, Lafer argues that when high school dropouts work in nonunion jobs, they are likely to increase their earning potential by $2.25 an hour by finishing high school. If, instead, they stay on the job and help to organize their workplace, their earning potential is likely to increase by more than $5.50 an hour. High school graduates who contemplate some college training short of a bachelor's degree would do three times better by organizing their workplace than going back to school.[17] This should be of particular interest to poor and working-class students and their teachers at a time when government programs designed to support low-income students' efforts to finish college have been slashed.

For decades after World War II, minimum wage laws maintained low-paid workers' income at about one-half the median for industrial workers. Today, nearly ten million workers (9 percent of the population) work minimum-wage jobs where pay is so low that year-round, full-time employees live in poverty. In 2000 half of Wal-Mart's full time employees were eligible for food stamps.[18] Making matters worse, taxpayers who subsidize businesses that pay low wages by picking up the tab on food stamps and health care for their workers don't blame the businesses; they blames the workers.

The predominant antipoverty program of the federal government is job training, but graduates cannot find jobs. Entry-level jobs have migrated to the suburbs, frequently because federal development money goes to suburbs, enabling them to lure employers away from cities with tax incentives. There is little public transportation linking the cities to the suburbs, and of course the availability of public transportation is determined by federal policy.[19]

Government policy and law could provide a progressive tax structure, protection for unions and union organizing, protection from job discrimination, equal pay for equal work, and better public transportation connecting workers with jobs. They could provide a minimum wage that would lift full-time workers out of poverty, medical insurance, and financial aid to students in higher education. These reforms would relieve the financial stress on working-class families and remove some of the obstacles to school success for their children. They are not radical ideas; they are, in fact, modest proposals. Many of them have worked in the United States in the past, and all of them are commonly accepted throughout the industrialized world. Most importantly, all these government policies could be brought about by an informed and organized electorate.

But most Americans do not participate much in politics. Paul Osterman reports that only 14 percent of us belong to political organizations, and only 20 percent of this 14 percent (about 3 percent) attend meetings.[20] Fewer than 10 percent have ever been asked to and agreed to participate in community political activity. Even Americans who engage in politics have become isolated citizens on the receiving end of mailings and TV commercials. We are involved only insofar as we elect candidates to do the real work of politics and government. Political "activity" is limited to writing checks and voting on Election Day. Osterman reports that even Henry Waxman, a liberal California congressman whom I admire, does not have a grassroots organization. His campaign is run out of a public relations office owned by another congressman's cousin.[21]

Working-class Americans were not always so politically inactive. During the New Deal voting rates increased across the board. In 1972, when civil rights and the Vietnam War were on the agenda, 60 percent of Americans in the bottom 25 percent economically voted, while in 2000 only 51 percent of this same group voted.[22]

Contemporary politics is characterized by falling participation and a "tilt toward the top"—the rich participate more than the poor. Barber aptly describes it as a "thin democracy."[23] Seventy-four percent of the members of Common Cause have at least a four-year college degree; 42 percent have a graduate or professional degree; 14 percent have some graduate school; 18 percent have a four-year degree. Average family income of members of Common Cause is nearly double the national median.[24]

In 2000, 54 percent of Americans in the bottom 20 percent economically voted, while 88 percent of Americans in the top 20 percent economically voted. In 1989, when compared to people whose family income was under $15,000 per year, Americans whose family income was $75,000 or more were three times more likely to be involved with informal community activities, two-and-a-half times more likely to be affiliated with a political organization, four times more likely to have worked in a campaign, and two times more likely to have engaged in protest activities.[25]

Ordinary citizens are protected from the callousness, greed, and self-interest of the powerful, and in some cases from honestly held conservative values and beliefs, only by legal rights on paper, not by healthy citizen participation. Improving government has become a matter of increasing the satisfaction of clients as consumers of government largess.[26]

Working-class schools expend nearly all their energy on preparing students to improve their lot by individual advancement—border crossing, which reinforces the meritocracy myth—while, in fact, the route to acquiring social rights for a vast majority of their students is collective struggle, not individual advancement. In fact individual advancement depends in many cases on the collective uplifting of entire classes of people. There would be no Condoleezza Rice or Barack Obama without the collective gains of the civil rights movement and no Madeline Albright or Hillary Clinton without the collective gains of the women's rights movement in the twentieth century. There would be no Professor Patrick Finn without the collective efforts of my parents' generation, who through union organizing and old Democratic Party politics lifted the economic and social status of Chicago's Irish working class.

Laws, rules, and regulations interpreted and enforced by a professional class of politicians have proven inadequate in securing and protecting the social rights of ordinary citizens. Rather than expending all their energy on the few border crossers and consigning the rest to the category of those who failed because they couldn't or wouldn't do what's natural, teachers of poor and working-class students should offer those who choose to go to work after high school an education that will better prepare them to improve the status of the workers they will become.

When we acknowledge the inherent conflict between citizens' rights on the one hand and the social class system and free-market economy on the other, we must acknowledge that interior technical school reform is not enough. The education that protects the interests of a vast majority of the poor and working class will look more like the Corresponding Societies of late eighteenth and early nineteenth centuries than Marshall's meritocracy.

TWENTIETH- AND TWENTY-FIRST CENTURY HEIRS TO THE CORRESPONDING SOCIETIES AND A NEW PARADIGM FOR EDUCATING WORKING-CLASS STUDENTS

<u>M</u>ost teachers represent the interests of the dominant group and the status quo without being aware of it. They imagine themselves to be apolitical because maintaining the status quo appears to be natural—not politics at all. I believe this to be true of all of Anyon's teachers, the lad's teachers, and the Freeway teachers. In fact, I would argue, this is true of nearly all American teachers and school administrators.

Such teachers see themselves as having two jobs in working-class schools. They identify border crossers and help them, well, cross borders. Their second job is to keep the lid on the rest of the students, that is—to paraphrase an early nineteenth-century advocate of reading instruction for the poor—to train them up in habits of industry and piety.[1] It's a tough job. No wonder it's so hard to attract or retain teachers in urban schools. Neither of these jobs has anything to do with justice. Border crossers join the more affluent classes, leaving the status quo unchallenged. The others are left with the counterproductive forms of resistance observed by Anyon, Willis, and Weis that contribute to teachers' desire to flee.

However, there are teachers whom Aronowitz and Giroux refer to as "transforming intellectuals," who are self-consciously critical of inequities in our society.[2] They see their mission as helping students "develop a deep faith in struggle to overcome injustices and change themselves." They aim to help their students become "critical agents" who can "speak, write, and assert their own histories, voices, and learning experiences." They view their students not as individuals but as "collective actors" within culture, class, racial, historical, and gender settings and with particular problems, hopes, and dreams. They try to help these collective actors become "agents of civic courage"—that is, to help them acquire knowledge and to act in their collective self-interest.[3] Understandably, the label "transforming intellectuals" never caught on, perhaps because it sounds a little too self-aggrandizing. More commonly used labels are "social justice teachers" or "social justice educators."

There is, in fact, a long history, dating back to the Corresponding Societies, of attempts by teachers of working-class people (chiefly adults) to provide powerful literacy to the vast majority of their students, the non–border crossers. In 1900, when the British Labour Party was gaining strength, Ruskin College was started as a "labor college" at Oxford University. The idea was that unions would send their best and brightest to be educated to be leaders in political and economic struggles on the side of labor. Oxford University subverted the plan, however, and turned Ruskin College into a conduit for labor's best and brightest to matriculate into the University and join the side of owners and managers. Potential working-class leaders were turned into border crossers.[4]

In 1912 teachers from Ruskin College who wanted to keep it a real labor college started The Central Labour College in London. It produced many Labour Party leaders and members of Parliament, but most of its students returned to their home unions, provided leadership, and shared their knowledge by teaching night-school courses in union halls on economic and political theory and labor history. Unfortunately, after a few years British labor decided to put its money and energy into local, union-hall, night-school education, which was enjoying great success, rather than into what seemed to be an elitist residential college in London. The college closed, and thirty years later union-hall education came to consist of public speaking, parliamentary procedure, and bookkeeping. The truly empowering courses on economic and political theory and labor history had disappeared because the graduates of the Central Labour College had moved on or died off. Without the residential labor colleges, with their focus on social, political, and economic theory and visions of a new social order, fewer new labor leaders and educators were being prepared with the knowledge and analytical ability "indispensable to the intellectual equipment of the workers for the conquest of political power."[5]

Two labor colleges were started in the Unites States in the 1920s—Commonwealth College in Arkansas in 1921 and Brookwood Labor College in New York State in 1925. Of the two, Brookwood was the better known. It used reflective, participatory, action- and experience-based methods that are most effective with workers.[6] Traditional methods were seen as a form of oppression because "the more completely students accepted the passive and subservient role imposed upon them by the traditional classroom, the more they would adapt to . . . society instead of functioning as active agents for social change."[7] John Dewey observed that Brookwood, "more than most educational institutions of whatever sort, [had] been truly educational in living up to its effort to lead students to think—which means, of course, to think for themselves."[8] Although Brookwood was championed by such people as John Dewey, Jane Addams, H. L. Mencken, Albert Einstein, and Louis Brandeis, it was driven out of business by the early 1940s by the political right and by American Federation of Labor leaders who were afraid of being labeled "red."[9]

Paulo Freire, a Brazilian educator, attracted worldwide attention in the 1960s and 1970s for his ideas concerning teaching literacy to poor adults.[10] He was a professor of philosophy and education at the University of Recife, a city where there were eighty thousand children between the ages of seven and fourteen who did not attend schools, where adult literacy was estimated at 30 to 40 percent, and where literacy campaigns had been repeatedly mounted with no effect. Freire saw that literacy campaigns were bound to fail as long as the "students" viewed

literacy as part of a culture that was alien to them. To translate this into the vocabulary that I have been using in this book,
Freire understood the concept of oppositional identity and resistance. He understood that for the poor in the slums of Recife,
literacy was seen as part of the identity of the "other" in a society
where the gap between the rich and poor is ever so much more
obvious than it is in the United States.

Freire understood that if they thought about it, the poor of
Recife would have concluded that any effort they put into adopting the culture of the rich, including literacy, would be in vain,
since they would not be accepted among the rich and would not
get the benefits that literacy gave the rich. The only result would
be that they would become alienated from their own people. I
say "if they thought about it" because Freire understood an even
more fundamental fact about the lives of the illiterate Third
World poor: they don't think about it. They are so submerged in
their daily lives that they have little or no awareness of the possibility for change, much less what they might do to bring about
change. They view their condition as natural, the will of God, or
determined by fate.

Freire developed an approach to adult literacy that gave a
whole new meaning to the old-fashioned concept of "student
motivation." In initiating a literacy campaign in an area, he first
sent in investigators to find the people to whom others turned
for help. He invited them to become the first members of his
"class," which he referred to as a "culture circle."

The first step in a culture circle was to help members think
about the differences between nature and culture. "Coordinators" introduced the following pictures or "codifications" and led
discussion about them, an activity referred to as "decoding."[11]

For the first picture the coordinator asked, "Who made the
well?" "Why?" "What material did he use?" "Who made the tree?"
"How is the tree different from the well?" "Who made the pigs,
the bird, and the man?" "Who made the house, the hoe, the book?"

The discussion was not designed to teach the people that there
is a difference between nature and culture and that culture is
created when people use natural materials to create and change
their environment. They already knew these things. The discussion (decodifying) was designed to encourage the participants
to talk about these things, something that in their submerged

Figure 15.1

Figure 15.2

state they rarely did, something, in fact, that their culture did not encourage. Freire referred to the culture of Brazil's illiterate poor as a "culture of silence."

The discussion surrounding the second picture is designed to elicit the following ideas: People can make culture; animals cannot. People can communicate both orally and graphically. *The proper role of people is to be active and to communicate with others—not to be passive or to be used by others. Proper communication between people is dialogue between equals.*

Is this getting into an ideology? Does Freire have a point of view? Is it a democratic ideology? Does it come into conflict with the reality of the lives of the poor people of Recife? Does it come into conflict with the reality of the lives of Shirley Brice Heath's Roadvillers, of Ogbu's involuntary immigrants, of Anyon's working-class schoolchildren (or her middle-class schoolchildren, for that matter), of Willis' lads or Weis' Freeway high school students? It sure does.

Figure 15.3

Figure 15.4

Figure 15.5

Figures 3, 4, and 5 facilitate a further discussion of culture and how it is transmitted to the young. In Figure 3 the bow and arrow represent culture. The Indian teaches his son to make a bow and arrow and to hunt with it through direct experience. In Figure 4 the gun represents culture. This tool is so complex that the technology for making it must be written down. Only those who can read can learn to make it. The more advanced a people's technology is, the greater the power they have to transform the world. Education, technology, and power are closely related.

In the fifth picture we have another hunter, but since cats cannot make tools (cannot make culture) this hunter can never modify her hunting activities. She is limited by nature. The hunters in Figures 3 and 4 are not. These observations lead to a discussion of instinct, intelligence, liberty, and education.

Figure 6 shows people whom those in the culture circle recognize as their peers making clay pots. The message: You too

Figure 15.6

Figure 15.7

are creators of culture. Figure 7 shows a pot from Figure 6 with flowers in it. People in the circle see another way that they make culture—by arranging flowers. Also, in Figure 7 there are representations of flowers on the vase put there by the workers. These flowers are symbols, graphic representations that stand for something else. Symbols are created by people as part of their culture. They have something in common with writing. Figure 8

Figure 15.8

shows a popular song written in a book. The people in the circle discuss the possibility of learning to read these words—words to a song which they already know.

Figure 9 shows two cowboys, one from the south of Brazil dressed in wool and the other from the northeast dressed in leather. The concepts developed from this codification are that clothing is part of culture. Availability of material, climate, and the work people do have an effect on clothing. Culture responds

Figure 15.9

Figure 15.10

to necessity, but sometimes culture remains the same after the conditions that influence it change. Tradition has an effect on culture.

Figure 10 shows a culture circle. Participants are asked to think about themselves and what they are doing—to reflect. The phrase "democratization of culture" is introduced by the coordinator. The group's culture is its own. It is created by them. It is engaged in by them. It can be modified by them. They can step back and think about it and how they create it and engage in it. By now Freire hoped the people would see literacy in a new light, not exclusively as part of the culture of the rich, but as something that might be part of their culture. If they can make pots and symbols, they can make books.

In case you missed the introduction of the concept of class struggle in relation to Figures 3, 4 and 5, let me point it out to you. Power is partly derived from advanced technology, and advanced technology relies on literacy. The lesson for participants in the circle is hard to miss: The literate are powerful and you're not. What are you going to do about it? This theme is continued as the circle turns its attention to "generative words." Generative words were words with two qualities. First they would generate impassioned discussions of the social and political realities of the lives of the people in the district. Secondly, they had spelling-sound relationships that could be learned and recombined to form other Portuguese words. The Portuguese words for *plow, slum, land, food, work, salary, government, brick,* and *wealth* were generative words chosen for one community.

Just imagine the discussion that words like *slum, land, food, work, salary, government, brick,* and *wealth* would have engendered in the slums of cities like Recife or Rio de Janeiro. *Plow* might prompt a discussion of the value of human labor, the process of transforming nature, and relations between labor and capital. *Food* might prompt a discussion of malnutrition, hunger, infant mortality, and disease. *Work* might prompt a discussion of people's value in relation to their work and of the relationship between manual, technological, and mental work. *Slum* might prompt a discussion of housing, food, clothing, health, and education in the slums, and these might be seen as problems that needed solutions rather than conditions that must be silently accepted.

After the discussion of each word the coordinator would focus on the written form of the word. He would write it in syllables and teach the sounds of the letters in the syllables. Then he would combine the consonant letters in the syllables they had learned with vowel letters and teach them to pronounce these invented syllables.

For example, the word *tijola* ("brick") would appear under a drawing (a codification) showing the use of bricks on a construction site. The circle would discuss the concept of "brick." What is it? How do we relate to it through work? How is it used in our lives and in the lives of other people? The coordinator would then focus on the written word *tijola*.

The word *tijola* has three syllables: *ti*, *jo*, *la*. The coordinator would arrange the syllables as follows:

ti ta te *ti* to tu
jo ja je ji *jo* ju
la *la* le li lo lu

Then the participants would be taught the idea that consonants followed by vowels form syllables and once you know how these syllables are spelled and how they are pronounced, you can read and write many words like *luta* ("struggle"), *loja* ("stove"), *lula* ("squid") and *lata* ("tin can").

By learning a small number of well-chosen words and the syllables you can make from these words with vowel substitutions, a Portuguese-speaking Brazilian can learn to read and write many words.

Before Freire agreed to bring his literacy program into an area, he insisted that all the authorities understand that he was educating for liberation and agree not to interfere. Meetings were held every week night for one hour for six to eight weeks. As soon as generative words were introduced, participants began to write their ideas. Soon they were examining local newspapers and discussing local issues. Those who finished (about three-fourths of those who started) could read and write simple texts, could get some understanding from local newspapers, and could discuss political and social problems.

The heart of Freire's program was its basic method—*dialogue*. Think back to the ten codifications and the discussion that might ensue from viewing them. One idea the second codification is designed to elicit is that "proper communication among people is *always* dialogue between equals." But culture circle participants might not agree. Should communication between parents and children always be dialogue between equals? Between men and women? Husbands and wives? Landlords and tenants? Police and people apprehended in the act of committing a violent crime? Prisoners and prison guards? Teachers and students?

Coordinators in Freire's culture circles were trained to engage in honest dialogue with the participants. The entire enterprise depended on it. Freire was not interested in propaganda. He was not interested in replacing one set of slogans (the oppressors') with another (the doctrinaire left's). Dialogue in a culture circle meant that the participants could express opinions different from those of the coordinators, and the coordinator resisted using his or her position of authority to carry the day. This is not easy to do. In several attempts to use Freirean methods in Third World literacy campaigns, the weakest link in the process has been when coordinators engaged in antidialogue.[12] We've seen several examples of antidialogue, like the teacher who said, "Do it my way, or it's wrong."

I have come to think that an essential difference between working-class and more affluent schools is the degree to which teachers are willing to negotiate and dialogue with their students, both in the sense of negotiating the moment-to-moment conduct of the school day and in the sense of negotiating meaning in the conduct of lessons. Teachers in working-class schools are usually unwilling; teachers in more affluent schools are increasingly more willing the more affluent their students are.

I've done an exercise in some of my classes to introduce the idea of dialogue to my students. I found it in a book by Alfred Alschuler, a Freirean educator. He called it "The Discipline Game."[13] I call it the Negotiation Game. The players are *a teacher*, *students*, and *a jury*. The teacher or a student chooses a card with a "situation." For example, *A student makes the following request to the teacher: "The class is tired after lunch and wants to talk instead of work."* The teacher and student(s) negotiate for three minutes. The jury decides whether there was a successful negotiation and awards points to the teacher, the students, or both.

The game has endless variations and possibilities. The teacher can have advisors and take time out to consult with them. Negotiations can be followed by discussions of how realistic the situations and solutions are, of the advisability of negotiating with students, and categories of situations that are negotiable and those that are not. Students can bring in situations from their classroom experience to use in playing the game. Alschuler suggests that playing it gives teachers and students a vocabulary for negotiation—something that is notably lacking on the part of teachers and students in schools like Anyon's working-class school and Freeway High School.

At the outset, almost all my students playing the part of teachers totally capitulate. "OK, I'll give you fifteen minutes to talk quietly and then we'll begin class." They are all surprised when I tell them that in my opinion giving the students fifteen minutes was not good negotiating. Presumably the teacher had something planned for those fifteen minutes that needed to be done. How can the teacher's work get accomplished and the students' need for rest be met? Negotiate *that*! Once they get the idea that negotiation is not giving in and expecting students to cooperate because you were nice to them (a very big mistake, as any experienced teacher in any school can tell you), and it does not mean you will automatically be taken for a patsy, my students begin to get into some interesting negotiations.

The best student I ever saw in the teacher's part was, not surprisingly, a teacher in the most upscale Catholic high school in the Buffalo area. On the first day of playing the game, in response to the "rest request," he answered without skipping a beat, "OK, take fifteen minutes and during that time I'll put a homework assignment on the board so we can still cover everything I planned for today." This was greeted with shocked dismay on the part of the "students." His next offer was, "OK, look at the headings in today's chapter and write a single sentence that states what the chapter is about. I'll give you ten minutes so you can catch your breath while you're doing it. I'll collect it and grade it." There was some interest in this offer. I don't remember how the negotiation came out, but I do remember that this student understood that *negotiate* does not mean *capitulate*, and I'll never forget the stunned expressions on the faces of the "students" (all teachers in real life) when he made the homework offer.

As the semester progresses and we play the game for about twenty minutes each week, some students become pretty good at negotiating. They acknowledge that teachers cannot accommodate students' requests without having their own needs met, and those who insisted that any negotiation will lead to chaos (those whom I suspect are authoritarian in their own classrooms) at least express some understanding of the concept and agree that less authoritarian discipline (and teaching) has some possibilities.

The closest thing to a dialogue in the descriptions of classrooms I've presented in this book was the discussion between the teacher and her students in Anyon's affluent professional school regarding a teachers' strike. The teacher was clearly out-gunned by her fifth graders, who were children of affluent professionals, and Anyon observed wryly that the teacher "may have made some impression on them." Here we had something like dialogue between equals. Teachers in gentry schools often engage in dialogue with their students, not because the teachers "empower" the students, but because the students are already powerful by virtue of the power their parents can bring to bear.

I do not believe teachers of working-class children refuse to negotiate with students because of some flaw in the teachers' character. It's more likely that the discourse of working-class communities and classrooms makes dialogue very difficult (but not impossible) and the discourse of more affluent communities and classrooms makes dialogue almost unavoidable.

Many of the attitudes, values, and beliefs of the discourse of powerful communities revolve around negotiation. If, for example, an individual middle- or upper-class homeowner has a problem with a city inspector, the values and attitudes of her discourse community prompt her to look for leverage and negotiate. She looks for instances where inspectors made judgment calls quite the opposite of the one made on her home. She looks for other homeowners who feel wronged by inspectors and teams up with them. She hires a lawyer.

The homeowner's attitude toward authority in her own home would tend to mirror her attitude toward the authority of the inspector: people in positions of power ought to be willing to negotiate. Making alliances with strangers who might become allies because they have the same problem is simply what's done in her discourse community. She's comfortable in a society of strangers. But if your students' discourse community values authoritarianism and sees negotiating with children as resulting in bratty children, negotiating with people in stronger positions does not come easy for them. If their discourse community is a society of intimates where conformity is important, making alliances with "outsiders" doesn't come naturally.

The attitudes, values, and skills that underlie negotiation are embedded in middle-class discourse, the discourse of the real school model. As I have argued again and again, border crossers are willing to buy into this discourse, but the majority of poor and working-class students are not. So what to do? What to do?

Our old friend James Gee comes to the rescue. Gee makes an important distinction between *acquiring* a discourse and *learning* one.[14] Our acquisition of discourses is mostly done unconsciously. We acquire the attitudes, values, beliefs, and ways of talking of our primary discourse at our mother's knee, so to speak. As we venture into the world, we acquire new discourses and join new discourse communities. As long as there is no serious conflict between the values, beliefs, and so on that we have come to accept through experiences in previous discourse communities, this is all done without much conscious effort.

We can also *learn* new discourses, as Anyon, Bernstein, and Heath learned the discourses of the communities they studied. In order to learn a discourse, you must become consciously aware of the values, attitudes, ways of learning, and so on that comprise it. Once having learned a discourse, we can critique it, as Anyon, Bernstein, and Heath did in their studies. We can compare it to other discourses we have learned. Once having learned a discourse, we can suspend judgment and operate within it for our own ends, even if we do not accept its values, such as a male chauvinist selling computer software to the National Organization of Women. Working-class students can operate within the discourse of an affluent professional classroom in the same way. They don't need to accept it as their own. They can operate within it for their own ends. The challenge to educators is to find out how to motivate them to want to.

When I was a teacher-education student, I was taught that there are two kinds of motivation. If you want to learn something because you are interested in it, the way some people are just fascinated by science, history, or literature, that's called intrinsic motivation. If you want to learn something to get a good grade, or go to a good college, but otherwise you're not much interested in it, it's called extrinsic motivation.

After the social upheavals of the 1960s and 1970s, a third kind of motivation was suggested. Oller and Perkins, two "Teaching English as a Second Language" educators, suggested that the motivation for Spanish-language speakers to become proficient in English need not be to "become Anglo" and read Shakespeare; it can be to deal more powerfully with the Anglo power structure.[15] The aim of working-class literacy doesn't have to be about border crossing exclusively. It can be about creating a more powerful working class that is prepared to demand its citizens' rights, especially its social rights.

Suppose you are a student who goes to an overcrowded high school where fewer than half the teachers are fully certified and where half the students drop out before graduation. Suppose unemployment in your neighborhood is double the national average, and housing is substandard, and nearly everyone is without health insurance. You can just get angry and expend every effort to frustrate the efforts of teachers who are operating in good faith on meritocratic assumptions.

But, what if your teachers addressed these issues while teaching history, English, art, music, and even math and science? What if your parents and teachers were involved in grassroots organizations that demanded better schools, a living wage, or universal health care? What if they were active in their unions and supported other union campaigns such as Justice for Janitors or organizing housecleaners, nannies, and car wash workers? What if your teachers taught the history of democratic movements such as abolition, suffrage, and labor and helped you to see that you and your fellow students could become more powerful if you appropriated the discourse of power and prepared to become union members or community activists or organizers or teachers or lawyers or elected officials with a passion for social justice so you can fight to get a better deal for yourself and families like yours?

Oller and Perkins called this kind of motivation "Machiavellian motivation." But I believe it has more to do with Paulo Freire than with Niccolo Machiavelli, and so I prefer to call it _Freirean motivation_. It's motivation with an attitude. It's motivation to acquire literacy with an attitude.

Teachers who understand this and act on it help their students acquire the knowledge and skills they need to act in their collective self interest—that is, to fight for such benefits as a livable wage, universal health care, decent public transportation, and equal pay for equal work. And that includes high-status knowledge and skills like algebra and calculus and Shakespeare and analysis of how power is exercised in our political system, by whom, and for whose benefit.

Working-class students with Freirean motivation want what the teacher has, and they will cooperate and work to get it. We will have the real-school model going, but it will be a rather different kind of school and classroom than the ones working-class students have attended in the past.

Most teachers in poor and working-class schools do not think much about intrinsic motivation (except, perhaps, to wish their students had it), but they talk a lot about extrinsic motivation (and also wish their students had it). They repeatedly refer to learning things because they will be on the test. When they find outstanding students, they encourage them with the promise of going to college and by inference joining the middle class. These are, of course, potential border crossers, students who are willing, perhaps eager, to adopt middle-class values, attitudes, behaviors, beliefs, and ways of communicating and abandon their own.

This is far different from Freirean motivation. Working-class students with Freirean motivation may learn middle-class values, attitudes, behaviors, beliefs, and language, but not to replace their own. Instead, they learn to operate in middle-class or even executive elite discourse communities in order to beat the middle-class and executive elite at its own game and to address the inequities and injustices suffered by their own communities the way organized labor and the old Democratic Party once did in order to effect government policy and to stand up to corporations and big-money interests. Teachers who understand this and act on it are social justice teachers who view their students not only as individuals but also as "collective actors" who learn to act in their collective self-interest.

The argument I am making here is not that the discourse of more affluent communities is superior to working-class discourse. But if you are working class and you want a better deal, I believe you have two options: If you want to join the middle class, then pay attention in school, *acquire* middle-class discourse and abandon your own. Border crossers have been doing this for generations. On the other hand, you can *learn* those parts of middle class discourse that will enable you to negotiate for a better deal, and go on being working class. One choice does not make you a better person than the other, but for the majority of the working class the second option is a whole lot more realistic. In either case, you will need the knowledge and negotiating skills that your school ought to be teaching you. If they are not, you should demand them.

Since the earliest days of free public education in America the answer to working-class aspirations for a better life has been "if you don't like the working-class deal, become middle-class through schooling." Let's examine that "answer" in two parts, (1) become middle-class and (2) do it through schooling. As for number one, *become middle-class*, just do the arithmetic. Anyon's rough-and-ready class categories are derived from the family incomes of the students in the classrooms she studied: Families whose income is below the fiftieth percentile for the nation are working class,[16] from the fiftieth to ninetieth percentile middle-class, and above the ninetieth percentile affluent professional or executive elite. If intrinsic motivation and border crossing worked, the 50 percent of Americans who now have working-class jobs and incomes would join the 40 percent of Americans who now have middle-class jobs and incomes. The availability of such jobs would have to more than double, and no one would have the jobs and incomes that the working class once had. It's clear to most working-class youngsters that they will not be joining the middle class, and they know it. It's incredible to me that so many of the rest of us seem unable to understand this.

As for number two—become middle-class *through schooling*—this has worked for a small number of border crossers generation after generation. Their numbers are small because they need to be academically gifted; it's harder to acquire middle-class status through education than it is to maintain middle-class status through education. Border crossers must also be willing to adopt the values, attitudes, interests, ways of talking, and so on, of the middle class and more or less abandon those of their community. Most working-class students are not academically gifted (as most students in general are not, otherwise *gifted* would have no meaning), and as the lads and Freeway students demonstrate, many of them are indifferent or hostile to the values, attitudes, and so on, of the middle class. This is often true of academically gifted working-class students as well.

If we are to truly educate the vast majority of working-class children, we need a major paradigm shift. We must replace the Old Paradigm of extrinsic motivation and individual border crossing with a New Paradigm of Freirean motivation and powerful literacy, the literacy that will enable the majority of poor and working-class children (who will no doubt continue to leave school at the end of high school or sooner) to become better able to exercise their civil, political, and social rights. This is the literacy of the Corresponding Societies, of Ruskin and Central Labour Colleges, and of Commonwealth and Brookwood Colleges. It's the literacy of "thick democracy," where citizens don't rely on elected politicians to secure and protect their rights. Instead, citizens organize to secure and protect their own rights.

Followers of Paulo Freire are redefining the job description of "teacher" in working-class schools. They continue to identify the small number of border crossers and help them accomplish their goal, but they educate them to become executives and professionals with a sense of justice and working-class solidarity in the spirit of London's Central Labour College. And they don't try to keep the lid on the remaining majority. Using Freirean motivation, they offer the remaining majority of the students the powerful literacy that is necessary in the struggle for better schools, better health care, enriched emotional and spiritual lives, powerful political organizations, stronger unions, and greater appreciation of their own culture and the culture of others. Freirean motivation gives working-class students a reason to cooperate and work hard, like rich students, and for the same reason: It's in their self-interest.

Chapter 16

TEACHERS WHO AGITATE
Freirean Motivation in the Classroom

During the civil rights upheavals of the 1960s and 1970s, Chicago mayor Richard J. Daley repeatedly blamed unrest in the city on "outside agitators." For him *agitator* was a bad word. It turned out that the agitators he had in mind included people like Martin Luther King Jr. I agreed with Mayor Daley up to a point. Martin Luther King Jr. was definitely from outside Chicago, and he was definitely an agitator. But for me and those with my political outlook, *agitator* is a good word. In fact the *Merriam-Webster Online* dictionary defines *agitate* as "to attempt to arouse public feelings [as in] *agitate* for better schools." This chapter is about teachers who agitate—in the good sense of the word.[1]

I love the class where my students read Robert Peterson's "How to Read the World and Change It."[2] They come in with their eyes as round as saucers. "What did you think of it?" I ask innocently.

"You can't do that!" they reply, almost in unison. "It's too political! I'd never get away with it."

Peterson is a self-proclaimed social justice educator and a disciple of Freire who teaches in a fourth- and fifth-grade inner-city classroom in Milwaukee, Wisconsin, where most of his students are Latino. He starts off the school year with a unit on the students' families and backgrounds, starting with a time line showing their birth dates and those of their parents and grandparents. They then put pins in a world map showing places of birth, and each child talks to older relatives to collect one story, joke, or memory from their family to write or tell orally.

Peterson teaches "cultural journalism" of the sort that produced the Foxfire books and made Eliot Wigginton famous.[3] Wigginton had his Georgia high school students interview old-timers to discover and preserve for future generations folk skills that were disappearing, such as broom making, quilting, and even moonshining. The result was a series of best-selling books published by Doubleday. The proceeds were plowed back into the writing program, which is still operating.

Great! My students love this. It's creative, child centered, and progressive. But then Peterson tells us that "Freire assumes that what will most inspire the learners is discussion and reflection on his or her own experiences, particularly his or her own oppression. In my eyes, many children in urban America are oppressed by a few key institutions: school, family, and community."[4]

Whoa! Warning bells sound! But Peterson goes on calmly to discuss the "difficult problems" he has addressed in focusing on such oppression. The first way he does this is to bring the world into the classroom, so that children start reflecting on their own lives. For example, one year during a boycott against grapes he showed a tape produced by the United Farm Workers and followed it up by taking students to hear César Chávez, then president of the United Farm Workers, speak at a nearby college. By chance there was a strike at a local factory a few days later, and Peterson took six students armed with a tape recorder to the factory to interview the strikers.

He believed these six students learned more in that half-hour than they had in years of social studies lessons. His class began to discuss their parents' jobs—where they worked and whether they belonged to a union. *Grievance* became a spelling word, and soon there were grievances about all sorts of things in the students' lives. The essence of his approach, says Peterson, "lies in the connections it builds between the topic at hand, the students' lives and the broader world around them." By this criterion the strike episode worked well.

Another way Peterson focuses on oppression in the lives of his students is to deal with power relations in his classroom. This seems as if it should be easy enough to handle. If your students are oppressed, stop oppressing them. Just go in tomorrow and say, "You decide what we'll learn, how we'll learn it, and how grades will be determined. I am no longer your oppressor." Unfortunately, this approach is tried with some regularity by new teachers, followed uniformly by what Willis referred to as "horrific breakdowns."

At the time he wrote this article, Peterson worked in a working-class school similar to the one described by Anyon, where students were allowed little autonomy. The dominant theme was control on the part of the teachers and resistance on the part of the students. Teachers who want to deal with such students in anything but an authoritarian manner have to, in Peterson's words, "be prepared for an enormous struggle."[5]

But still he realized that as long as he ran his classroom in a despotic manner, his students would not learn to make decisions, to be responsible, or to take charge of their learning and their lives. His aim was to construct "a classroom in which students have the maximum amount of power that is legally permitted and that they can socially handle."[6] He engaged in the "enormous struggle" on several fronts.

First he created a positive atmosphere in the classroom through activities that stressed self-affirmation, mutual respect, communication, group decision making, and cooperation. Many middle-class teachers think these values and skills are "natural," and when children do not possess them, they throw up their hands and revert to an authoritarian style. Peterson took a different approach. He believed that if his students didn't have these values and skills, it was his job to teach them. And so he used lessons and activities such as the following.

He did circle activities where each student was asked to share a personal fact or opinion, and he insisted on the following ground rules. No put-downs. Listen. Don't interrupt. Everyone gets a turn (including the teacher). Everyone gets equal time. Everyone has the right to pass. Once they were understood, these ground rules became classroom rules for the entire school day—for the teacher as well as the student.[7]

He did small-group problem-solving sessions with four or five students and himself in front of the class. He talked about the sessions afterward with the entire class. Did everyone understand the problem right away? Who helped others understand? Who asked helpful questions? Who suggested solutions? When the problem was solved, did someone sum up? Were there any put-downs? Did everyone listen? Did anyone interrupt?

The point is that you don't give a bunch of fifth graders a topic to discuss and throw up your hands when it turns into a free-for all, as Ms. S. did in the vandalism "discussion."[8] Teachers are supposed to teach, not blame children for what they don't know how to do. But when the make-believe school model is in effect and resistance is the dominant theme, don't expect this to be easy. Get ready for an "enormous struggle."

On other fronts, Peterson teaches history lessons designed to engage his students and improve their self-esteem. The history of the education of girls and women's fight for the vote, for example, helps girls see that people have fought for their rights and perhaps they should take advantage of those they have and fight for others. I wish someone had shown me and my fifth-grade classmates a documentary such as "Out of Ireland," which recently ran on PBS.[9] There were struggles in the history of my own ancestors that I never really understood. It sure gave my self-esteem a lift, a lift I could have used when I was twelve.

Peterson has a method for dialoguing with his students in a manner reminiscent of Freire's culture circles. He shows them a drawing, photograph, or cartoon, or he reads them a poem or story, and he asks: What do you see? What's happening to your feelings? Relate it to your life. Why do we face these problems? What can we do about, it?

And when I say Peterson dialogues, I mean he dialogues; he doesn't demagogue. His aim is not simply to incite students but to help them think through possible and productive responses to injustice. When his students don't like something that the president has said or done, their solution is to kill him. They want to solve the problem of gangs in their neighborhoods by machine-gunning gang members or sending them to the electric chair. He challenges these "solutions" (which he believes, incidentally, are the result of media saturation) and tries to get the children to think about why they think the way they do, and he tries to bring these topics up in other contexts for further dialogue. The thing about dialogue is that it's never over.

He helps students question the truth of print. He gives them a story from a third-grade reader crediting an anonymous police-man for the invention of the traffic light and a short piece from a book on African American inventors that credits a black scien-tist with inventing the traffic light,[10] and he asks, "Is everything you read in books true? Which of these do you believe? Is there a way to find out which is true?"

He asks his students to count the number of pages in their five hundred–page history textbook that are devoted to the his-tory of labor in the United States. It turns out the number is five. He asks what that means. Why might it be so? He teaches some of the history of labor strife in Milwaukee and asks students to question their parents about it. When they discover that their parents, who are working people, don't know the history of labor strife in their own city, he asks why that might be so.

He uses controversial posters and quotations to encourage writing and discussion. For example, the following comes from Desmond Tutu: "When the missionaries first came to Africa they had bibles and we had the land. They said, 'Let us pray.' We closed our eyes. When we opened them we had the bibles and they had the land."[11]

Peterson models social responsibility. He believes it's impor-tant to understand the world, and when injustices are uncov-ered to act, not simply complain. He attends meetings, goes to marches, lobbies politicians, and belongs to social justice orga-nizations. He is, in fact, an editor of one of the best and most progressive educational publications in America, *Rethinking Schools*.[12]

On another front he teaches—not only about the history of injustices suffered but about victories over injustice. Women's suffrage and the civil rights struggle are examples of people com-ing together and getting positive results. Peterson believes such histories "nurture civic courage."[13] Peterson valorizes not "rug-ged individuals" who rose to gentry status through their own monumental efforts but groups of people who through collective efforts changed the system and became better off as a group.

On one occasion, a number of years ago, he invited a speaker to address his class on the "sanctuary movement," in which

Americans were openly harboring illegal aliens from Central America whom they believed were political refugees from dictatorships that our government supported. The speaker described government bombings of villages with weapons supplied by the United States. The upshot of this was that Peterson took twelve students after school on public transportation with parental consent to a protest rally at the federal building with signs they made saying such things as "Support the poor! Not the 'freedom fighters'—they're the rich" and "Give Nicaragua Some Food Instead of Weapons."[14]

Since they were the only visible Latino group at the rally, the other demonstrators gave them a great reception and a prominent place in the proceedings. And so, in come my students, bug-eyed, saying, 'You can't do that; it's too political," or "I'd never get away with it." Of course, taking sides is political. It reflects a position, a point of view. When you valorize Clara Barton and ignore Mother Jones, it's political. Teachers make such decisions every day—or they are made for them.

A widely used United States history book appears to give Abraham Lincoln and John Brown (both white men) exclusive credit for the abolition of slavery. There is no mention of grass-roots abolitionists, many of them women, of slave revolts, or even of runaway slaves as contributing to the abolition of slavery. That's political.

"Isn't it political," I ask, "to teach the history of European missionaries bringing 'civilization' to Africa and never mention Bishop Tutu's assertion that in the end the Europeans had the land and the Africans had the bibles?

"Isn't it political to teach the history of the abolition of slavery or women's suffrage or the civil rights struggle as the work of larger-than-life heroes who simply appealed to American's better nature rather than as the accomplishment of common people who organized and took collective action and prevailed over angry and powerful resistance?

"Isn't it political to justify American foreign policy because it brings the benefits of industrialization to the Third World rather than suggest that our foreign policy exploits the people of the Third World and supports dictators?"

I point out that what shocks them about Peterson is not that he's political; it's that he's controversial. We engage in dozens of political acts and make dozens of political statements in our classrooms every day that support the status quo. We don't think of them as political because they are not controversial.

My students' next reason why they cannot follow Peterson's lead is, "It's not in the curriculum." Piffle! I've taught in public school at every level from elementary through graduate school, and no principal or chair or supervisor ever asked me whether what I was teaching on a particular day was in the curriculum. Furthermore, curricula always have broad objectives such as "learning to participate in a democracy," so that you'd have a pretty sorry command of logic and language if you couldn't justify everything Peterson did as meeting stated objectives.

What "I'd never get away with it" really means is, "If I tried it, I'd get into trouble." I'll go along with that 100 percent, but "I'd get into trouble" is not an ethical reason for making a professional decision. I'll agree it is the reason millions of professional decisions are made every day—that's why the status quo is the status quo—but we're talking justice here, not go-along-get-along.

William Bigelow and Linda Christensen are two high school teachers at Jefferson High School in Portland, Oregon, who have also determined to be on their students' side.[15] They too understand that dialogue is something other than more conversation in the classroom. One of their objectives in the Literature in U.S. History course that they co-teach is "to involve students in probing the social factors that make and limit who they are and . . . help them reflect on what they could be."[16]

Students studied the forced Cherokee Indian removal from the South to west of the Mississippi River during the Andrew Jackson administration. Following reading and role playing the parts of the Indians, plantation owners, bankers, and the Jackson administration, Bigelow and Christensen asked the students to write about a time when they had their rights violated, telling what they felt and what they did in response. They then shared their stories in a "read-around" format, and the students were asked to take notes on the kinds of rights people felt they had and what action they took when their rights had been violated.

Here are a few examples: A girl wet her pants in class because the teacher would not let her leave the room to go to the bathroom.

A girl encountered a lecherous teacher in middle school. Another was sexually harassed on her way to school, and she felt that she was mistreated by the school administration when she reported the incident. A boy was hassled by the school administration because he was wearing a political symbol on his jacket. A black boy was watched more closely by clerks at a convenience store than his companions who were white.

The students then spent time examining the "collective text." Almost half the violations of their rights took place in school. There were a surprising number of stories of sexual harassment.[17] A number of white students were surprised by the varieties of racism black students encountered.

Most students had not responded to these violations of their rights at all. Those who did responded as individuals. One student complained to a counselor; another told her mother; others told friends. No one they told followed through on their behalf.

Bigelow and Christensen felt this activity covered several of their objectives. It connected the curriculum (the Cherokee removal) to the students' lives. It helped them see that they can create knowledge from their own lives. It helped them reflect not only on their individual lives but on their society and how society shapes them in good ways and bad. It helped the students shift their focus from themselves as individuals with individual problems to themselves as members of groups who had problems in common that demanded collective solutions.

In another instance, Bigelow and Christensen had students read a novel, *Radcliffe*, wherein an upper-class boy (Radcliffe) begins to attend a predominantly working-class school in England. In one episode the teacher humiliates a boy who cannot answer a question by saying, "There's no reason for Victor to think at all. We all know where he is going to end up, don't we [pointing out the window at the factory chimneys.]? There are places out there waiting for him already."[18]

"What are the boys in this classroom learning?" Bigelow and Christensen asked their students. The answer was that the teacher expected children of laborers to be laborers and children of bosses to be bosses, that students had no power to respond to insults directed at one of them but intended for all of them, and that the school endorsed the social hierarchy and the status quo.

Most teachers, even those who consider themselves social justice teachers, would probably be satisfied with these responses from their students, but Bigelow and Christensen were just getting warm. They asked their students, who were predominantly working class, to observe what went on in their classes similar to what they read about in Radcliffe's class. Did the teachers promote questions and critiques or obedience and conformity? What kind of knowledge and understanding was valued? What kind of relationships were encouraged among students? Here is one student's response.

> In both biology and government, I noticed that not only do boys get more complete explanations to questions, they get asked more questions by the teacher than girls do. In government, even though our teacher is a feminist, boys are asked to define a word or to list the different parts of the legislative branch more often than the girls are. . . . I sat in on an advanced sophomore English class that was doing research in the library. The teacher, a male, was teaching the boys how to find research on their topic, while he was finding the research himself for the girls. Now, I know chivalry isn't dead, but we are competent of finding a book.[19]

When Bigelow and Christensen asked students to reflect on who benefited from the methods of education to which they were subjected, Connie wrote the following.

> I think that not only is it the teacher, but more importantly, it's the system. They purposely teach you using the "boring method." Just accept what they tell you, learn it and go on, no questions asked. It seems to me that the rich, powerful people benefit from it, because we don't want to think, we're kept ignorant, keeping them rich.[20]

Bigelow and Christensen comment that Connie's hunch that her classes benefited the rich and powerful was incomplete, but it did put her on the road to understanding that the character of her education was not simply accidental.

Were Bigelow and Christensen content? Not at all. They gave the students a short excerpt from a classic in the sociology of education that states that there is differential schooling in America such that poor children are prepared to become poor adults and rich children are prepared to become rich adults, and that although this is done to a certain extent through different content being taught in different schools and "high" and "low" classes in the same schools, it is accomplished largely through the way classes are conducted.[21] This is, of course, what Anyon's study was all about.

After introducing this "theory," Bigelow and Christensen provided an opportunity for their students to test it. They arranged for their students to visit a high school (which they refer to as "Ridgewood High") in a wealthy community.

Bigelow confesses to being disappointed that his students noticed differences in atmosphere rather than differences in classroom dynamics, but they did make some eye-opening observations: More money is spent per pupil at Ridgewood. The cafeteria food is better. Students are allowed to eat outside and anywhere in the building. Teachers at Ridgewood ask students, 'What college are you going to?" Teachers at Jefferson ask, "Are you going to college?" Students at Jefferson are more highly supervised and rule governed.

Were Bigelow and Christensen ecstatic at their success? No, instead they noted a failure. They had encouraged their students to see themselves as victims. Although the theory they offered their students gave them an analytical framework with greater power to interpret their school lives than anything they had ever encountered, ultimately, it suggested hopelessness. The students' sociological detective work had only underscored their powerlessness.

But Bigelow and Christensen did not leave it there. Like Peterson, they include in their curriculum times when people built alliances to challenge injustice. They teach the history of abolition, the labor movement, women's suffrage, and the civil rights movement, not as the story of heroic individuals such as Elizabeth Cady Stanton, John L. Lewis, Rosa Parks, and Martin Luther King Jr., but as the history of people who organized and took the collective action that made the contributions of these heroes and heroines possible.

Teachers like Bigelow and Christensen are not likely to teach the Rosa Parks myth that she was a tired seamstress who was too tired to give her seat to a white man and so she was arrested, and so the black people boycotted the bus and got the law changed—one heroic act done almost by accident by an individual acting alone and an easy victory over essentially kindhearted whites. They are more likely to teach the history of the Montgomery bus boycott as a victory of rank and file people acting collectively.

Rosa Parks was not a tired old seamstress. She was an activist, the secretary of the local NAACP. She and many other black people had been discussing discrimination against them and ways they might fight against it in churches and organizations for some time. When she was arrested (she had been ejected from buses before for refusing to give up her seat, but never before arrested), the people were ready to act. They organized the boycott. They organized meetings and rallies and alternative transportation. They fought off lawsuits and dirty tricks such as having insurance canceled on church vehicles used as alternative transportation. They kept each other's spirits up until they had their demand for the end of bus segregation—381 difficult days after the boycott began.[22]

Bigelow and Christensen go back to the "collective text" exercise and remind students that they can learn to understand seemingly personal problems as societal problems and act with others to solve them. And like Peterson, Bigelow and Christensen are active in political movements outside the classroom. This demonstrates to students that they believe fundamental change is possible and desirable. Linda Christensen has written an excellent book filled with ideas for social justice teaching entitled *Reading, Writing, and Rising Up*.[23] One reviewer of the first edition of this book says she uses Christensen's book in combination with *Literacy with an Attitude* in one of her courses and they complement each other perfectly.

Bigelow concedes that because of the unequal power of teacher and student, the classroom can never truly mirror the democratic society that he works toward. He does not hold "a plebiscite on every homework assignment,"[24] nor does he pretend that he has no more expertise and knowledge than his students. He does not abdicate his authority. But he does try to employ dialogue and work for conscientization, and he attempts to enable his students to become "collective actors" and "agents of civic courage"[25] who will act in their collective self interest.

In 2003 Mary Finn and I sat in on a "teacher inquiry group" that Jeff Duncan-Andrade was working with at an elementary school in south-central Los Angeles.[26] It was a group of seven teachers who were reading the literature on liberating education and meeting weekly after school to reflect on it and how it applied to their teaching practice. Anyon, Finn, Freire, and MacLeod were among the readings.[27] A common theme across meetings was that much of the teaching practice of the participants was indeed domesticating; how were they to become liberating teachers and meet all the challenges presented in this typical urban school?

Mr. Kinsman and Ms. O'Reilly were first- and second-grade teachers who participated in the group. In honor of the fiftieth anniversary of the *Brown v. Board of Education of Topeka, Kansas* decision, they devised a unit on the history of American education. Since the Open Court reading program was mandated in this school, they showed the reading supervisor how they would accomplish each of the Open Court objectives using other materials. Mary and I visited Kinsman's class one day when he was reading *The Story of Ruby Bridges* to the class.[28] It's the story of a six-year-old who was the first black child to integrate an all-white school in Louisiana in 1960. Each time he mentioned a new character, the children raised their hands, and Kinsman wrote it on the board. At the end of the session they used the names as a guide to retell the part of the story Kinsman read that day.

As a culminating task the students wrote and performed a dramatization of what they had learned, including Ruby's entering school accompanied by U.S. marshals through a disapproving crowd of white citizens. There were no fill-in-the-blanks worksheets or rote learning, characteristics of domesticating education. Kinsman and O'Reilly believed this was liberating education, particularly when compared to the Open Court script they would have had to use if they had not taken the initiative to demonstrate that they were meeting all the objectives of the scripted program. Although they had data showing greater growth among their students on every objective compared to other classes in the school, Kinsman and O'Reilly thought the crowning achievement of the unit was the students' self-motivation and engagement. One group of students got together at recess to fine-tune their script and rehearse for the dramatization! That level of commitment and organization surprised even the teachers.

Laurence Tan, a fifth-grade teacher in the teacher inquiry group, has a degree of local fame in Los Angeles, in part because of the ice cream truck boycott his class organized. The meaning of *oppression*, and how it affected his fifth-grade students, was a frequent topic of discussion in Tan's class. One day students reported that the driver of the ice cream truck that pulled up to the school every day at dismissal time had begun selling toy guns along with ice cream. Since having toy guns in school was grounds for suspension, the students thought that was wrong. And so they organized a protest, right out of the 1960s, with signs, chants, and marching, that descended on the hapless driver, who closed up shop and drove off. This is all captured on video tape. There were no more toy guns sold outside the school.

Tan is frequently invited to speak, and audiences always want to hear about the ice cream truck episode. But to his credit, he insists on speaking about his teaching practice as well. He admits that in his first year of teaching he gave passing grades on themes when students critically reflected on their lives as long as he could make out their meaning "through a litany of grammatical errors and spelling mistakes," but he realizes he had "crippled them and was socially unjust for doing so."

Tan reports that his students are generally afraid to speak up because of their previous experiences when they were misunderstood or their words were misrepresented.[29] He helps them realize that, especially because they are from Watts, in order to be heard and taken seriously they need to communicate effectively through writing as well as through speech. He helps them find their voices and to use writing not only for expression but to effect change. He has many examples where the students' writing was instrumental in school and community action. His students' writing becomes less about grades and more about survival, struggle, and change.

Tan takes a similar approach with reading, math, science, and other subjects. His students use critical skills to analyze stories they read in the school-mandated anthologies. They used math to collect data and to act on their results. They learn how to impact their communities and lives by being competent in standards-based learning. Tan's students also perform as well or better than other fifth-grade students in the school on standards-based measures. Like Kinsman and O'Reilly, Tan understands the real-school model, Freirean motivation, and empowering education.

City Voices, City Visions is a project conceived of and directed by Suzanne Miller at SUNY Buffalo. From a kernel idea—give digital video cameras to students in the city, let them record their lives and experiences, and use the footage as material upon which to build lessons that would accomplish learning standards—the idea grew and was refined with experience. Some of the earliest results efforts were encouraging, but there were at the same time there were too many "wedding videos" that seemed to go nowhere. After eight years of experience, reflection, strategizing, and hard work by Miller, numerous SUNY Buffalo graduate students and Buffalo (and suburban) teachers, the project has developed guidelines and a more disciplined, structured approach. Teachers now ask students to produce sixty- to ninety-second videos in four well-defined genres: iSpeak/poetry videos (narration of a text based on music videos); un-commercials (using an advertising format to sell a concept); movie trailers ("coming soon to a science class near you"); and news segment (based on *60 Minutes* or E! True Hollywood).

Keith Hughes has been part of City Voices, City Visions almost from its inception. He teaches social studies in a Buffalo high school where 18 percent of the students qualify for free lunch and special education students (approximately 12 percent) are mainstreamed. When doing City Voices, City Visions projects in his classes (it is just one of many teaching-learning strategies), Hughes's students work in teams starting with brainstorming, storyboarding, and pitching their proposals to Hughes, who takes the role of the executive producer. He questions aspects of their projects in order to push them towards more sophisticated thinking.

"For Coloreds Only" is a digital video produced by two popular girls in Hughes's eleventh-grade social studies class. Tia is African American and Liz is white. Both are average students with about average enthusiasm for social studies. The class was studying the Progressive era, and after debating whether to take up the status of women or Jim Crow, the girls decided on Jim Crow. They produced a powerful video—judge for yourself—depicting the history of separate facilities for blacks and whites and the horror of lynching set to Billy Holliday's "Strange Fruit." While making the film, the students researched various forms of segregation, the use of literacy tests for voting, and the greatest horror, lynching. They were surprised and disturbed by the discrepancies in the number of lynchings reported. Commenting on the fact that some sources apparently underreported the number, one of the girls commented, "It's like bad enough that they were killed for no reason, but then, it's like they never existed." They discussed the project outside class with friends and family. It was Tia's mother who suggested using "Strange Fruit." Tia actually intervened in a lunchroom altercation, saying those involved needed to "know where they came from," and if they did, they would never be fighting over sneakers.

Hughes reports that students work harder and are more engaged when working with digital video than when working with a more traditional literacy medium. Writing is individual; digital video is community oriented. Students become collaborative problem solvers. They use advanced problem-solving methods and alternative ways of communicating meaning, such as montage, skits, and statistics. Digital video gives students the power to express themselves in a powerful medium about a societal issue *that is important to them*. It gives students access to a medium used by corporations and government to raise their voices about something that concerns them—it raises students' consciousness that that's what democracy is about. Hughes's social studies students do four or five digital videos a year. Ninety-nine percent of his eleventh-grade students have passed the U.S. History Regents Exam over seven years.

Paul McPartland also teaches in an urban, working-class high school. He became interested in using digital video in his social studies classes when he happened to observe a class deeply involved in the process as he passed by the door. The students were very active but at the same time the class seemed orderly and purpose driven (a distinctly unusual situation in an urban, working-class school) that McPartland later talked to the teacher and decided to try digital video himself. When he did, he found it was very labor intensive, and the results (videos) were discouraging until he came to a spectacular product produced by a usually low-performing student. He decided to try again, but this time with more guidance. City Voices, City Visions requires not only technical know-how but an understanding of the educational principles that underlie the process. McPartland enrolled in one of City Voices, City Visions' twenty-eight-hour training programs and has been using digital video as one teaching-learning strategy ever since.

Digital video production is a composing activity similar to, but often more engaging than, writing text. Students must produce an introduction, body, and conclusion. They must edit and revise and scrutinize the work spatially, musically, socially, emotionally, and technically. They must proofread and spell-check. It demands looking, thinking, seeing, planning, reflecting on past projects, and thinking about future ones. Although publication is emphasized in writing workshops (see chapter 12), it is almost unavoidable in digital video production. There are not only class and school-wide opportunities to publish, there are city-wide venues and the Internet. I wonder how many City Voices, City Visions products are *not* on YouTube, Facebook, or MySpace.

City Voices, City Visions focuses on what students have to say rather than on gatekeeping—the practice of demanding standard English and formal correctness first that is typical of instruction in poor and working-class classrooms. Correctness is attended to during the process, as it typically is in affluent professional and executive elite classrooms. Students work in teams and develop a sense of community. Students must negotiate with the teacher (as TV producer), one another, and in a somewhat more abstract but very important sense the concept and the material. Conformity and docility are not highly prized here; inquisitiveness and assertiveness are. Students become members of an active, creative, reflective community of learners. They begin to use language you don't usually hear in a working-class classroom: "I decided"; "I opted"; "I wanted"; "I chose"; "I needed more control of the project." Video production makes students *directors* of their own learning. Recall Willinsky's definition of New Literacy in chapter 12: *strategies . . . which attempt to shift the control of literacy from the teacher to the student.*[30] City Voices, City Visions promotes powerful literacy.

Powerful literacy, the writing process, and progressive methods go hand in hand. Writing workshops have the writing process and progressive methods down. City Voices, City Visions adds the two neglected and "essential elements of savvy citizenry—media literacy and political/social awareness." There is an abundant body of research showing the effectiveness of City Voices, City Visions.[31]

There are two important points that have yet to be made: First, Freirean motivation is not simply about consciousness raising. Peterson did not take his fifth-graders to interview strikers and get them riled up and then figure his job was done; he used the experience as a basis for lessons in reading, writing, and social studies for the next several days. All of the teachers I've described here use Freirean motivation to teach the basic standard curriculum. Second, since the methods I've described here are progressive methods that encourage initiative and assertiveness rather than docility and obedience, those academically gifted students who want to be traditional border crossers are likely to be more successful because they are getting a better education than they would have in a traditional working-class classroom.

Social justice teachers believe in Freirean motivation, and so they believe it's their job to provide powerful literacy to their poor and working-class students, and if they are going to succeed, they must get the real school model working in their classrooms. The students must want the knowledge they are offering badly enough to cooperate and work hard to get it. They believe they must make their students aware of what's at stake on a conscious, political level, and therefore, they must relate literacy to their students' struggle for citizens' rights, including social rights. They believe they must run their classrooms in a way that gives their students reasons to engage in explicit, context-independent language and school discourse. Visiting picket lines, speaking out on race relations through digital video, and joining living wage demonstrations are as much a part of their literacy curriculum as the spelling rule "*i* before *e* except after *c*." They believe there's no point, in fact, of teaching "*i* before *e* except after *c*" unless they do the rest. Why should the majority of their students care?

Chapter 17

AGITATING STUDENTS AND STUDENTS WHO AGITATE

Freirean motivation can appeal to the majority of students in poor and working-class classrooms. It has the potential to transform poor and working-class schools from make-believe schools into real schools, but with rather different objectives than educators usually think about. Such schools are not meant to enable students to become either Alfred Marshall's gentlemen (and gentlewomen) or T. H. Marshall's citizens who have had their rights passed down to them and who are willing to accept unequal status and wealth because they accept the myth that they lost out in a fair-and-square competition. It is meant to enable the majority of poor and working-class children (who will no doubt continue to leave school at the end of high school or sooner) to become better able to exercise their social, civil, and political rights. It's the literacy of "thick democracy," where citizens don't rely on elected politicians to secure and protect their rights. Instead, citizens organize to secure and protect their own rights, often without the help of, or in opposition to, elected officials.

In their appropriately titled book *Learning Power: Organizing for Education and Justice*, Jeannie Oakes and John Rogers describe a project they and other UCLA faculty were involved in with administrators, teachers, and students at a California school they called Wilson High School.[1] Wilson students were drawn from the wealthy north side of town and from the poor and working-class south side of town. The northsiders saw to it that Wilson was well funded and well staffed. Per-pupil expenditures were about $900 higher than the state average and about $2,000 higher than in neighboring districts.

Wilson student test averages were among the highest in the state. About two-thirds of its students qualified for admission to four-year colleges and universities, twice the state average. However, the school experience, achievement, and college opportunities of honors-track students, predominantly affluent northsiders, were dramatically different from those of regular-track students, predominantly poor and working-class southsiders.

Although 85 percent of Wilson graduates went on to college, northsiders tended to go to four-year colleges and universities, while southsiders attended two-year colleges, and, compared with northsiders, a larger percentage of southsiders did not go on to college at all. Southsiders were no more likely to attend four-year colleges and universities than their peers who attended neighboring high schools.

In the middle 1990s the district superintendent and principal at Wilson High School called on Oakes, Rogers, and other UCLA faculty for help with what they called "the two school problem." A group made up of UCLA and Wilson faculty began to work with Christopher Antonopoulos, who taught a ninth-grade humanities course designed for freshmen with academic potential but who needed extra support and encouragement. Thirty students participated. They were all poor and working class. The project came to be called the Futures project, the students involved Futures students, and the Wilson and UCLA faculty Futures adults.

As freshmen, Futures students undertook what they called the "student pathways" project in Antonopoulos' class. They studied seniors from both the regular and honors tracks. They interviewed them about their post–high school plans and how their experience at Wilson had influenced them. They examined transcripts and shadowed students through the day. They learned to collect and code data, conduct interviews, and do observations. With the help of Futures adults, Futures students also studied the published literature on social stratification, distribution of educational opportunity, and efforts to achieve equity on both the local and national levels. They tried to make sense of the data they collected in light of their own knowledge and experience and in light of the research and theory that seemed to bear upon it.

Many of the Futures students began to understand for the first time that pupils—roughly speaking, those from the northside versus those from the southside—took vastly different paths through high school and that these paths had a profound effect on their future lives. At the end of the school year the Futures adults and students decided to continue the project. Antonopoulos agreed to keep the students as a social studies cohort for the next three years. Besides committing to continue the "student pathways" research, the students committed to supporting one another as they chose pathways for themselves.

Affluent parents know how to navigate the system, how to get their children into the classes of the best teachers, how to get honors placements even when their child does not fit the criteria, and more. Futures adults brought this kind of know-how to Futures students, along with the sociological research that enabled them to better understand their place in an unequal pattern of high school success and college preparation. Futures students began to appear in college prep and advanced placement courses.

As they worked together on Futures research and their regular school work, they developed strong relationships. The project provided computers and Internet access so they could maintain contact outside the school day with both each other and Futures adults. During summers they attended seminars at UCLA, where they worked with university faculty as apprentices investigating the sociology of education. They studied the influence of family on education, the links between popular culture and school curriculum, student resistance, the living wage movement, civic engagement in cities, and how the media portrays youth. The UCLA summer seminars culminated in student presentations to audiences of UCLA faculty, graduate students, school administrators, school board members, state officials, community organizers, and parents. They also made presentations to groups of students, teachers, and parents at Wilson as well as graduate education classes and national conferences. They became agents with voices, and they learned the value of acquiring and sharing what Oakes and Rogers call "disruptive knowledge," knowledge that exposes injustice and demonstrates that it is the results of societal structures that can be changed through struggle.

Futures students soon noticed and commented on the differences between Antonopoulos' class and classes in the "general track." One girl observed, "In Futures we had freedom to go beyond the textbook. . . . In the other classes, you can't really do that. . . . You just had to go with whatever the textbooks say to get a good grade in the class."[2] Compare this observation with Anyon's that in working-class classrooms students are rewarded for docility and obedience; in more affluent classrooms students are rewarded for initiative and assertiveness.

Increasingly, students drew connections between personal stories and larger patterns and structures of inequality. One student commented that she had no idea she was being tracked or that tracking existed. She came to appreciate the value of drawing on both personal experience and knowledge generated through systematic inquiry.

Futures students, like most of the rest of us, bought into mainstream social, political, and economic thinking. They had accepted the assumptions that individualism, competition, and merit constitute an "even playing field" in American democracy. If you wind up with less, it's because you entered a fair contest and you lost. Those who won were smarter or worked harder. The Futures Project allowed them to consider alternate explanations of inequalities between different groups of students. For whatever reason and whoever was at fault, the playing field was most certainly not level.

By the time they were seniors, Futures students developed a strong skepticism regarding "facts" concerning school achievement, college preparation, and college admissions. They arrived at a critique of meritocracy similar to the one I presented in chapter 13. They were able to recognize structural and historical contexts that underlay their educational experiences. One student reported,

It really opened my eyes. . . . Because I was a recent immigrant . . . I wasn't aware of how the school system works. . . . From the theories we studied, I was more understanding of other students' experiences, I looked at it differently. . . . Before, I would have first blamed the students. Second, I'd blame the school system. Now, not just the school system, but the whole society.[3]

Futures students consciously began to appropriate the strategies used by more affluent students to reach their goals, but they did not give up their neighborhood identities or become indistinguishable from middle-class students. One girl joined the newspaper, and despite some opposition from the student editors she began the first Spanish-language column in the paper's 105-year history. Futures students were elected to student government, facilitated sessions at a retreat on race relations, and founded a new organization for indigenous students. Two of them started a tutoring program at an inner-city middle school that they called Club Unitos.

As their academic skills increased, their understanding of the system deepened. They began seeing themselves as college bound. They found college prep courses demanding, and they suffered from an abiding and realistic lack of self-confidence. They relied not on self-confidence but on courage to persevere on their own behalf and on the behalf of others like them. They encountered resistance, but still "they elbowed for themselves narrow spots at the tables of power from which they would not budge."[4] Futures student enrollment in advanced placement classes went from seven in tenth grade to twenty-two in eleventh grade and to forty-one in their senior year. They believed that they had blazed the trail for other students like themselves.

In spring 2000 all but one Futures student graduated. Twenty-five of the thirty had offers from four-year colleges. In fall 2001, 90 percent were enrolled at institutions of higher learning. Sixteen were enrolled at four-year colleges, nine were at two-year colleges, and two were in technical or vocational schools. Most of them were involved in campus or community organizations of a political or social service nature. Many of them remained in touch with each other, and many had built networks in their colleges similar to the Futures network.

These were not traditional border crossers. They were New Paradigm border crossers with Freirean motivation who were learning school discourse not to replace their own but to critique it and use it to further the collective self-interest of their class. They had learned that, unlike oppositional identity, resistance need not be self-defeating. In fact, several came to see themselves explicitly as "critical college-going students seeking to prepare themselves to give back to their communities and help recreate schools as democratic institutions."[5]

But the Futures experiment faced resistance from northside parents. In the course of the experiment, the English Department relaxed restrictions on admissions to eleventh- and twelfth-grade English honors classes, and Futures students felt they were at least partly responsible for this. They were shocked when the Parent Teacher Student Association (mostly affluent northsiders) demanded that the English Department create a track between regular and honors English so that students could move up from regular classes but not enter honors classes. The association also urged the social studies department, which had been proud of its economically and racially diverse sections of world history, to create a tenth-grade advanced placement world history class, which would result in further segregation. Futures students tried to take this matter to the student government, but "the advantaged students who thought they had much to lose by de-tracking classes . . . successfully filibustered the dialogue with plans for the prom, Krispy Kreme Day, and the fashion show."[6]

Like the Brownstoners, affluent parents of Wilson High School students apparently defined high-quality education as *exclusive* education. They did not want "other" students in the same classrooms as their children. I put a slightly different interpretation on these events: Apparently, there already had been southside students in honors and AP classes.[7] These were no doubt Old Paradigm border crossers, and so they were few in number and had the "right attitude" from a northsider's prospective. Futures students had an attitude, all right, but it was one of feeling they had a right to the kind of education their student pathways project had shown them was in their self-interest. It was not the attitude northside parents were looking for from upstarts who wanted to share their children's previously exclusive classes.

Oakes and Rogers observe that the status quo is maintained by "powerful cultural narratives or logics."[8] There is the logic of merit: The rich and powerful get that that way through a fair and square contest for which everyone is equally prepared and in which everyone understands and participates willingly. This is closely related to the logic of deficit: Poor and working-class students remain at the bottom of the heap regardless of the opportunities afforded them because of their laziness and cultural and intellectual infirmities.

When projects like Futures demonstrate that, with support, poor and working-class students are able to make remarkable progress in school, even in the face of powerful opposition, protectors of the status quo appeal to the logic of scarcity: We cannot afford programs like Futures because global competition is putting tremendous pressure on business to lower the cost of production. Taxes add to the cost of production and take money away from new investments, and so universal health care, child care, clean air, public transportation, and education must compete for tax dollars in a climate of tax cuts, war spending, and ballooning deficits.

Many Americans who benefit from the status quo appeal to the logic of the rugged individual: We might have the money, but it is wrong to spend it on social programs because they weaken the moral fiber of the less fortunate among us. When the government supplies quality child care for children of working parents, for example, it takes away the parents' incentive to arrange for the care of their own children. This makes them more dependent and less able to compete in the rough-and-tumble economy. This logic applies to programs like Futures as well. Wilson High School had always offered honors courses, and, in fact, some poor and working-class students (those with true grit, some would argue) took advantage of them. Programs that assist more poor and working-class students to take advantage of these courses only make them more dependent. And so you cut taxes, create scarcity, and prevent do-gooders from hurting the poor. This is particularly appealing to many conservatives who believe they got where they are in a fair contest and the poor got what they deserve—falling back on both the logics of merit and deficit but adding, "By protecting them from a 'Nanny State,' we're helping the poor."

Bill Moyers believes that "class war was declared a generation ago . . . [when] William Simon, who was soon to be [Reagan's] Secretary of the Treasury . . . called on the financial and business class, in effect, to take back the power and privileges they had lost in the depression and new deal."[9] This class answered Simon's call "to trash the social contract" and to "starve the beast"—the "beast" being a government too interested in the general welfare and what remained of New Deal programs such as Social Security. The idea was to cut taxes to the point where there simply was no money to devote to the general welfare. In 2003 the fifty states collectively faced a sixty-billion dollar deficit. They did not raise taxes; they cut services. Our parks, forests, levies, libraries, bridges, pure food and drug enforcement, and product safety enforcement, to name just a few, are in shambles.

But tax cuts do more than suck money from the public sphere. They widen the class divide. The gap in wealth between the top 20 percent and the bottom 20 percent, which was thirtyfold in 1960, was seventy-five-fold in 2000.[10] To put the Bush tax breaks into perspective, the average worker who took home $517 per week got about $400 a year in tax breaks, while the average CEO who took home $155,769 per week received well over $50,000 a year in new tax breaks.[11] In 1980 the ratio of CEO pay to average worker compensation was 41 to 1; in 2002 it was 531 to 1. Adjusted for inflation, the minimum wage was higher between 1940 and 1970 than it was in 2000.[12] The tax rate paid by wealthy citizens for the first sixty years of the twentieth century has been cut in half, while taxes paid by the working poor and middle class have increased. Recent tax policy has enabled 60 percent of U.S. corporations to pay no taxes at all, and in some cases corporations receive millions in rebates.[13]

In 2001 44 percent of Americans described the country as a nation of haves versus have-nots. In the late 1980s only 26 percent described the country that way. In 1972 52 percent said the government was run by big interests that looked out only for themselves. In 2000 that figure rose to 65 percent. In 1999 75 percent of Americans said they believed benefits of economy were unevenly distributed.[14] The high-paying jobs of heavy industry have all but disappeared. The lack of jobs or access to jobs by public transportation, the closing off of opportunities for higher education for more and more middle- and low-income

Americans, a disastrous war of choice in Iraq, and the disastrous state of urban schools, exacerbated and exaggerated by conservatives in order to justify the privatization of schooling through vouchers, are the kinds of things that often trigger a movement.

Jean Anyon[15] has argued that educators would have more success in their classrooms if they were to focus on developing a "new civil rights movement," one that demands changes in the federal government's economic policy that over the past thirty years has created the enormous number of urban families in poverty, squeezes the middle class, and at the same time has drastically increased the wealth of the wealthiest. Not all of our poor and working-class students can get a high-status, high-paying occupation, but they can get a hell of a lot better deal than they're getting now. This takes us into a sphere beyond that where educational reformers operate historically. That's the civil sphere, the political sphere.

Chapter 18

AGITATING PARENTS AND PARENTS WHO AGITATE

Gillian Richardson used the first edition of this book as the basis for focus groups with self-identified working-class parents of children in the schools of a one-company town in Western New York.[1] The town was not unlike Freeway in that the company had cut back on workers and was rumored to be on the verge of closing. All the parents were high school graduates, including one who earned a general equivalency diploma (GED); none held a postsecondary degree. There were three stay-at-home mothers, three factory workers, one welder, and one road maintenance worker. Richardson wanted to know what these working-class parents thought about research that had been done on them—so to speak—and she wanted to know if their attitudes toward their own and their children's schooling would change as they reflected on these studies.

She gave each participant a copy of the book, but she did not require that they read it. Each focus group began with a thirty-minute videotape summarizing the pertinent chapters. However, all the participants said they read the entire book and frequently made reference to it. Richardson facilitated each session using a predetermined set of questions that she had developed in an earlier pilot study.

Session One. In discussing Anyon's studies, participants noted that it was common knowledge that there were separate working-class and upscale schools in their town and that working-class schools were inferior. They identified rote learning and authoritarian control, both intellectual and physical, as characteristic of working-class schools. They all remembered having had little power as students and incidents of punishment, sometimes physical punishment. One man said, "That's what sticks out most in my mind—is the punishment."[2] Participants also said their children were often disrespected and humiliated by teachers. Every participant shared at least one such incident.

Session Two. In discussing Freeway High School and the Brownstoners, they said they were not happy with their children's schools, but they didn't like the way more affluent parents tried to influence schools—"brown nosing," pressuring the system through social and political networks, and becoming overly involved in the school. All of these were viewed negatively. This is, of course, the perennial plight of working-class people. They see that middle class discourse works to the advantage of those who use it, but they are repelled by the values, attitudes, behaviors, and beliefs that comprise middle-class discourse. Parents as well as students can have oppositional identity.

They acknowledged the fact that working-class students rejected high-status knowledge. One man said that he knew in high school he wanted to be a welder like his father. As a result, he found English boring and meaningless, but he wanted to learn math because "it was part of my future." However, he did not like the math teacher's rote learning methods, and when he spoke up, he was disciplined for being disruptive. He said, "That experience sort of put a shell on me when it came to math. I had a problem with math from then on."[3]

Third Session. The participants related to Shirley Brice Heath's description of literacy in working-class homes. Most participants did not remember being read to as a children or seeing their parents reading or writing very often. They did read to their own young children, but like Heath's Roadvillers, they concentrated on literal interpretation of stories and were surprised that "how," "why," and "what if" questions helped prepare children for school-learning. Six of the eight participants reported their children had been placed in remedial reading programs at an early age.

Participants "instantly recognized" Bernstein's descriptions of working-class homes and communities, particularly authoritarianism within the family. They agreed that in their parents' homes they had had few opportunities to practice negotiation and there were not many occasions where explicit language was necessary. Decisions were not made collaboratively, and so there was little need for explicit explanations. They acknowledged feelings of powerlessness, particularly as individuals, but they also insisted they had power through group solidarity, particularly related to union tactics in the factory.

While participants agreed that working-class people tend to have less contact with strangers than do middle-class people and therefore less practice in using explicit language, the main focus of discussion was on the caution with which the working class approaches outsiders in terms of communication, particularly those from the upper or better-educated classes.

Fourth Session. Participants were very approving of Freire's methods and those of social justice teachers in the United States like Peterson, Bigelow, and Christensen. They were particularly attracted to the ideas that children need to be given frequent opportunities to express their own ideas and that creativity, expression, and analysis should be encouraged beyond knowing the answers or knowing where to find them. This had become a theme throughout the focus groups, and they recognized that teachers need parents' support to make such methods possible.

Fifth Session. In discussing community organizing around school issues and parent involvement, the group felt outside organizers are needed to raise working-class consciousness and to provide training in organizing strategies. They reiterated the idea that teachers will need the backing of parents to ensure that they can implement changes without jeopardizing their careers.

All the participants expressed a willingness to become involved in organizing efforts to better the educational situation of their children; however, all but one specified that they would be willing to act only behind the scenes—attending meetings, making phone calls, and doing mailings.[4] None of them would be willing to participate in a group that advocated breaking laws or violence.

Richardson found development in the parents' attitudes across the five focus groups from "magical conforming" to "naïve reforming" to "critical-transforming." Magical conforming says there's no problem, or there's a problem, but nothing can be done. Naïve conforming says that the problem is individuals—incompetent principals, teachers, or parents, and recalcitrant students. Fix them, one by one, and it will be OK. The critical transforming attitude that is needed says the problem is in the system. Change unjust and unproductive power relationships between parents, teachers, students, and taxpayers, for example. If you don't change those power relationships, that is change the status quo, it'll never be OK. In the first focus group, problems were seen as caused by historical inevitabilities (e.g., the state has always controlled the curriculum) or uncontrollable external forces—meaning politics. In the last session, the group's attitude towards taking action to confront problems in education was dramatically transformed. They expressed the assumption that change is possible and that success lies in collective action.

Between 2000 and 2002, Mary Finn, Lauri Johnson, and I conducted workshops for parents, teachers, and administrators in one of Buffalo's low-performing schools.[5] The New York State Education Department had mandated site-based management teams for all schools several years earlier—a mandate that, when followed at all, was followed to the letter, rather than the spirit of the law. In 1999, seventeen of the nineteen parents on a Buffalo Public Schools district-wide "parent involvement committee" resigned en masse when the district failed to make promised changes in the local plan for state-mandated site-based management.

Our workshops had three objectives: to familiarize parents with progressive, child-centered, collaborative methods of teaching reading and writing so they could provide effective support at home; to encourage teachers to use more progressive, child-centered, collaborative methods in their classrooms; and to empower parents for effective advocacy in their children's education and participation in school governance. Mary Finn and I planned and facilitated the workshops; Lauri Johnson, a colleague, ethnographer, and mother of two students in the Buffalo Public Schools, participated in the workshops and observed, documented, and evaluated them.

We conducted the workshops at Lakeview Elementary School (a pseudonym), located on State Street (a pseudonym), a major thoroughfare that separates a poor and working-class, largely black and Hispanic community on the east from a poor and working-class, largely white community on the west. These communities had a history of deliberate avoidance, if not animosity, toward one another. They maintained separate community centers, churches, and community organizations. Lakeview students were approximately one-third white, one-third black, and one-third Latino. Ninety-three percent of the students received free and reduced-price breakfast and lunch. Average standardized test scores were well below national norms.

Our workshops lasted two hours and met weekly for six weeks. Graduates of basic workshops were invited to take a follow-up workshop in later cycles. We paid all participants—administrators, teachers, and parents alike—to attend, and we provided childcare. We tried to include twelve parents, two teachers, and one school administrator (principal, social worker, or counselor) in each basic workshop but were not always successful. We soon ran out of administrators who were willing to participate.

Our first objective was to involve parents in children's literacy learning by showing them progressive, child-centered, collaborative methods of teaching reading and writing so they could provide effective support at home. We hoped teachers in the workshops who were not using progressive methods in their classrooms (most of them, we had reason to believe) would be encouraged to do so.

For example, we demonstrated what primary teachers call a Directed Listening and Thinking Activity. The facilitator holds up a picture storybook, reads the title, directs participants to look at the cover picture, and asks "What do you think will happen in this story?" Participants make suggestions and the facilitator asks, "What makes you think that? What are the clues in the title and cover picture?" After a few suggestions, the facilitator opens the book and reads several pages showing the pictures as she/he goes along. Then she/he asks, "Were we right about what the story is about? What clues helped us?" This cycle is repeated until the end of the book.

At the end of the exercise we gave each participant a copy of the book so they could do the exercise at home with their child and write in their journal about the experience. The following week they shared their journal entries in small groups. It was truly amazing to watch these parents come to realize that there were ways to read to their child beyond "sit still and listen"— the typical "literacy event" in most working-class homes.[6] One mother described how her interaction with her five-year-old daughter had changed by the sixth session.

> Before this workshop it was, just do your homework, I'm cooking dinner. Now it's I'll help you with your homework . . . we'll share together . . . and I watch [her more] . . . she's a teacher too. I let her make more decisions than I would normally have. . . . [Before it was] this is the way its going [to be]. And [now] it is more teaching her to think.[7]

We addressed parent empowerment in every workshop as well. One parent empowerment activity was called *Ask the Right Question*.[8] We gave participants seated in small groups copies of an essay with missing punctuation, misspellings like *tigrs* for *tigers* and *lite* for *light*, and with sentences like *My dad and me went to the circus*. The letter *C* on the paper was obviously the teacher's grade, but there were no other marks. We asked, "If your fifth-grade child brought home this paper, what question would you want to ask the teacher?"

The following are some typical responses:

- "Did you notice the spelling (and other) errors? Why didn't you correct them?"
- "How many Cs did you give on this assignment?"
- "How did you arrive at this grade? What would my child have had to do to get a B?"

We repeated this activity using other "props" such as a fourth-grade arithmetic homework assignment that would have been more appropriate for second grade. As a final step, participants role-played parent-teacher conferences. The fact that there were teachers and sometimes administrators in the workshops made for some interesting role plays.

Of course, nothing teaches the numerous skills needed to negotiate with powerful people like experience, and so near the end of each series of basic workshops we introduced the criteria for a good issue: It's easy to understand, it affects a lot of people, and there's a reasonable chance that you will get good results fairly quickly. We asked participants what issue they would be willing to work on at Lakeview School. There was a ground swell of agreement that the lunchroom presented two problems that fit the description of a good issue. Some of the meals were nearly universally detested. Macaroni and cheese was one such meal. It wasn't that the children and teachers didn't like macaroni and cheese; they didn't like *that* macaroni and cheese. Secondly, children who qualified for free lunch (most of the children in the school) were required to pay for chocolate milk most days, and parents were aware that at some other schools chocolate milk was free every day.

When we talk about this episode, a frequent reaction is "Macaroni and cheese? Chocolate milk? Are these the most important problems facing Lakeview Elementary School?" Of course they are not, but experienced organizers know that the first issues parents organize around tend to be less profound then you might expect, and that's good from an organizing point of view. When low test scores is the issue, for example, parents are intimidated by their lack of knowledge and specialized vocabulary. But parents feel entitled to their opinions about macaroni and cheese and free milk. Such issues allow them to enter their first negotiations on familiar turf. Successes here give parents experience and confidence to address more significant issues.

With very little advice from the facilitators, the parents formed a committee and made an appointment with the lunchroom manager. The first meeting was a huge success. The lunchroom manager said that if they didn't want macaroni and cheese, she wouldn't order it any more. As for the chocolate milk—a previous principal believed that chocolate milk was not good for children, and she made the rule that the lunchroom could only offer it free with free lunches one day a week. On the other four days, children would have to pay for it. That principal left, but no one told the lunchroom manager to change the rule. She checked with the current principal, and the next day it was announced that henceforth chocolate milk would be free with free lunch every day, and there would be no more macaroni and cheese. The parents, especially those who met with the lunchroom manager, were elated and were fully ready to take on another issue.

Lauri Johnson made the following observations:

> As workshop participants took up the issue of changing the school lunch program, they began to speak up and feel more empowered as parents. Sarah, a young White woman who worked nights and attended the workshops the next morning without sleep, noted that others had begun to listen to what she had to say: I would normally just let my kid go to school, meet the teacher, she's passing her, OK. But now . . . I'm jotting down meetings and. . . . my voice does count, and I can, you know, it might not be right, but at least I can get in there and share my views . . . it just made me feel really good. . . . [9]

The teachers who participated in the workshops also noticed a change in the parents. As Deborah [a teacher] stated it, "The thing I liked most was seeing the parents interact and seeing them become empowered as the weeks went on. . . . And just the way they expressed themselves. Sitting up straighter in their chair and making more eye contact and you could just see a growth in self-esteem. . . . More people are being involved now with the school and making changes. Like with the lunches, that's a big thing. I mean people have complained for a couple of years about that and nothing has ever been done. . . . So to see the parents go, hey, I can talk about this. This is wonderful."[10]

Using money from Parents for Public Schools, Buffalo, I invited everyone who had completed a basic and follow-up workshop to sign up for a three-session series of workshops based on the first edition of this book.[11] None of the teachers or administrators responded, and so the participants were all parents.

I gave each parent a copy of the book and told them which chapter we would be talking about at each session if they chose to read it, but the reading was not required. In the first workshop, I divided participants into small groups and gave each group a stack of thirty-six cards. On about half the cards there was a statement describing Anyon's working-class schools (for example: "Work consists of copying teacher's notes from the board and writing answers to text questions."), and on the remaining cards there was a statement about her affluent professional schools (for example, "Products are stories, essays, plays, poems, murals, film, craft projects, surveys, and graphics.") The cards were in random order.

I asked participants to divide the cards into two stacks labeled "Describes schools like ones in Amherst" (an upscale suburb) and "Describes schools like Lakeview." The parents had no trouble sorting the cards into piles that matched Anyon's working-class and affluent professional schools. They expressed anger and frustration in the discussion that followed. They blamed the school and the teachers for what was clearly an unfair system.

We did exercises and discussions covering the beginnings of compulsory education, complete with the "big boys" turning the teachers out of the schools, which they loved, the lads, whom they found hilarious, Freeway High School students, whom they recognized as their own children, and class-related attitudes toward authority, conformity, power, and communication styles as observed by Bernstein and Heath. As each new topic was addressed, I asked participants to relate it to differences Anyon found in working-class and affluent professional schools. We compared the efforts of Freeway parents (which failed) and the Brownstoners (which succeeded) to improve educational outcomes for their children to our efforts at organizing parents at Lakeview. By the end of the workshops, parents were no longer blaming teachers, their children, or themselves exclusively for the poor achievement of Lakeview students. They began to see that the whole system (including their part and their children's part in it) was working to their disadvantage. I tried to help them see that changes were needed all around and that such changes needed to be negotiated among all the parties.

One parent asked, "Have the teachers in this school had this set of workshops?" A second said, "They ought to." And a third said, "And we ought to facilitate it for them." This, of course was not the toadying (or "brown nosing") that Richardson's focus group participants believed middle-class parents do to get better schools for their children. And it was not the toadying that parent involvement advocates often seem to expect, however unconsciously. Just as Freirean motivation produces a different kind of border crossers among students, it produces a different kind of "involved parents," and ones for which schools, particularly working-class schools, are not, generally speaking, prepared.

I like to think of Richardson's focus groups and the Lakeview School parent workshops as Corresponding Society meetings and Freire's culture circles. I associate them more directly with the work of Saul Alinsky (1909–1972), a sociology student at the University of Chicago, who in the late 1930s created a new role in the public arena, that of "community organizer." Alinsky died two years after *Pedagogy of the Oppressed* was published in English, and so he may never have heard of Freire, but he was a master of what I have described here as Freirean motivation.

Alinsky applied the art and science of labor organizing to community problems such as inferior public services in working-class neighborhoods. He started the Back of the Yards Council in the white working-class neighborhood adjacent to the Chicago stockyards and the Woodlawn Organization in a black neighborhood near the University of Chicago. He also founded organizations in Rochester, Buffalo, New York City, and California. He trained numerous organizers including César Chávez. Over the years he helped form the Industrial Areas Foundation, which became a nationwide network of organizations that took on such issues as civil rights, job discrimination, and education.

Unlike organizations like Common Cause, whose members tend to be affluent and whose only communication with supporters is to raise money or ask members to e-mail government officials, Industrial Areas Foundation members are recruited from those who are less affluent and affected by injustice, and its explicit goal is to teach people to do politics.

As we shall see, educating working-class children in their own self-interest will involve social justice teachers working both with their students and with parents and community organizations including unions. The schools will produce citizens ready to struggle for a better deal for the majority of working-class citizens, and the organizations will fight for government policies that improve the lives of working-class citizens through universal health care, living wage legislation, quality child care, and so on. This better quality of life will, of course, better prepare poor and working-class children for school and assist in the work of social justice teachers.

Following Alinsky's organizing principles, we had planned to continue to build on our success so that Lakeview parents would take on bigger and bigger issues like the school curriculum, teaching methods, the school budget, discipline, and parents' role in school governance, but this was not to be. The school board announced that several schools would have to be closed because of declining student numbers and budget considerations. Lakeview Elementary School was one of the schools that was closed, but not before a small number of parents from our workshops organized themselves, got a thousand names on a petition, and turned out two hundred parents for a meeting with the superintendent and some school board members. The decision, of course, had been irrevocable before it was announced. So much for the rhetoric of shared decision making that the school board had espoused during the previous five years. Lakeview Elementary School was closed, its students and teachers scattered across the city in a new "choice" program adopted by the board of education.

The fact that Lakeview Elementary School was closed was a big disappointment, but we learned some useful things about parent power and literacy and our roles. Participants overcame their isolation and came together as a community. Parents learned about the benefits of progressive methods of improving literacy and formed new relationships with their children around literacy. They were adopting new attitudes toward authority, and learning to replace authoritarian styles of exercising authority with negotiated styles. They experienced some success in exercising their newfound power. Our biggest regret is that we did not succeed in our efforts to involve workshop participants with VOICE Buffalo, a city-wide Alinsky-inspired multi-issue community organization. We would have drawn strength and longevity from an association with a larger coalition focused on broader social justice issues and might have kept some of our parents involved in school reform.

Of course, there are countless occasions where parents organize on their own. Oakes and Rogers tell the story of one such occasion.[12]

In 1993, Mary Johnson lived in a 950-unit low-income housing complex in South Gate, California, just outside Los Angeles.[13] During a "sweep" of her housing complex following the Rodney King verdict, the police threatened to arrest Johnson's eleven-year-old daughter because she was holding a video camera.[14] They didn't arrest the child, but they did confiscate the camera.

The next day Johnson called the ACLU and the NAACP, and she and a neighbor, Dora Long, began knocking on doors asking residents to sign a petition criticizing the South Gate Police Department. They collected nine hundred signatures in two weeks. This, along with considerable further effort, led to several town hall meetings attended by police, politicians, and the owner of the complex. In the end there were much improved relations between the police and the community; there were improvements in the housing complex, and a standing committee of residents was formed to bring complaints to the owner of the complex.

In 1997, Johnson and several of her fellow activists took part in thirteen weeks of workshops conducted by the Institute for Democracy, Education, and Access (IDEA) Parent Curriculum Project at UCLA. The purpose of the UCLA workshops was similar to one of our objectives for the Lakewood Elementary School workshops—to demonstrate to parents what good teaching and learning look like. The meetings themselves were conducted along progressive lines. Participants studied state standards in every subject and learned how they could be met using progressive methods. They conducted "learning walks" through classrooms and compared what they saw with the way the Institute classes were run. For many the contrast between the Institute classes and the way their children were being taught (which was the same way they had been taught as children) was a revelation. One parent commented, "Is this really possible? Can we do this? Do we have a right to be taught this way?"[15]

Understanding the standards, how methods of teaching can affect learning, and how these were affected by school policy, these parents began to ask questions in the schools. School officials were happy to think that the project would create a new pool of volunteers, but they were wary of "complainers." In other words, they were not happy with the prospect of "involved parents" with Freirean motivation; therefore, they were not forthcoming with information. The parents realized they needed more information before they could effect school change, and so in 2001 Valarie Munoz, Mary Johnson, and Emma Street started an organization called Parent U-Turn, and they joined a UCLA Seminar on accessing information on the distribution of educational opportunities across the schools of greater Los Angeles. They learned that things were even worse than they suspected in the schools their children attended and that their district was not unique. Widespread reform was in order, and they began to imagine how the disruptive knowledge they had discovered could become a catalyst for change.

Parent U-Turn learned numerous lessons in gaining and exercising power and has had numerous successes. When they tried to force the schools to comply with the No Child Left Behind mandate for parent involvement in school governance, they were met with such tactics as having the schools hold "public" meetings that were never announced or that were announced after the meetings were held. One member was threatened with being removed from a meeting for complaining that a council had been elected without notifying the parents that an election was to be held. They advertised their complaints in *Teaching to Change LA*, a UCLA online journal, and that attracted the attention of a local newspaper. They used this attention to get advice from a civil rights lawyer. They sent a seven-page letter to the head of complaints at the California State Department of Education documenting thirty-four violations of NCLB legislation. This finally "resulted in a detailed agreement providing parents with access to information and assurances of full inclusion in district and school-site planning and decision making."[16] Mary Johnson remarked, "The document we have has power in it. When I call the assistant superintendent and say, 'You are out of compliance,' they respond in two or three days."[17]

Many schools in Los Angeles are on a "three-track, year-round" school system in order to address overcrowding. Two-thirds of the students are in school and one-third are off on a rotating twelve-month schedule. When Parent U-Turn learned that some schools would go to a four-track system, they were up in arms, in part because of the child care complications this would create for working parents. However, they reframed the debate to make their position more powerful politically. They argued that the four-track plan was simply a way to enable the district to avoid addressing the real problem: More schools needed to be built. Furthermore, they argued the plan had been announced without community consultation. And, why, they asked, was there no three-(or four-) track, year-round system in more affluent areas of the district?

Parent U-Turn's campaign culminated in a 50 percent effective one-day boycott of Johnson's local school and a parent demonstration. Due, no doubt, to her long-standing relationship with them, the city sent portable toilets, and the local police sent a squad car to ensure the demonstrators were not harassed. The following day four busloads of parents converged on the school board meeting. Johnson demanded a solution that would end overcrowding, not prolong it. The school board agreed to delay the implementation of the four-track schedule, and Parent U-Turn resolved to continue to put pressure on the board.

Over time, Parent U-Turn won concrete improvements in their local schools and developed a collective identity as researchers and activists that enabled them to tackle increasingly difficult challenges. They have become a force to be reckoned with in local education politics. How's that for parents who agitate?

Chapter 19

SCALING AGITATION UPWARD

In 2004, Alex Caputo-Pearl, a Los Angeles teacher-activist, invited Mary Finn and me to a meeting of the Coalition for Educational Justice, where opposition to the California High School Exit Examination would be under discussion. I went with serious reservations.

Since my first teaching job in 1959, I have believed that standardized tests based on national norms are a good thing. I taught seventh grade in Woodlawn, the black neighborhood south of the University of Chicago where Alinsky founded the Woodlawn Organization. Woodlawn was a "port of entry" for blacks who were moving north for the first time, and I would frequently get new students from the Deep South. They would typically come in with report cards from their previous schools with all Cs, but their standardized test scores would typically reflect a third- through fifth-grade level of achievement. The report cards told their parents that the children were doing OK. "OK compared with what?" I asked myself.

I thought, and I still think, such parents were being conned. Therefore, I believe in standardized testing based on national norms. I think parents should want to know where their children stand, where their children's schools stand, and where their economic, ethnic, or racial groups stand *compared to all children in the nation*. If the answer to any of those questions is not so good, I think they should be mad as hell and want to do something about it. The solution should not be to stop the schools from giving the tests that tell us what we need to know.

The No Child Left Behind Law originally mandated that there would be a single set of standardized tests, with norms based on large national samples of students for each subject in each of the grades tested. Minimum scores would be established for each test to determine whether students had met the standard. Schools would be compared with every other school in the nation. School systems could be compared with every other school system in the nation. States could be compared with every other state.

Whoa! The mandate was almost immediately changed so that each state would create its own tests, with norms based on a sample of students within the state, and each state would set its own minimum standards. As a result, I'm almost certain, based on years experience as a professional educator and political observer, that some schools in northeastern states that are being "decertified" because of low student scores are doing better than some schools in southeastern states that appear to be meeting the "standards." That is because when there is a single test with norms based on a large national sample, average standardized test scores in the northeast have historically been above national averages while average standardized test scores in the southeast have historically been below national averages.

Anyone familiar with the literature of standardized testing over the last fifty years knows this is true, and yet the folks in the United States Department of Education hypocritically rattle on about tough standards while backing away from the only process that would tell us who is meeting standards and who isn't. Once again, political considerations dictated what we would all like to believe is dispassionate, apolitical, public school policy.

As it turned out my anxiety about attending the Coalition for Educational Justice meeting was unwarranted. They were miles ahead of me. No Child Left Behind legislation not only mandates testing and standards, it sets standards for what schools must provide to enable all children to meet the standards set for them: a certified teacher in every classroom teaching in the subject they are certified for (no more social studies teachers teaching algebra, for example), reasonable class size, adequate supplies, and clean and safe learning environments, among other things.

It costs nothing to blame victims: to shame children, their parents, their teachers their schools, their neighborhoods, their class, their race, or their ethnic group. But it's unfair to impose a high-stakes standardized test that would have resulted in stripping mostly working-class students and students of color of diplomas when the state has not come near providing the minimal standard for schools described in No Child Left Behind legislation. The demand under the discussion at the meeting was that the state provide decent schools first, and then the Coalition would be eager to talk about a high school exit exam.

The Coalition for Educational Justice originated in 1999. It was a key player in a grassroots victory in 2003, when groups pressured the Los Angeles Unified School District Board of Education and, eventually, the California State Board of Education, to delay implementation of the California High School Exit Examination. It was initially a group composed mainly of teachers, many of whom had cut their teeth organizing against California state propositions targeting poor and working-class citizens.[1] Many of these teachers had been a part of producing *A Second Opinion*, a progressive newsletter published within United Teachers of Los Angeles, the Los Angeles teachers' union, and distributed to five thousand to ten thousand teachers. Over time, through grassroots organizing, the Coalition for Educational Justice became a coalition of hundreds of teachers, students, and parents.

Teacher-members of the Coalition for Educational Justice are what Anyon refers to as "bi-cultural brokers."[2] They are in a position to become intimately involved as organizers with their students, their student's parents, and their communities as the Coalition for Educational Justice has done, and at the same time they can leverage both their middle-class status and their power as members of a powerful union. Teachers' unions and collective teacher action hold enormous and largely untapped potential to bring about social change.[3]

The Coalition has developed a political education curriculum that includes structural analysis, organizing, and social movement building. They teach it in their classrooms, and they urge other teachers to do likewise. On the day I write this, the Coalition for Educational Justice has representatives and chapters in over thirty schools in Los Angeles Unified School District. In 2002, Coalition for Educational Justice played a lead role when people associated with *A Second Opinion* formed Progressive Educators for Action. By 2005, Progressive Educators for Action became part of a coalition that swept the union elections, winning four of seven city-wide offices and the majority of the union's board of directors. Coalition for Educational Justice teacher leaders remain an integral part of Progressive Educators for Action and its work of showing teachers how to organize other teachers around progressive issues.

Today's social justice teacher-educators are acting outside the walls of academe as well. In May of 2000 a group of California students and their parents sued the governor, the State Department of Education, and State Superintendent of Schools, claiming that the students attended schools that lacked "trained teachers, necessary educational supplies, classrooms, even seats in classrooms, and facilities that meet basic health and safety standards."[4] The case became known as the Williams case, named after one of the plaintiffs.

Jeannie Oakes and John Rogers, Directors of the Institute for Democracy, Education, and Access at UCLA, were among more than a dozen nationally known educators who were brought in to examine evidence related to the Williams case.[5] Together with teams from the American Civil Liberties Union, Public Advocates, and the Mexican American Legal Defense and Educational Fund, they showed that deficiencies in teachers, materials, and facilities were clustered in schools attended by low-income students. They argued that in order to meet state standards and pass state tests, students needed to learn certain content and skills, and schools that lack basic resources are unable to teach this content and these skills. Not only does the California state constitution define education as a fundamental right, California law requires basic educational equality; and so the plaintiffs argued that the state was failing to meets its constitutional and legal obligations not only to them but to more than one million other students who attended schools like theirs. The state did not dispute the plaintiffs' claims. Instead, it argued that even if it provided more resources to this population of students, their test scores would not improve. The logic of deficit yet again!

The Williams case caught the attention of grassroots organizations interested in such issues as the minimum wage, affordable housing, immigrant rights, and affirmative action. They began to see their issues as integral to school achievement of poor and working-class students, and they saw the possibility of forming coalitions around school achievement that incorporated all their issues. Several such groups joined forces to press the Williams case and to agitate for implementation of the court decision if the case was decided in the plaintiff's favor.

Gary Blasi, a professor involved in UCLA's Public Interest Law and Policy Program and a consultant on the Williams litigation team, convened a meeting of professional organizers, leaders of grassroots groups, education reform advocates, teachers, civil rights lawyers, and activists, and he invited Oakes and Rogers to discuss their interests in the Williams case and share the research they had done in relation to it. At the meeting the organizers and activists learned that UCLA faculty could provide data and analysis that would be useful in furthering the cause, and the UCLA faculty learned that because of their relationship to the aggrieved parties (in many cases they were the aggrieved parties), their political savvy, and their commitment to action, organizers and activists asked the right questions.[6] After several such meetings, about half a dozen organizations joined with the UCLA team in what became the Educational Justice Collaborative. By 2006 (four years later) thirty organizations had joined. Families and communities of students most adversely affected by unequal schools were at the forefront.

As the project evolved, the UCLA team's main role was to do research, produce data and analysis, and teach organizers and activists how to do this work themselves. Much of what they produced was disruptive knowledge. This led to a two-way flow of information between grassroots organizers and activists who understood and experienced the inequities in the schools on the one hand, and legal and policy experts who were trained to collect data and fashion arguments to address these inequities on the other. The experts and academics joined with the organizers and activists in reassessing their knowledge and adjusting their arguments in light of the knowledge and experience of the other.

This is what typically happens when people work and negotiate across discourse communities. Each borrows the knowledge, values, and even ways of talking from the other as it suits their purposes.

Throughout the duration of the Williams case, grassroots organizations used their organizing know-how and media savvy to raise public awareness of the conditions in California schools. They built relationships and took direct action to persuade the state to respond to the case through behind-the-scenes legislative advocacy, confrontations in public meetings, getting media attention, mobilizing members for mass actions, and doing research in communities. They shared disruptive knowledge in community forums, in formal reports, on T-shirts and banners, and in speeches at public demonstrations and testimony before policy makers. They used press releases, editorial board meetings, op-ed pieces, talk-show appearances, and ongoing relationships with reporters as vehicles for what Dewey would have called "a new public intelligence."[7]

The Educational Justice Collaborative was able to reframe the issues in the Williams case. The state wanted to talk about the insurmountable deficits of the students and their families; the Educational Justice Collaborative members argued that the problem was not that the students had deficiencies but that they were denied "opportunities to learn."

When Governor Schwarzenegger took office in 2003, he ordered the attorney general to settle the Williams case. In a statement regarding his position on the case, Schwarzenegger said, "I've seen how inner city schools are falling behind because they're not getting the equal teaching and the equal books, and equal learning material."[8] We learn here that the Terminator may in fact be a compassionate conservative, or at least an intelligent conservative, and that the Educational Justice Collaborative's "opportunities to learn" framing of the problem carried the day.

The state agreed to adopt new standards and new accountability mechanisms to ensure qualified teachers and decent facilities and instructional materials in all California public schools. Parents, teachers, and community members were given mechanisms to complain if the standards were not met, and the state agreed to firm timelines for taking corrective action.

Finally, the state agreed to devote a billion dollars to address the terrible conditions that Williams plaintiffs identified. Sadly, the billion dollars was not "new money." It was taken from money already earmarked for education.[9]

There is no doubt that the Educational Justice Collaborative was instrumental in the outcome, through both their research and their argument, but perhaps more importantly by agitating—lobbying legislators, orchestrating confrontations at public meetings, getting media attention, and turning out people in mass actions. Oakes and Rogers believe that the state's ultimate willingness to settle the Williams case turned more on the political power of grassroots advocacy than on any findings of fact. It is certain that neither would have prevailed without the other.[10]

Although its focal point was originally the Williams case, the Educational Justice Collaborative is not a single-issue organization. It has developed new leaders, increased the number of people who participate in public engagement, altered the course of legislation and policy, and forced policymakers to recognize and legitimize their organizing strategies as a proper, even necessary, form of public engagement.

The Williams Case was one manifestation of a nationwide movement for fiscal equity in public schooling. Since 1973 lawsuits have been filed in forty-four states.[11] The first wave of such cases was argued on the basis of "equal protection." By 1990, however, with the beginning of the standards movement, the basis of the suits shifted. Nearly every state constitution guarantees citizens "a sound basic education," "a thorough and efficient education," or "an ample education," and when state education departments and professional teachers' organizations such as the International Reading Association and the National Council of Teachers of Mathematics began establishing minimum subject-matter learning standards for each grade, these standards gave plaintiffs and the courts a way to define "a sound basic education." Standards written by state departments of education put the emphasis on *sound* rather than *basic*, and so the basis of fiscal equity lawsuits shifted from equal protection to holding states responsible for providing constitutionally guaranteed sound basic education. Students' social right to a sound education was recognized by the courts in state after state.

In New York, for example, the Campaign for Fiscal Equity educated the court on the history of the national standards-based reform movement and the development of standards in New York State. The court ruled that a sound basic education is one that prepares students to vote and serve on juries intelligently. That would include the ability to read and understand propositions and constitutional amendments on ballots and to understand scientific evidence presented in trials. Having defined the state's responsibility to students in terms of standards, the court defined remedies in terms of what public schools must provide in order for students to have a reasonable chance to meet the standards. These included sufficient qualified teachers and principals, appropriate class size, adequate school buildings, sufficient up-to-date books, supplies, libraries, technology, laboratories, and a safe, orderly environment.

However, legislatures with a "starve the beast" agenda routinely subvert attempts to enforce court-ordered remedies for fiscal inequity. In West Virginia the legislature simply ignored the court-ordered remedies, and the court backed down. In New Jersey the legislature challenged the court's order, and the court and legislature have yet to resolve the issue as of this writing.

The Coalition for Fiscal Equity put together a panel of the nation's leading economists and school finance experts to determine the resources that will be needed to provide all New York State's students a reasonable opportunity to meet the state's education standards. The panel found that it will take between $7.7 billion and $8.5 billion of *additional* funding—$5.3 billion for New York City Schools alone. That money has not been forthcoming.

In every struggle for citizens' rights—abolition, women's suffrage, the labor movement, civil rights, and women's rights—court decisions are crucial, but it takes agitation, struggle, and "thick" grassroots democracy to make legal rights (de jure) into rights citizens enjoy (de facto). As we have seen, those who benefit from the status quo will fight every erosion of their privileges at every step along the way. We can learn something from the fact that when the Campaign for Fiscal Equity brought its suit in New York, the state was not represented by a team from the more than three hundred attorneys in the state's attorney's office. Instead, the state paid $11 million to a law firm from Atlanta, Georgia, that it claimed was nationally recognized as an expert in education law. Its expertise was, in fact, in fighting school desegregation.[12]

I would venture to guess that in 2008 we are about as far along in the struggle for real schools for poor and working-class students (which must include motivation to learn as well as opportunities to learn) as the civil rights movement was in 1958. Those most affected—poor and working-class students, their parents (and their unions), and their teachers (and their unions)—must organize many, many more people and form larger and larger coalitions. This movement is already under way.

Research for Action, a Philadelphia-based nonprofit organization engaged in education research and reform, has documented the activities and accomplishments of four community-based, multi-issue organizations working in low-to-moderate-income communities to improve public education.[13] They are the Logan Square Neighborhood Organization in Chicago, Austin Interfaith in Texas, New York ACORN, and the Oakland Community Organizations in California. Like the Education Justice Collaborative organizations, these four are multi-issue organizations that work on educational justice issues outside the school establishment.

The Logan Square Neighborhood Organization, for example, was started a by group of local churches, businesses, and homeowners in the Logan Square area of Chicago who were worried about the rapid suburbanization and deindustrialization of the Chicago metropolitan area in the early 1960s. Their goals were to develop youth leadership, enhance neighborhood safety, maintain affordable housing, and revitalize the local economy. Its membership now includes both individuals and representatives of forty-seven neighborhood organizations.

When Illinois state law created local school councils in 1988, the Logan Square Neighborhood Organization turned its attention to assisting parents to improve schools. Among its accomplishments are new school buildings, evening community learning centers, mortgage incentives to encourage teachers and principals to buy houses and live in the area, parent training as tutors and mentors, and a teacher-preparation program where Chicago State University offers free courses in the neighborhood for parents interested in becoming teachers.

The Logan Square Neighborhood Organization Parent Mentor program has trained over 840 parents in leadership skills and brought them into classrooms where they provide extra social and academic help to children. Their presence in the classroom has led to more individualized student attention, better parent-teacher communication, and an increasingly more orderly and respectful atmosphere within the schools. Graduates of the Parent Mentor Program have been key actors in developing community centers at Logan Square Neighborhood Organization schools and in leading the fight against gentrification and maintaining Logan Square as a mixed-income neighborhood. Logan Square Neighborhood Organization initiatives and the parent involvement project have resulted in gains in student achievement in neighbor schools. In 1990 the percent of students reading above the national average ranged from eleven to twenty-two percent at the six core Logan Square schools. By 2000 those figures ranged from twenty-four to thirty-six percent.

The Logan Square Neighborhood Organization has obtained district and city funds for facility improvements and after-school programs that provide academic enrichment. They have sponsored new kinds of professional development for teachers and principals, including visits to other schools with parents to observe innovative programs, in-service training driven by the needs of teachers and principals, home-visit training, and workshops with parents to design schools and curriculum, and they have increased the presence of parents in schools and the roles parents are playing, making parent-school negotiation and collaboration a reality. It has also obtained funding to build new schools and facilities in overcrowded districts to the tune of five new annexes at elementary schools and two new middle schools.

The other three organizations included in the Research for Action report achieved similar results. These organizations demonstrate the power of grassroots organizing outside the school establishment to effect real change in the schools. Technical, interior educational reforms that come about through negotiations

with organized parents and communities can make a difference—
they may be the only kind that do.

Colleges of teacher education could do a lot better job of preparing their students to become social justice educators and
bicultural brokers.[14] Nearly all colleges of teacher education
teach their students to use progressive methods of instruction,
quite reasonable on the basis of learning theory. But as the lads
and Freeway High school students demonstrate, introducing
progressive methods into working-class classrooms involves
an enormous struggle. And so we find our students who go to
working-class schools using traditional curricula and methods
of instruction almost the day they start to teach.

It makes better sense to advocate progressive methods on
the basis of the work of sociologists such as Anyon, Ogbu, Weis,
Heath, and Oakes, and sociolinguists such as Bernstein and
Gee, and on examples of earlier empowering education such as
Corresponding Societies, Ruskin College, The Central Labour
College, Commonwealth College, and Brookwood College. Progressive methods are empowering. Traditional methods are
domesticating. If your aim is to enable poor and working-class
students to demand and protect their citizenship rights, you
must use progressive methods, but in poor and working-class
classrooms, progressive methods must be used in combination
with Freirean motivation.

On the other hand, it's easy to get carried away by the idea
that if you understand the sociology, history, and politics of education, you're ready to be progressive teacher. I taught middle
and high school in 1960s, mostly on the south side of Chicago,
and I saw many "flower children" come to teach in the schools
where I was teaching. They had the struggle for justice part of it
down pretty well, but apparently no knowledge of teaching and
not much interest in the hard work of teaching, and it was not
a pretty picture. You've got to know quite a lot about the nuts
and bolts of teaching to become a teacher like Peterson, Christensen, or Tan. And so progressive methods of teaching must be
taught, not simply referred to with the assumption that anyone
can teach if her or his heart is in the right place.

Most teachers believe in meritocracy, that there's a level playing field, and so those who don't make it have only themselves to blame. Teachers who teach in poor and working-class schools must have a realistic picture of who their students are and who their students' parents are. Social science and labor studies departments in colleges offer such courses as History of the Working Class; History of the Labor Movement; History of Social Change: Abolition, the Labor Movement, Women's Rights, and Civil Rights; Economics of Poverty in America; and Class-Related Discourse Theory. Humanities, American studies, and working-class studies departments offer courses in working-class literature, drama, film, art, and music. It would be ideal if undergraduate teacher-education students could satisfy their core requirements with these courses and organize them into a program leading to an undergraduate minor in working-class studies.

But to ensure that teacher education faculty and students can learn who working-class people are at their best, they need to engage in projects like Futures, the Lakeview Parent Workshops, Coalition for Educational Justice, Educational Justice Collaborative, or Logan Square Neighborhood Association. Had Ruby Payne taken part in any one of these projects, she might not have perseverated on the sordid details of cases with which she "had become acquainted" and noticed instead the admirable qualities and potential of the poor and working-class people with whom she *would have* become acquainted. She might have made better sense of the concept of discourse and made more effective suggestions as to how to teach powerful discourse to working-class students. True enough, the people engaged in these projects are only part of the working-class community, but so are the people in the tabloid scenarios Payne offers us and from which too many of us are eager to generalize. Ideally, New Paradigm teacher education students would fulfill part of their requirements by working with grassroots organizations and labor unions.

Finally, New Paradigm teacher education students must be placed for their supervised teaching experience with veteran teachers who have a proven track record in New Paradigm teaching and student achievement. Finding veteran New Paradigm teachers is not easy, but it is possible. They can be found in organizations like the Coalition for Educational Justice, and they can be created in projects like Duncan-Andrade's teacher inquiry group at an elementary school in south-central Los Angeles.[15]

The twenty-first-century version of last century's civil rights movement will be a citizens' rights movement, particularly a social and economic rights movement for all Americans—both the poor and working classes, which have always been under siege, and increasingly the middle class, which has come under siege by government policies beginning with Reagan. It will be waged within classrooms like Peterson's, Christensen's, Bigelow's, and Tan's. It will be waged in communities involving teachers, parents, and students like the Coalition for Educational Justice. It will be waged within schools and involve university faculty, teachers, and parents like the Lakeview Elementary School Workshops and Parent U-Turn. It will involve university faculty, teachers, and students like in the Futures Project. It will involve teachers, teacher unionists, parents, and students like those in the Coalition for Educational Justice. And it will be waged in the streets, the legislatures, and the courts with organizations like the Educational Justice Collaborative and the Logan Square Neighborhood Association.

There must be two related, symbiotic, and simultaneous movements. The first will be a movement to educate working-class students (using Freirean motivation) to fight for social rights effectively as students and as future citizens—whether as New Paradigm border crossers committed to social justice for everyone or as the vast majority of working-class students who will not become middle-class when they leave school but will have a better life as a working-class adults with full citizenship rights. The second will be a movement among older students and adult citizens for universal social rights through campaigns for such things as unions, living wages, universal health care, and decent schools. As the second movement gains ground, poor and working-class children will arrive at school better prepared and in better health, as well as better fed, housed, and cared for. This will make the work of the schools (the first movement) more effective.

Chapter 20

IMPORTANT CONCEPTS AND A FEW LINES
FROM *LES MISERABLES*

The following are the important concepts from the book in an order that outlines the central argument of the book.

Domesticating/empowering education. Domesticating education is associated with working-class (and, in fact, middle-class) classrooms. Methods are traditional and teacher centered. Discipline and control of students is authoritarian. Ideal students are docile and obedient.

Empowering education. Empowering education is associated with affluent professional and executive elite classrooms. Teachers are in charge, but they negotiate with students regarding discipline and control, and even curriculum and methods at times. Methods are progressive and student centered. Ideal students are inquisitive and assertive.

Negotiation. I believe the single most important characteristic that explains differences between Anyon's working-class, middle-class, affluent professional, and executive elite classrooms is the degree to which teachers are willing to negotiate with students about discipline, curriculum, methods, and meanings of subject matter learned. Starting with near zero in working-class classrooms, the more affluent the students, the more negotiation there is. Negotiation also marks the differences between traditional and progressive methods, informational literacy and powerful literacy, discourse communities of the least affluent and powerful to the most affluent and powerful, and Old Paradigm and New Paradigm working-class classrooms.

Progressive / Traditional Methods of Teaching. In progressive classrooms, curriculum guides are viewed not as something that must be covered by each child in a fixed and thorough manner but as guides for facts, concepts, skills, understandings, and attitudes that might be developed as the teacher deems appropriate for the class and for individual students. Teachers make an effort to relate what is being taught to the students' lives outside school. The teacher and textbook are not the sole sources of knowledge. Pupils go on field trips, utilize the library and audiovisual presentations, interview local citizens, and so on. Memorization and drill are replaced with efforts to lead students to discover general principles. The ideal is not discipline from above but self-discipline. Students are rewarded for inquisitiveness and assertiveness. Progressive education is empowering. Progressive methods are conducive to powerful literacy and action.

In traditional classrooms instruction typically consists of memorization and drill, copying teachers' notes, and writing answers to textbook questions. The teacher and the textbook are almost the sole sources of knowledge. There's little attempt to relate what is being taught to the students' lives outside school. Teachers tend to be authoritarian. Control of the students is paramount. Students are rewarded for docility and obedience. Traditional education is domesticating. It often results in only functional literacy or possibly informational literacy. Traditional methods are not conducive to acquiring powerful literacy. In fact they interfere with the acquisition of powerful literacy.

Oppositional identity and student resistance. Minorities with a history of oppression feel that adopting the identity of their oppressors and abandoning their own is a form of betrayal to their ancestors and community, and so they form their identities in part as being "not like them," and, as acts of defiance, they accentuate parts of their identity that the majority find offensive. A similar mechanism is found in working-class identity formation in opposition to more affluent classes. Since schools are the purveyors of dominant culture, working-class students tend to resist the attempts of the school to educate them.

Border crossers. Border crossers are poor and working-class students who are willing work hard and adopt the values, attitudes, interests, ways of talking, and so on, of the middle class and more or less abandon those of their community in order to become middle class through schooling. This has worked for a small number of poor and working-class students generation after generation. Their numbers are small partly because of oppositional identity.

New Paradigm border crossers work hard in school and learn school discourse not to replace their own but to use it to further their self-interest and the collective self-interest of their class.

Discourse Community. A community where members share values, attitudes, behaviors, beliefs, ways of learning, and ways of talking is a discourse community. Working-class discourse communities are characterized by authoritarianism, conformity, feelings of powerlessness, and a society of intimates. These characteristics underlie a tendency toward implicit communication and absence of negotiation skills.

More affluent discourse communities are characterized by collaborative exercise of authority, less conformity, feelings of power, and a society of strangers. These characteristics underlie a tendency toward explicit language, negotiation skills, and a willingness to negotiate.

We *acquire* a new discourses (a largely unconscious process) as we become members of a new community as long as its beliefs, values, and attitudes do not seriously conflict with those we already have. We can *learn* a new discourse (a conscious process) and adopt certain of its characteristics if we find them it useful to our purposes, as do New Paradigm border crossers.

Levels of Literacy. There are four levels of literacy: performative, the ability to "sound out" words and turn sentences that are typical of informal face-to-face conversation into writing; functional, the ability to meet the reading and writing demands of an average day of an average person; informational, the ability to read and absorb the kind of knowledge that is associated with the school and to write examinations and reports based on such knowledge; powerful, the ability to evaluate, analyze, and synthesize while reading and listening and to persuade and negotiate through writing and speaking. It is literacy used to understand and control what's going on around you. It is the literacy of persons who are conscious of their own power and self interest. It's the literacy of negotiation.

Autonomous model of literacy. The autonomous model of literacy refers to a belief that if you teach people to read as well as, say, the average fourth grader, all of the knowledge, wisdom, and culture in print is available to them, and they will just naturally pursue it in the style of Abe Lincoln. It's not so. If students are not taught powerful literacy and if it is not the typical literacy of their discourse community, they are not likely to acquire it. If students are taught by traditional methods, they are not likely to acquire powerful literacy.

Citizenship Rights. Citizens' Social Rights are the rights to a decent standard of food, housing, clothing, health care, childcare, and education and to live the life of a cultivated human being according to the prevailing standards of the society. Without social rights, people are not able to fully exercise their civil and political rights. Poor, uneducated people are hardly in a position to assert their right to free speech or to run for office, for example.

Marshall believed that all citizens had civil and political rights in the mid-twentieth century and that through meritocracy in public schools all *deserving* citizens would have social rights by the end of the twentieth century.

The clash between citizenship rights, particularly social rights, on the one hand and the free-market economy and social class on the other. Modern citizenship is a system of equality. The free market and social class are systems of inequality. These institutions struggle with one another for ascendance. When legislatures pass minimum wage laws, for example, they enhance social rights and, therefore, citizens rights, and they limit the freedom of the market. When legislatures repeal minimum wage laws, they unleash free-market forces that curtail social rights. It's a rare bird who thinks the free market or social class can, or even should, be abolished, but most people in the center and on the left believe efforts should be made to moderate the unequal distribution of wealth that is inherent in social class and a free-market economy and that infringes on the citizens rights, particularly the social rights of workers.

Starve the beast. William Simon, President Reagan's Secretary of the Treasury called on the financial and business class to take back the power and privilege they had lost in the New

Deal, to "trash the social contract," and to "starve the beast"—
the "beast" being a government too interested in the general welfare and such programs as Social Security.[1] The idea was to cut
taxes to the point where there simply was no money to devote to
the general welfare. This philosophy worked, and it is at work
still. It's a clear-cut case where the forces of the free market and
social class were enhanced at the expense of citizen's rights,
especially social rights.

Merit/meritocracy. Meritocracy is the belief that all children
naturally want high-status, high-paying occupations (extrinsic
motivation) and so while all students are invited compete for
high-status educational programs on the basis of examinations,
students are not equally willing to put forth the effort in school
to prepare for such occupations. Therefore, students who are
smart and work hard earn high scores, get places in high-status
school programs, enter high-status, high-paying professions, and
end up with more money and status than the average citizen
regardless of the socioeconomic status of their parents; students
who are not smart or don't work hard earn low scores on examinations, are assigned to low-status school programs, enter low-
status, low-paying occupations, and must be satisfied with less
status and a more modest standard of living *regardless of the
socioeconomic status of their parents.*

This is nonsense, of course, because (a) poor and working-
class children are not as well prepared for elementary school as
middle-class, affluent professional and executive elite children;
(b) poor and working-class children attend different schools from
middle-class, affluent professional, and executive elite children,
and poor and working-class schools are inferior; (c) poor and
working-class children who earn high test scores do not have the
same access to higher education, especially high-status higher
education, as more affluent students who earn similar or even
lower test scores; and (d) middle-class, affluent professional,
and executive elite children who are not very bright or lazy or
both still find their way into higher education (often high-status
higher education).

Logic of Deficit. The logic of deficit is the belief that poor and
working-class students remain at the bottom of the heap regardless of the opportunities afforded them because of the laziness,
bad behavior, and cultural and intellectual infirmities of poor

and working-class people. It enables us to believe that meritoc-racy is a just system in the face of overwhelming evidence that whether one rises or falls depends almost entirely on the socio-economic status of his or her parents.

Social justice educators. Social justice educators are self-con-sciously critical of inequities in our society. They engage in the New Paradigm for the education for poor and working-class stu-dents, which relies on Freirean motivation to urge students to learn traditional school discourse not to replace their discourse but to acquire powerful literacy, the literacy that will enable the majority of poor and working-class children to become better able to exercise their social, civil, and political rights.

Freirean motivation. Poor and working-class students with Freirean Motivation understand that cooperating and working hard in school does not have to be about border crossing. It can be about becoming powerful and remaining working-class.

It requires that teachers (a) address social justice issues while teaching history, English, art, music, and even math and science and (b) teach the history of democratic movements such as abo-lition, suffrage, and labor not as messiah stories but as stories of average citizens who organized and stood up for themselves.

It requires (a) that students understand how power is exer-cised in our social, economic, and social systems, by whom, and for whose benefit and (b) that they can appropriate the discourse of power not to join the middle class but to negotiate to get a bet-ter deal for themselves and their families.

This is the motivation of the Corresponding Societies, of Ruskin and Central Labour Colleges, and of Commonwealth and Brookwood Colleges. It's the motivation found in projects like Futures and in classrooms of teachers like Peterson, Bigelow, Christensen, Tan, and Kinsman.

Disruptive knowledge. Disruptive knowledge is knowledge that exposes the injustice of the status quo.[2] It is a key element in Freirean motivation. Examples of disruptive knowledge are what Futures students learned in their student pathways proj-ect, the statistics that the UCLA team supplied the plaintiffs in the Williams case regarding unequal funding and conditions that "shock the conscience" in California's poor and working-class schools, and the information parents in Parent U-Turn sought from the schools, were denied, and had to ferret out for themselves.

Old Paradigm / New Paradigm. The Old Paradigm for the education for poor and working-class students relies on extrinsic motivation and learning traditional school discourse in order to become middle-class, that is, to border cross in the traditional sense. It is heavily invested in the validity of the concept of meritocracy and the logic of deficit.

The New Paradigm for the education for poor and working-class students relies on Freirean motivation to urge students to learn traditional school discourse not to replace their discourse but to acquire powerful literacy, the literacy that will enable the majority of poor and working-class children (who will no doubt continue to leave school at the end of high school or sooner) to become better able to exercise their social, civil, and political rights.

Literacy with an attitude. Powerful literacy in the possession of poor and working-class people is literacy with an attitude. It is the literacy of the Corresponding Societies, Freire's cultural circles, the Central Labour College, Brookwood and Commonwealth Labor Colleges, the Futures project, and classrooms like those of Peterson, Bigelow, Christensen, Tan, and Kinsman. It is the literacy of the Coalition for Educational Justice, the Educational Justice Collaborative, and the Logan Square Neighborhood Organization. It's the literacy of thick democracy.

Thin democracy / thick democracy. A thin democracy is one like ours in America where citizens depend on laws, rules, and regulations interpreted and enforced by a professional class of politicians to secure and protect their rights, including social rights, and where college-educated, affluent citizens are a whole lot more likely to engage in protest activities, to work in a political campaign, to be affiliated with a political organization, to be involved with informal community activities, or to vote than less affluent, less educated citizens. In thick democracy citizens don't rely on a elected politicians to secure and protect their rights; they organize to secure and protect their own rights. This is particularly true of citizens who feel they are unjustly denied their rights.

Characteristics of colleges of teacher education to prepare New Paradigm teachers. In colleges that prepare New Paradigm teachers, (a) the concepts enumerated in this chapter are thoroughly explored; (b) progressive methods are advocated on the basis on the basis of the work of sociologists and sociolinguists and examples of earlier empowering education for the working class; (c) progressive methods are advocated based on the recognition that education is political and that traditional methods are domesticating and progressive methods are empowering; (d) progressive methods are taught in combination with Freirean motivation in poor and working-class schools; (e) progressive methods are *taught*, not simply referred to with the assumption that anyone can teach if her or his heart is in the right place; (f) undergraduate teacher-education students minor in working-class studies; (g) students work with grassroots organizations and labor unions; (h) students are placed with veteran teachers who have a proven track record in new paradigm teaching and student achievement; and (i) after graduation students are encouraged to participate in teacher self-study groups with support from the college.

A new civil rights movement. Since the Reagan administration, while we have relied on the old paradigm and internal, technical school reforms to eliminate or ameliorate poverty, government policy has drastically increased the number of families in poverty, squeezed the middle class, and drastically increased the wealth of the wealthiest.[3] Internal, technical school reforms are not enough. We must look for remedies in the civil sphere, the political sphere.

This will include two related, symbiotic and simultaneous movements, a movement to educate working-class students (using Freirean motivation) to fight for social rights effectively as students and in the future and a movement among adult poor and working-class citizens and their allies for social rights through campaigns for such things as unions, living wages, universal health care, decent schools.

As the schools produce better prepared graduates, the second movement will prosper as its members are better prepared for the struggle. As the second movement gains ground, poor and working-class children will arrive at school better prepared and in better health, as well as better fed, housed, and cared for. This will make the work of the schools (the first movement) more effective. At last we will have a "thick democracy," where citizens organize to demand and defend their hard-won rights rather than hope that elected professional politicians will do it for them.

Nothing less will force and maintain the necessary concessions from the powerful institutions of social class and free-market economy—which are based on inequality—to find a just equilibrium with full citizenship—which is based on equality.

If you get the idea, you ought to be hearing in your mind something like the lines from the musical *Les Miserables*:

> Will you join in our crusade?
> Who will be strong and stand with me?[4]

Notes

Preface to the Second Edition

1. T. H. Marshall, "Citizenship and Social Class," in *Citizenship and Social Class*, ed. T. H. Marshall and Tom Bottomore (London: Plutobooks, 1992). This essay was printed originally in 1950.

Chapter 1. Title, Author, and Hard-Bitten School Teachers

1. Maurice Levitas. *Perspectives in the Sociology of Education* (Boston: Routledge & Kegan Paul, 1974).

2. Jonathan Kozol. *Savage Inequalities: Children in America's Schools* (New York: Harper Perennial, 1992).

3. I've fictionalized the name of the school. In fact, I taught at two Chicago elementary schools and refer to incidents that occurred in both of them later in the book.

4. John Stewart Carter. *Full Fathom Five* (Boston: Houghton Mifflin Co., 1965).

5. But it's thirty years later now, and we no longer refer to teachers as hard-bitten; we refer to them as "hard-assed." Let's admit it. Language lost a certain elegance in the sixties, and it has not recovered.

Chapter 2. A Distinctly Un-American Idea:
An Education Appropriate to Their Station

1. Jean Anyon, "Social Class and the Hidden Curriculum of Work," *Journal of Education* (1980): pp. 67–92 and "Social Class and School Knowledge," *Curriculum Inquiry* (1981): pp. 3–42.

2. A rebus story is one where pictures and letters are brought together to form words. For example, a cartoon picture of a hand, a plus sign, and the letters *some* make up the word *handsome*.

3. S. Bowles and H. Gintis, *Schooling in Capitalist America: Educational Reform and Contradictions of Economic Life* (New York: Basic Books, 1976); M. W. Apple, *Ideology and Curriculum* (Boston: Routledge and Kegan Paul, 1979); P. Bourdieu and J. Passeron, *Reproduction in Education, Society, and Culture* (Beverly Hills: Sage, 1977).

4. Robert B. Reich, *The Work of Nations: Preparing Ourselves for 21st Century Capitalism* (New York: Vintage Books, 1991). See also Thomas W. Fraser, *Reading, Writing, and Justice: School Reform as if Democracy Matters* (Albany: State University of New York Press, 1997).

5. The grant proposal is described in J. Cynthia McDermott, "An Institute for Independence through Action, Process, and Theory." In John M. Novak, ed. *Democratic Teacher Education: Programs, Processes, Problems, and Prospects* (Albany: State University of New York Press, 1994).

6. Jonathan Kozol, *Savage Inequalities: Children in America's Schools* (New York: Harper Perennial, 1992).

7. Megan Elizabeth Connolly, *Paper 1, LAI 563 Language, Society, and Language Arts Instruction* (Photocopied, Department of Learning and Instruction, State University of New York at Buffalo, 1998).

8. Susan Marie Sampson, *Paper 1, LAI 563 Language, Society, and Language Arts Instruction* (Photocopied, Department of Learning and Instruction, State University of New York at Buffalo, 1998).

Chapter 3. Harsh Schools, Big Boys, and the Progressive Solution

1. Daniel P. Resnick, "Historical Perspectives on Literacy and Schooling," *Daedalus* (1990): pp. 15–32.

2. *Baltimore Catechism: A catechism of Christian doctrine, prepared and enjoyed by order of the Third Plenary Council Baltimore; with explanations in the form of short notes and of sections in simple question and answer. Published by ecclesiastical authority* (Chicago: The John P. Daleiden Company, 1918).

3. David W. Swift, *Ideology and Change in the Public Schools: Latent Functions of Progressive Education* (Columbus: Charles E. Merrill Publishing Company, 1971). The argument that progressive ideals were instrumental in developing our present, arguably unjust school system is taken almost entirely from Swift.

4. Ellwood P. Cubberly, *Public Education in the United States* (Boston: Houghton-Mifflin Company, 1919), p. 328 rev. ed. Quoted in David W. Swift, *Ideology and Change in the Public Schools: Latent Functions of Progressive Education*, p. 35.

5. Clifton Johnson, *The Country School in New England* (New York: D. Appleton and Company, 1893), pp. 47–52. Quoted in David W. Swift, *Ideology and Change in the Public Schools: Latent Functions of Progressive Education*, p. 36–37.

6. Clifton Johnson, *Old Time Schools and School Books* (New York: The Macmillan Co., 1904), pp. 123–126. Quoted in David W. Swift, *Ideology and Change in the Public Schools: Latent Functions of Progressive Education*, pp. 33.

7. Ruth Freeman, *Yesterday's Schools* (Watkin's Glen, N.Y.: Century House, 1962), p. 77. Quoted in David W. Swift, *Ideology and Change in the Public Schools: Latent Functions of Progressive Education*, p. 34.

8. Ruth S. Freeman, *Yesterday's Schools*, pp. 78–79. Quoted in David W. Swift, *Ideology and Change in the Public Schools: Latent Functions of Progressive Education*, p. 34.

9. U. S. Commissioner of Education, *Annual Report of the Commissioner of Education Made to the Secretary of the Interior for the Year 1870* (Washington, D.C.: 1875), p. 273. Quoted in David W. Swift, *Ideology and Change in the Public Schools: Latent Functions of Progressive Education*, p. 42.

10. Lawrence A. Cremin, *The Transformation of the School* (New York: Random House, Inc., Vintage Books, 1964), p. 22. Quoted in David W. Swift, *Ideology and Change in the Public Schools: Latent Functions of Progressive Education*, p. 19.

11. John Willinsky, *The New Literacy: Redefining Reading and Writing in the Schools* (New York: Routledge, Chapman and Hall, Inc. 1990), p. 8.

Chapter 4. Oppositional Identity: Identifying "Us" as "Not Them"

1. The concepts of "involuntary minorities," "oppositional identity," and the details supporting these concepts are taken from John U. Ogbu, ed., "Cultural Diversity and School Experience," in Catherine E. Walsh, Literacy as Praxis: *Culture, Language, and Pedagogy* (Norwood, N.J.: Ablex Publishing Corporation, 1991), pp. 25–50.

2. In fact, West Indian blacks who immigrate to the United States outperform American-born blacks in terms of levels of education, income, and occupational status. See Thomas Sowell, ed., *Essays and Data on American Ethnic Groups* (Washington, D.C.: Urban Institute, 1978), pp. 41–49.

3. John U. Ogbu, "Cultural Diversity and School Experience."

4. Kerby Miller and Paul Wagner, *Out of Ireland: The Story of Irish Immigration to America* (Washington, D.C.: Elliott & Clark Publishers, 1994).

5. Perry Gilmore, "'Gimme Room': School Resistance, Attitude, and Access to Literacy," in Candice Mitchell and Kathleen Weiler, eds., *Rewriting Literacy: Culture and the Discourse of the Other* (New York: Bergin & Garvey, 1991), pp. 57–76.

6. Perry Gilmore, p. 66.

7. Perry Gilmore, p. 67.

8. Robert Coles, *The Spiritual Life of Children* (Boston: Houghton Mifflin, 1990).

9. Robert Coles, p. 24.

10. R. Scollon and S. B. K. Scollon, *Narrative, Literacy and Face in Interethnic Communication* (Norwood, N.J.: Ablex Publishing Corporation, 1981).

11. Bob Herbert, "In America: Workaday Racism" (New York: The New York Times Company, 1996). http://www.dorsai.org/~jdadd/texaco3.html. See also Jim Fitzgerald, "Jury Hears Tapes in Texaco Case" (Associated Press: April 29, 1998). http://www.blackvoices.com/news/98/04/29/story07.html.

12. Gary Natriello, Edward L. McDill, and Aaron M. Pallas, *Schooling Disadvantaged Children, Racing Against Catastrophe* (New York, Teachers College Press: 1990).

Chapter 5. The Lads

1. Paul E. Willis, *Learning to Labor: How Working Class Kids Get Working Class Jobs* (Westmead, England: Saxon House, 1977).

2. Willis, p. 1.

3. Recall the discussion of my black eighth graders on Chicago's south side with high reading scores in 1965 and a group of eighth graders in Winnetka, Illinois, with the same scores and where they probably are in terms of socioeconomic status today.

4. Willis, pp. 11–12.

5. Willis, p. 12.

6. Willis, p. 29.

7. Willis, p. 54.

8. Willis, p. 57.

9. Willis, p. 62.

10. Kozol, Jonathan, *Savage Inequalities: Children in America's Schools* (New York: Harper Perennial, 1992).

11. Samuel Bowles and Herbert Gintis, *Schooling in Capitalist America: Educational Reform and the Contradictions of Economic Life* (New York: Basic Books. 1976). Perry Gilmore, "'Gimme Room': School Resistance, Attitude, and Access to Literacy," in Candice Mitchell and Kathleen Weiler, eds., *Rewriting Literacy: Culture and the Discourse of the Other* (New York, Bergin & Garvey: 1991), pp. 57–76. S. Hamilton, "The Social Side of Schooling," *Elementary School Journal 83* (1983): pp. 313–334. E. Leacock, *Teaching and Learning in City Schools* (New York: Basic Books, 1969).

12. Willis, p. 77.

13. Willis, p. 78.

14. Willis, p. 70.

15. Willis, p. 80.

16. Willis, p. 74.

17. Willis, p. 59. Labov and Robbins observed that among black and Puerto Rican boys in New York a high level of acceptance on the street was a good predictor of poor school performance and reading score. W. Labov and C. Robbins, "A note on the Relation of Reading Failure to Peer-Group Status in Urban Ghettos," *The Record—Teacher's College* 70 (1969), pp. 395–405.

Chapter 6. Changing Conditions—Entrenched Schools

1. Lois Weis, *Working Class without Work: High School Students in a De-industrializing Economy* (New York: Routledge, 1990).

2. Weis, p. 19.

3. Weis, p. 23.

4. Weis, p. 27.

5. Weis, p. 68.

6. Weis, pp. 28–29.

7. Weis, p. 29.

8. Weis, p. 29.

9. Weis, p. 28.

10. Weis, p. 28.

11. Weis, p. 28.

12. Weis, p. 30.

13. Weis, p. 32.

14. Weis, p. 82.

15. Weis, p. 84.

16. Weis, p. 86.

17. Weis, p. 88–89.

18. David Bensman and Roberta Lynch, *Rusted Dreams: Hard Times in a Steel Community* (New York: McGraw Hill, 1987), p. 28.

19. Weis, p. 170.

20. Weis, p. 171.

21. Weis, p. 171.

22. Weis, p. 173.

23. Weis, p. 173.

24. Weis, p. 174.

25. Weis, p. 176.

26. I have been told by friends who taught in western New York when the mills were still open that a number of full-time male teachers in Freeway schools worked full-time jobs in the mills on the 4–12 shift and that this was well-known to the administration and school board.

27. R. T. Sieber, "The Politics of Middle-Class Success in an Inner City Public School," *Journal of Education* 164 (1981): pp. 30–47.

28. Sieber was studying the differences between an Episcopal, Catholic, and Public school in this ethnically mixed neighborhood in New York City. He did not anticipate finding the situation that had developed in the public school.

29. Recall that teachers in Anyon's working-class schools were often rude to students. One teacher remarked that she would not teach in the suburbs because the kids "thought they had rights." Insulting remarks by teachers to students were observed in both the lads' school and at Freeway high school. I recently met an upper-middle-class African American woman who lives in an affluent suburb of Atlanta. She told me she was sending her twin boys to a private school because, although she was committed to public education, she would not have her boys spoken to in the manner that both teachers and staff spoke to black boys in the local public elementary school.

Chapter 7. Class, Control, Language, and Literacy

This chapter is based largely on the observations of Basil Bernstein. Basil Bernstein, *Theoretical Studies Towards a Sociology of Education* (London: Routledge and Kegan Paul. 1971), *Applied Studies Towards a Sociology of Education* (London: Routledge and Kegan Paul, 1973), *Towards a Theory of Educational Transmission* (London: Routledge and Kegan Paul, 1973), and *The Structuring of Pedagogic Discourse* (London: Routledge and Kegan Paul, 1990).

1. Sociologists, particularly British sociologists, are thinking of a rather more affluent group of people than the average American when they refer to the middle class. Identifying class is a very complicated matter, but they are usually referring to people such as doctors and lawyers rather than policemen and white collar workers. In America, we all think we're middle-class. I'm certain the people in Freeway would think of themselves as middle-class, but sociologists would probably identify them, even most of the teachers at Freeway high school, as working-class.

2. L. Schatzman and A. Strauss, "Social class and communication," *American Journal of Sociology* 60 (1955): pp. 329–339.

3. T. Givon, *On Understanding Grammar* (New York: Academic Press, 1979), p. 287.

4. T. Givon, p. 297.

5. Students in Anyon's working-class school are a good example of a group of people who feel powerless. They resisted the school's authority, but their actions were implicit—mostly nonlinguistic, in fact. The reasons for their resistance were never stated. Contrast this with the affluent professional and executive elite students who routinely engaged in negotiations with their teachers, explicitly stating grievances and reasons for change.

6. Jeanne Chall and Vicki Jacobs, "Writing and Reading in the Elementary Grades: Developmental Trends Among Low SES Children," in Julie M. Jensen, *Composing and Comprehending* (Urbana, Ill.: ERIC Clearing House on Reading and Communication Skills, 1984), pp. 93–104.

Chapter 8. Where Literacy "Emerges"

1. J. Buckhalt, R. Rutherford, and K. Goldberg, "Verbal and Non-verbal Interactions of Mothers and their Down's Syndrome and Nonretarded Infants," *American Journal of Mental Deficiency* 82 (1978): pp. 337–343. T. Cross, "Mothers' Speech Adjustment: The Contribution of Selected Child Listener Variables," in C. A. Snow and C. A. Ferguson, eds., *Talking to Children: Language Input and Acquisition* (Cambridge: Cambridge University Press, 1977), pp. 151–188. C. E. Snow, "The Development of Conversation between Mothers and Babies," *Journal of Child Development* 4 (1977): pp. 1–22.

2. Gordon Wells, "Language as Interaction," in Gordon Wells, *Language through Interaction* (Cambridge: Cambridge University Press, 1981), pp. 22–72, 102.

3. Wells, p. 107.

4. Wells, pp. 24–25.

5. M. A. K. Halliday, *Learning How to Mean: Explorations in the Study of Language* (London: Edward Arnold Publishers, 1975), pp. 111–112.

6. M. King, "Speech to Writing: Children's Growth in Writing Potential," in J. Mason, ed., *Reading and Writing Connections* (Boston: Allyn and Bacon, 1989), pp. 7–30, 14.

7. M. King, p. 15.

8. J. C. Harste, V. A. Woodward, and C. L. Burke, *Language Stories and Literacy Lessons* (Portsmouth, N.H.: Heinemann, 1984).

9. Ashley Hartfield, "The Runaway Elephant," in Patrick J. Finn, *Helping Children Learn to Read* (New York: Longman, 1990), p. 175.

10. Shirley Brice Heath, *Ways with Words* (Cambridge: Cambridge University Press, 1983).

11. In fact, Heath studied three communities. I refer to only two of them in this discussion.

12. James Paul Gee, "What Is Literacy?" in *Rewriting Literacy: Culture and the Discourse of the Other.* Ed. C. Mitchell and K. Weiler. New York: Bergin & Garvey, 1991, p. 3.

Chapter 9. Where Children Are Taught to Sit Still and Listen

1. Shirley Brice Heath, *Ways with Words* (Cambridge: Cambridge University Press, 1986).

2. Heath, p. 143. The woman quoted actually said, " . . . we was cut from the same pattern. We all knowed what to expect." Such usages as "we was" and "we knowed" are commonly identified as dialect and are actually classified as "illiteracies" by some authors. My experience is that "dialect" is too often blamed for the educational, economic, and social woes of those who engage in it. Rather than focus on what she is saying about her community's attitude toward conformity, which is the real issue here, teachers too often want to go right to work to teach such

women subject-verb agreement and the standard form of the past tense for the irregular verb *to know*, thinking that she, now "literate," would march unwaveringly toward mainstream values, behaviors, and status. For that reason, I've edited the woman's remarks.

3. Shirley Brice Heath, "Separating 'Things of the Imagination' from Life: Learning to Read and Write," in W. H. Teale and E. Sulzby, eds., *Emergent Literacy* (Norwood, N.J.: Ablex Publishing Corporation, 1986), pp. 156–172, 161–162.

4. Jean Anyon, "Social Class and the Hidden Curriculum of Work," *Journal of Education* (1980): pp. 67–92 and "Social Class and School Knowledge," *Curriculum Inquiry* (1981): pp. 3–42. David W. Swift, *Ideology and Change in the Public Schools: Latent Functions of Progressive Education* (Columbus, Ohio: Charles E. Merrill Publishing Company, 1971). Paul E. Willis, *Learning to Labor: How Working Class Kids Get Working Class Jobs* (Westmead, England: Saxon House, 1977). Lois Weis, *Working Class without Work: High School Students in a De-industrializing Economy* (New York: Routledge, 1990).

Chapter 10. The Last Straw: There's Literacy and Then There's Literacy

1. E. A. Havelock, *Preface to Plato* (Cambridge, Mass.: Harvard University Press, 1963).

2. From the earliest literacy campaigns, the idea was to teach the poor to read, not to write. Teaching writing to the poor implies that they might have something to say, an idea that does not often occur to domesticating educators, and if it does, it frightens them. Hannah More, a late-eighteenth-century advocate of literacy for the poor, asserted, "I allow of no writing for the poor. My object is not to make them fanatics, but to train up the lower classes in habits of industry and piety." More is quoted in B. Simon, *Studies in the History of Education: The two Nations and the Educational Structure 1780–1870* (London: Lawrence and Wishart, 1960), p. 133.

3. The concept of four levels of literacy is taken from Gordon Wells, "Apprenticeship in Literacy," in C. E. Walsh, ed., *Language, as Praxis: Culture, Language, and Pedagogy* (Norwood, N.J.: Ablex, Publishing Corporation, 1991). Wells calls the highest level of literacy "epistemic literacy." Gee discusses levels of literacy as well and refers to the highest level as "essay-text literacy." James Gee, "Orality and Literacy: From *The Savage Mind* to *Ways with Words*," in J. Mabin, ed., *Language and*

Literacy in Social Practice (Clevedon, England: Multilingual Matters Limited, The Open University, 1994).

4. James Gee, "Orality and Literacy."

5. Wells suggests that levels of literacy are associated with levels of social class. Performative and functional literacy are associated with discourse communities such as that of Roadville. Informational and powerful literacy are associated with discourse communities such as that of Maintown.

Chapter 11. Literacy with an Attitude

1. M. Spufford, *Small Books and Pleasant Histories: Popular Fiction and Its Readership in Seventeenth-century England* (Cambridge: Cambridge University Press, 1981).

2. J. Willinsky, *The New Literacy: Redefining Reading and Writing in the Schools* (New York: Routledge, 1990), p. 177.

3. Willinsky, p. 184.

4. E. P. Thompson, *The Making of the English Working Class* (New York: Vintage Books, 1963).

5. J. Donald, "How Illiteracy Became a Problem (and Literacy Stopped Being One)," in C. Mitchell and K. Weiler, eds., *Rewriting Literacy: Culture and the Discourse of the Other* (New York: Bergin & Harvey, 1991), pp. 211–228, 212.

6. E. P. Thompson, p. 103.

7. E. P. Thompson, p. 154.

8. E. P. Thompson, p. 156.

9. E. P. Thompson, p. 103

10. E. P. Thompson, p. 151.

11. An idea promulgated by Paine and continued by Thoreau, Gandhi, Martin Luther King, Jr., and Paulo Freire.

12. E. P. Thompson, p. 155.

13. E. P. Thompson, p. 155.

14. E. P. Thompson, p. 108.

15. B. Simon, Studies in the History of Education, p. 133.

16. J. Donald, 214.

17. P. Colquhoun, *A New and Appropriate System of Education for the Labouring People.* (London: J. Hatchard, 1806), pp. 11–12.

18. J. Donald, p. 220.

Chapter 12. Not Quite Making Literacy Dangerous Again

1. M. McCurdy, "Writing on Their Own: Kindergarten and First Grade," in N. Gordon, ed., *Classroom Experiences: The Writing Process in Action* (Portsmouth, N.H.: Heinemann, 1984).

2. Note similarity to Ashley's Runaway Elephant Story in chapter 8. These writers are a little further along than Ashley.

3. N. Atwell, *In the Middle: Reading, Writing, and Learning with Adolescents* (Portsmouth, N.H.: Heinemann, 1987).

4. J. Willinsky, *The New Literacy: Redefining Reading and Writing in the Schools* (New York: Routledge, 1990), p. 8.

5. D. Graves, *Writing: Teachers and Children at Work* (Portsmouth, N.H.: Heinemann, 1983).

6. J. Bechtel, "Videotape Analysis of the Composing Process of Six Male College Freshman Writers." Paper presented at the Annual Meeting of the Midwest Regional Conference on English in the Two Year College (ERIC Document ED 177 558) and S. H. Pianco, "A Description of the Composing Process of College Freshmen Writers," *Research in College Teaching 13*: pp. 5–22.

7. S. Michaels, "Narrative Presentations: An Oral Preparation for Literacy with First Graders," in J. Cook-Gumperz, ed., *The Social Construction of Literacy* (Cambridge: Cambridge University Press, 1986), pp. 94–116.

8. S. Michaels, 1986, p. 105.

9. S. Michaels, 1986, pp. 108–109.

10. S. Michaels, 1986, p. 110.

11. J. Collins, "Hegemonic Practices: Literacy and Standard Language in Public Education," in C. Mitchell and K. Weiler, eds., *Rewriting Literacy: Culture and the Discourse of the Other* (New York: Bergin & Garvey, 1991), pp. 229–254, 239.

12. For a review of the research on the relationships between social class and ability grouping, teacher expectations, and unequal treatment in reading groups see Patrick Shannon, "Reading Instruction and Social Class," in Patrick Shannon, ed., *Becoming Political: Readings and Writings in the Politics of Literacy Education* (Portsmouth, N.H.: Heinemann, 1992), pp. 128–138.

13. M. Sola and A. Bennett, "The Struggle for Voice: Narrative, Literacy, and Consciousness in an East Harlem High School," in C. Mitchell and K. Weiler, eds., *Rewriting Literacy*, pp. 35–56.

14. M. Sola and A. Bennett, pp. 44–45

15. S. Michaels, "Hearing the Connections in Children's Oral and Written Discourse," in C. Mitchell and K. Weiler, eds., *Rewriting Literacy*, pp. 103–122, 110.

16. S. Michaels, 1991, p. 114.

17. S. Michaels, 1991, p. 116.

18. Willinsky and Hunniford discovered a group of young adolescent girls in two new literacy classrooms who read nothing but "young adult romance novels." J. M. Willinsky and J. O. Hunniford, "Reading the Romance Younger: The Mirrors and Fears of a Preparatory Literature," *Reading-Canada-Lecture* 4(1): pp. 16–31.

19. The 1 classes in the Brownstoners school were very traditional and directive when the Brownstoners arrived. That was the cause of the consternation of the Brownstoners.

20. Shirley Brice Heath, *Ways with Words* (Cambridge: Cambridge University Press, 1983).

21. Recall that Anyon found the middle-class school more like the working-class school than the affluent professional or executive elite school.

Chapter 13. Schools and a Square Deal for Working People

1. A. Marshall, "The Future of the Working Class," in *Memorials of Alfred Marshall*, ed. A. C. Pigou (London: Macmillan, 1925), quoted in *Citizenship and Social Class*, ed. T. H. Marshall and Tom Bottomore (London: Plutobooks, 1992).

2. T. H. Marshall, "Citizenship and Social Class," in *Citizenship and Social Class*, ed. T. H. Marshall and Tom Bottomore. (London: Plutobooks, 1992), 5.

3. Ibid.

4. Ibid.

5. Ibid., 3–51.

6. Ibid., 18.

7. M. Friedman, "The Role of Government in Education," in *Economics and the Public Interest*, ed. Robert A. Solo (1955; repr., by permission of Rutgers University Press), http://www.schoolchoices.org/roo/fried1.htm.

8. T. H. Marshall, "Citizenship and Social Class," 34.

9. M. Young, *The Rise of the Meritocracy* (London: Thames and Hudson, 1958).

10. N. Lehman, *The Big Test: The Secret History of the American Meritocracy* (New York: Ferrar, Straus and Giroux, 1999).

11. R. G. Stauffer, *The First Grade Reading Studies: Findings of Individual Investigations* (Newark, DE: International Reading Association, 1967).

12. V. Lee, and D. Burkham, *Inequality at the Starting Gate: Social Background and Achievement at Kindergarten Entry* (Washington DC: Educational Policy Institute, 2002).

13. R. Rothstein, *Class and Schools: Using Social, Economic, and Education Reform to Close the Black-White Achievement Gap* (New York: Teachers College Press, 2004), 51–56.

14. J. Anyon, *Radical Possibilities: Public Policy, Urban Education, and a New Social Movement* (New York: Teachers College Press, 2005). Anyon's book is rich with this kind of data.

15. J. Oakes and J. Rogers, with Martin Lipton, *Learning Power: Organizing for Education and Justice* (New York: Teachers College Press, 2006), 151.

16. Lee and Burkham, *Inequality*, 3.

17. W. Symonds, "College Admissions: The Real Barrier Is Class," *Business Week*, April 14, 2003, 68–69.

18. G. Sheehy, "The Accidental Candidate" *Vanity Fair*, October 2000, http://www.gailsheehy.com/Politics/politicsindex_resp.html.

19. W. Symonds. "College Admissions," 68–69.

20. R. Payne, *A Framework for Understanding Poverty*, 4th rev. ed. (Highlands, TX: aha! Process, Inc., 1996); I am indebted to an excellent

critique of Payne's work by Randy Bomer, Joel E. Dworin, Laura May, and Peggy Semingson, "Miseducating Teachers about the Poor: A Critical Analysis of Ruby Payne's Claims about Poverty," *Teachers College Record*, 2008.

21. B. Keller, "Payne's Pursuits," *Education Week*, May 3, 2006, 30–32.

22. P. Tough, "The Class-Consciousness Raiser," *New York Times Magazine*, June 10, 2008, 52–58.

23. Payne, *Framework*, 3.

24. Ibid., 9.

25. Scholars such as Sarah Michaels and Shirley Brice Heath have described this phenomenon. They have recognized the importance of teaching students to add the linear narrative typical of school discourse to their repertoire and described techniques for doing it. S. Michaels, "Hearing the Connections in Children's Oral and Written Discourse," in *Rewriting Literacy: Culture and the Discourse of the Other*, ed. C. Mitchell and K. Weiler (New York: Bergin & Garvey, 1991. S. B. Heath, *Ways with Words* (Cambridge: Cambridge University Press, 1983).

26. Payne, *Framework*, 90.

27. C. Compton-Lilly, *Reading Families: The Literate Lives of Urban Children* (New York: Teachers College Press, 2003). A. Lareau and E. Horvat, "Moments of Social Inclusion and Exclusion: Race, Class, and Cultural Capital in Family-School Relationships," *Sociology of Education* 72 (1999): 37–53. H. J. Leichter, ed., *Families and Communities as Educators* (New York: Teachers College Press, 1978). L. Moll and others, "Funds of Knowledge for Teaching: Using a Qualitative Approach to Connect Homes and Classrooms," *Theory Into Practice* 31, no. 2 (1992): 133–41. E. Skilton-Sylvester, "Literate at Home but Not at School: A Cambodian Girl's Journey from Playwright to Struggling Writer," in *School's Out! Bridging Out-of-School Literacies with Classroom Practice*, ed. G. Hull and K. Schultz (New York: Teachers College Press, 2002), 61–90. D. Taylor and C. Dorsey-Gaines, *Growing Up Literate: Learning from Inner-City Families* (Portsmouth, NH: Heinemann, 1988). H. Varenne, and R. McDermott, "'Why' Sheila Can Read: Structure and Indeterminacy in the Reproduction of Familial Literacy," in *The Acquisition of Literacy: Ethnographic Perspectives*, ed. B. Schieffelin and P. Gilmore (Norwood, NJ: Ablex, 1986), 188–210. N. Gonzales, L. Moll, and C. Amanti, eds. *Funds of Knowledge: Theorizing Practices*

in Households, Communities, and Classrooms (Mahwah, NJ: Erlbaum, 2005).

28. N. Gonzales, L. Moll, and C. Amanti, eds., *Funds of Knowledge: Theorizing Practices in Households, Communities, and Classrooms* (Mahwah, NJ: Erlbaum, 2005). Also Taylor and Dorsey-Gaines, *Growing Up Literate*.

29. R. Bomer and others, "Miseducating Teachers about the Poor: A Critical Analysis of Ruby Payne's Claims about Poverty," *Teachers College Record* (2008). C. Edelsky, ed., *Making Justice Our Project: Teachers Working toward Critical Whole Language Practice* (Urbana, IL: National Council of Teachers of English, 1999). B. Fecho and J. Allen, "Teacher Inquiry into Literacy, Social Justice, and Power," in *Handbook of Research on Teaching the English Language Arts*, ed. J. Flood and others (Mahwah, NJ: Lawrence Erlbaum, 2003), 232–46. D. Hicks, *Reading Lives: Working-Class Children and Literacy Learning* (New York: Teachers College Press, 2002). D. Macedo, *Literacies of Power: What Americans Are Not Allowed to Know* (Boulder: Westview Press, 1994), P. McLaren, *Life in Schools: An Introduction to Critical Pedagogy in the Foundations of Education* (White Plains, NY: Longman, 1989). I. Shor and C. Pari, *Education Is Politics: Critical Teaching across Differences, K-12* (Portsmouth, NH: Boynton/Cook, 1999). J. Swenson, "Transformative Teacher Networks, On-Line Professional Development, and the Write for Your Life Project," *English Education* 35, no. 4 (2003): 263–321. R, Yagelski, *Literacy Matters: Writing and Reading the Social Self* (New York: Teachers College Press, 2000).

30. Payne, *Framework*, 115.

31. J. E. Dworin and R. Bomer, "What We All (Supposedly) Know about the Poor: A Critical Discourse Analysis of Ruby Payne's *Framework*," *English Education* 40 (2008), 101–21.

32. Not infrequently, after I've given a speech or conducted a workshop someone will ask me if I've ever heard of Ruby Payne and add, "She's saying the same thing you are." God help us.

Chapter 14. Citizens' Rights vs. Social Class and a Free-Market Economy

1. F. Douglass, letter to an abolitionist associate, quoted in J. Oakes and J. Rogers, with M. Lipton, *Learning Power: Organizing for Education and Justice* (New York: Teachers College Press, 2006), 93.

2. Oakes and Rogers, *Learning Power*, 30–31.

3. J. Anyon, *Radical Possibilities: Public Policy, Urban Education, and a New Social Movement* (New York: Teachers College Press, 2005).

4. Anyon, *Radical Possibilities*, 68; P. Morris and others, *How Welfare and Work Policies Affect Children: A Synthesis of the Research* (Washington DC: Manpower Development Research Corporation, 2001), 21–22.

5. A. Huston and others, *New Hope for Families and Children: Five-Year Results of a Program to Reduce Poverty and Reform Welfare* (New York: Manpower Development Research Corporation, 2003), 1.

6. Anyon, *Radical Possibilities*, 69; J. Bos and others, *New Hope for People with Low Incomes: Two-Year Results of a Program to Reduce Poverty and Reform Welfare* (New York: Manpower Demonstration Research Corporation, 1999).

7. Anyon, *Radical Possibilities*, 67; J. Costello and others, "Relationships between Poverty and Psychopathology: A Natural Experiment," *Journal of the American Medical Association* 290, no. 15 (October 2003): 1–2; A. O'Conner. "Rise in Income Improves Children's Behavior," *New York Times*. October 21, 2003.

8. Anyon, *Radical Possibilities*, 34.

9. Ibid.; D. Howell and E. Wolff, "Trends in Growth and Distribution in the U.S. Workplace, 1960–1985," *Industrial and Labor Relations Review* 44, no. 3 (1991): 486–502.

10. Anyon, *Radical Possibilities*, 34; G. Lafer, *The Job Training Charade* (Ithaca, NY: Cornell University Press, 2002), 84.

11. Anyon, *Radical Possibilities*, 34; Lafer, *Job Training Charade*, 84.

12. Anyon, *Radical Possibilities*, 32; L. Mishel and R. Teixeira, *The Myth of the Coming Labor Shortage: Jobs, Skills, and Incomes of America's Workforce 2000* (Washington, DC: Economic Policy Institute, 2001), 181.

13. Anyon, *Radical Possibilities*, 33; Lafer, *Job Training Charade*, 78.

14. Anyon, *Radical Possibilities*, 33.

15. D. Barboza, "China Drafts Law to Boost Unions and End Abuse," *New York Times*, October 13, 2006.

16. Anyon, *Radical Possibilities*, 34; Mishel and Teixeira, *Myth*, 153.

17. Anyon, *Radical Possibilities*, 33; Lafer, *Job Training Charade*, 78.

18. Anyon, *Radical Possibilities*, 21.

19. Lafer, *Job Training Charade*, 31.

20. P. Osterman. *Gathering Power: The Future of Progressive Politics in America* (Boston: Beacon Press, 2002).

21. Ibid., 172.

22. Ibid., 12.

23. Ibid., 172; B. Barber, *Strong Democracy: Participatory Politics for a New Age* (Berkeley: University of California Press, 1984).

24. Osterman, 11.

25. Ibid., 123.

26. Ibid., 172.

Chapter 15. Twentieth- and Twenty-First Century Heirs to the Corresponding Societies and a New Paradigm for Educating Working-Class Students

1. B. Simon, *Studies in the History of Education: The Two Nations and the Educational Structure 1780–1870* (London: Lawrence and Wishart, 1960), 133.

2. S. Aronowitz and H. Giroux, *Education Still Under Siege*, 2nd ed. (Westport, CT: Bergin and Harvey, 1993).

3. Aronowitz and Giroux, *Education*, 46.

4. M. E. Finn. "For Further Thought," in *Teacher Education with an Attitude: Preparing Teachers to Educate Working-Class Students in Their Collective Self-Interest*, ed. by P. Finn and M. E. Finn (Albany, NY: SUNY Press, 2007), 231–46; W. W. Craik, *The Central Labour College, 1909–1929: A Chapter in the History of Adult Working-Class Education* (London, UK: Lawrence & Wishart, 1964), 158.

5. Finn, "Further Thought," 238; Craik, *Central Labour College*, 156.

6. The Education Labor Collaborative is bringing together union educators and teacher educators to explore common interests. (For more information, visit their Web site at http://www.organizingthecurriculum.org.)

7. Finn, "Further Thought," 237; R. J. Altenbaugh, *Education for Struggle: The American Labor College of the 1920s and 1930s* (Philadelphia: Temple University Press, 1990), 130.

8. Finn, "Further Thought," 237; J. Dewey, "Labor Politics and Labor Education," *The New Republic*, January 9, 1929, 212–15.

9. Finn, "Further Thought," 231–46.

10. P. Freire, *Cultural Action for Freedom* (Cambridge: Harvard Education Review, 1970); *Pedagogy of the Heart* (New York: Continuum, 1997); *Pedagogy of the Oppressed* (New York: Seabury Press, 1970); *Teachers as Cultural Workers: Letters to Those Who Dare to Teach* (Boulder CO: Westview Press, 1998).

In 1963 Freire was asked to direct a national literacy project by a newly elected president of Brazil. In one province the number of registered voters increased by over 150 percent. Freire and his colleagues expected to have two hundred thousand culture circles operating throughout the country by 1964, but there was a military coup and the program was abruptly ended. Freire was placed under house arrest and imprisoned for ten weeks; he finally sought refuge in Chile. He was invited to Harvard as a visiting professor and later acted as an advisor on education to the World Council of Churches in Geneva, Switzerland. He returned to Brazil in 1980, where he died in 1997 at age 75.

11. C. Brown, *Literacy in 30 Hours: Paulo Freire's Process in North East Brazil* (London: Centre for Open Learning and Teaching, Writers and Readers Publishing Cooperative, 1975).

12. R. F. Arnove, "The Nicaraguan National Literacy Crusade of 1980," in *Perspectives on Literacy*, ed. E. R. Kintgen, B. M. Kroll, and M. Rose (Carbondale, IL: Southern Illinois University Press, 1988).

13. A. S. Alschuler, *School Discipline: A Socially Literate Solution* (New York: McGraw-Hill Book Company, 1980), 177–204.

14. J. Gee, "What is literacy?" in *Rewriting literacy: Culture and the Discourse of the Other*, ed. C. Mitchell and K. Weiler (New York: Bergin & Garvey, 1994), 3–11.

15. J. Oller and K. Perkins, "Intelligence and Language Proficiency as Sources of Variance in Self-Reported Affective Variables," *Language Learning* 28 (1978): 85–97.

16. Jean Anyon, "Social Class and School Knowledge," *Curriculum Inquiry* 11, no. 1 (1981); "Social Class and the Hidden Curriculum of Work," *Journal of Education* 162, no. 2 (1980).

Chapter 16. Teachers Who Agitate: Freirean Motivation in the Classroom

1. *Merriam-Webster Online*, s.v. "agitate," http://www.merriam-webster.com/dictionary/agitate.

2. R. E. Peterson, "Teaching How to Read the World and Change It: Critical Pedagogy in the Intermediate Grades," in *Literacy as Praxis: Culture, Language, and Pedagogy*, ed. C. E Walsh (Norwood, NJ: Ablex Publishing Corporation, 1991). 156–82.

3. E. Wigginton, ed., *The Foxfire Book: Hog Dressing; Log Cabin Building; Mountain Crafts and Foods; Planting by the Signs; Snake Lore, Hunting Tales, Faith Healing; Moonshining; and Other Affairs of Plain Living* (Garden City, NY: Doubleday, 1972); *Foxfire 2: Ghost Stories, Spring Wild Plant Foods, Spinning and Weaving, Midwifing, Burial Customs, Corn Shuckin', Wagon Making and More Affairs of Plain Living* (Garden City, NY: Anchor Press, 1973); *Foxfire 3: Animal Care, Banjos and Dulcimers, Wild Plant Foods, Butter Churns, Ginseng, and Still More Affairs of Plain Living* (New York: Doubleday, 1975); *Foxfire 4: Fiddle Making, Springhouses, Horse Trading, Sassafras Tea, Berry Buckets, Gardening, and Further Affairs of Plain Living* (Garden City, NY: Anchor Press, 1977); *Foxfire 5: Ironmaking, Blacksmithing, Flintlock Rifles, Bear Hunting, and Other Affairs of Plain Living* (Garden City, NY: Anchor Press, 1979); *Foxfire 6: Shoemaking, Gourd Banjos, and Songbows, One Hundred Toys and Games, Wooden Locks, a Water Powered Sawmill, and Other Affairs of Just Plain Living* (Garden City, NY: Anchor Press, 1980).

4. Peterson, "Teaching," 161.

5. Ibid., 164.

6. Ibid., 158. Compare this with Willinsky's definition of New Literacy: "Those strategies in the teaching of reading and writing which attempt to shift control of literacy from the teacher to the student."

7. There are a growing number of violence-prevention programs in schools that teach these skills. One, the Alternatives to Violence Program (http://www.AVPUSA.org), was started in the New York State prison system. It is now offered in schools and communities throughout the country and abroad.

8. M. Sola and A. Bennett, "The Struggle for Voice: Narrative, Literacy, and Consciousness in an East Harlem High School," in *Rewriting Literacy: Culture and the Discourse of the Other*, ed. C. Mitchell and K. Weiler (New York: Bergin & Garvey, 1991), 35–56.

9. K. Miller and P. Wagner, *Out of Ireland: The Story of Irish Immigration to America* (Washington, DC: Elliott & Clark, 1994).

10. Scott Foresman, *Golden Streets* (Glenview, IL: Scott Foresman, 1980); R. Adams, *Great Negroes: Past and Present* (Chicago: Afro-Am Publishing Company, 1969).

11. Peterson, "Teaching," 172.

12. Rethinking Schools, 1001 East Keefe Ave., Milwaukee, WI, 53212.

13. Peterson, "Teaching," 170.

14. Ibid., 179.

15. W. Bigelow, "Inside the Classroom: Social Vision and Critical Pedagogy," in *Becoming Political: Readings and Writings in the Politics of Literacy Education*, ed. P. Shannon (Portsmouth NH: Heinemann, 1992) 72–82.

16. Bigelow, "Inside the Classroom," 72.

17. Ibid., 73. Weis made the same observation about Freeway High School.

18. Ibid., 75. A teacher at Freeway High School made almost the identical comment.

19. Ibid., 75–76.

20. Ibid., 76.

21. S. Bowles and H. Gintis, *Schooling in Capitalist America: Educational Reform and Contradictions of Economic Life* (New York: Basic Books, 1976). J. Anyon, "Social Class and the Hidden Curriculum of Work," *Journal of Education* 162, no. 2 (1980): 67–92; "Social Class and School Knowledge," *Curriculum Inquiry* 11, no. 1 (1981): 3–42.

22. Herbert Kohl, "The Politics of Children's Literature: What's Wrong with the Rosa Parks Myth," in *Rethinking Our Classrooms: Teaching for Equity and Justice*, ed. B. Bigelow and others (Milwaukee, WI: Rethinking Schools, Ltd., 1994), 137–40.

23. L. Christensen, *Reading, Writing and Rising Up: Teaching about Social Justice and the Power of the Written Word* (Milwaukee, WI: Rethinking Schools, Ltd., 2000).

24. Bigelow, "Inside the Classroom," 72.

25. S. Aronowitz and H. Giroux, *Education Still Under Siege*, 2nd ed. (Westport, CT: Bergin and Harvey, 1993), 46.

26. J. M. R. Duncan-Andrade, "Urban Teacher Development that Changes Classrooms, Curriculum and Achievement," in *Teacher Education with an Attitude: Preparing Teachers to Educate Working-Class Students in Their Collective Self Interest*, ed, P. J. Finn and M. E. Finn (Albany, NY: SUNY Press, 2007).

27. Anyon, "Social Class and School Knowledge," 3–42; "Social Class and the Hidden Curriculum of Work," 67–92. P. Finn, *Literacy with an Attitude: Educating Working-Class Children in their Own Self-Interest* (Albany, NY: SUNY Press, 1999). P. Freire, *Pedagogy of the Oppressed* (New York: Seabury Press, 1970). J. MacLeod, *Aint No Makin' It* (Boulder, CO: Westview Press, 1995).

28. R. Coles, *The Story of Ruby Bridges* (New York: Scholastic Press, 1995).

29. L. Tan, personal correspondence.

30. J. Willinsky, *The New Literacy: Redefining Reading and Writing in the Schools* (New York: Routledge, 1990) 177.

31. Using movie-making software has fostered student agency and engagement as learners and higher school achievement, including success on the state high-stakes writing test. S. Borowicz, "Embracing Lives through the Video Lens: An Exploration of Literacy Teaching and Learning with Digital Video Technology in an Urban Secondary English classroom" (PhD diss., University at Buffalo, State University of New York, 2005); A. Costello, "Digital Video and Drama Production as Literacy Learning Tools in English Classrooms" (PhD diss., University at Buffalo, State University of New York, 2006); A. Lauricella, "Digital video Production as a Tool for Learning: Exploring Multiple Text Documents in an Urban Social Studies Classroom" (PhD diss., University at Buffalo, State University of New York, 2006); S. Miller, "Teacher Learning for New Times: Repurposing New Multimodal Literacies and Digital-video Composing for Schools," in *Handbook of Research on Teaching Literacy through the Communicative and Visual Arts, Volume II*, ed. J. Flood, S. B. Heath, and D. Lapp (New York: Lawrence Erlbaum Associates and the International Reading Association, 2008), 441–60; S. Miller and S. Borowicz, "City Voices, City Visions: Digital Video as Literacy/Learning Supertool in Urban Classrooms," in *Urban Education with an Attitude*, ed. L. Johnson, M. Finn, and R. Lewis (Albany, NY: State University of New York Press, 2005), 87–108; S. Miller and S. Borowicz, *Why Multimodal Literacies? Designing Digital Bridges to*

21st Century Teaching and Learning (Buffalo, NY: GSE Publications and SUNY Press, 2006); S. Miller and S. Borowicz, "New Literacies with an Attitude: Transformative Teacher Education through Digital Video Learning Tools," in *Teacher Education with an Attitude: Preparing Teachers to Educate Working Class Students in their Collective Self-Interest*, ed. P. J. Finn and M. E. Finn (Albany, NY: State University of New York Press, 2007), 111–26. (For more information on the CVCV project, go to the Web site at http://www.cityvoicescityvisions.org).

Chapter 17. Agitating Students and Students Who Agitate

1. J. Oakes and J. Rogers, *Learning Power: Organizing for Education and Justice* (New York: Teachers College Press, 2006), 43–70.

2. Ibid., 67.

3. Ibid., 59.

4. Ibid., 62.

5. Ibid., 61.

6. Ibid., 65.

7. Oakes and Rogers report that 5 percent of honors English students were southsiders at the beginning of the project (*Learning Power*).

8. Ibid., 158.

9. B. Moyers, "This Is the Fight of Our Lives" (keynote address, Inequality Matters Forum, New York University, June 3, 2004), http://www.commondreams.org/views04/0616-09.htm, cited in P. Finn and M. E. Finn, introduction to *Teacher Education with an Attitude: Preparing Teachers to Educate Working Class Students in Their Collective Self-Interest* (Albany NY, 2007), 5–6.

10. Ibid., 6.

11. United for a Fair Economy, "CEO Pay/Worker Pay Ratio Reaches 301-to-1," *Common Dreams Progressive News Service*, April 14, 2004, http://www.commondreams.org; Citizens for Tax Justice, "We're Paying Dearly for Bush's Tax Cuts," September 23, 2003, http://www.ctj.org.

12. J. Anyon, *Radical Possibilities: Public Policy, Urban Education, and a New Social Movement* (New York: Routledge, 2005), 30.

13. Ibid., 53.

14. P. Osterman, *Gathering Power: The Future of Progressive Politics in America* (Boston: Beacon Press, 2002), 8–9.

15. Anyon, *Radical Possibilities*.

Chapter 18. Agitating Parents and Parents Who Agitate

1. G. Richardson, "Structural Barriers and School Reform: The Perceptions of a Group of Working-Class Parents," in *Urban Education with an Attitude*, ed. L. Johnson, M. E. Finn, and R. Lewis (Albany NY: SUNY Press, 2005), 173–92; P. Finn, *Literacy with an Attitude: Educating Working-Class Children in Their Own Self-Interest*. (Albany, NY: SUNY Press, 1999).

2. Richardson, "Structural Barriers," 178.

3. Ibid., 180.

4. Ibid., 184.

5. P. Finn, L. Johnson, and M. E. Finn, "Workshops with an Attitude," in *Urban Education with an Attitude*, ed. L. Johnson, M. E. Finn, and R. Lewis (Albany NY: SUNY Press, 2005), 193–218.

6. S. B. Heath. *Ways with Words* (Cambridge: Cambridge University Press, 1983).

7. Finn, Johnson, and Finn, "Workshops with an Attitude," 203.

8. Ask the Right Question Project, Inc. www.rightquestion.org.

9. Finn, Johnson, and Finn, "Workshops with an Attitude," 211.

10. Ibid., 212.

11. P. Finn, *Literacy with an Attitude*.

12. J. Oakes and J. Rogers, *Learning Power: Organizing for Education and Justice* (New York: Teachers College Press, 2006).

13. Ibid., 111–31.

14. S. Maydans, "The Police Verdict: Los Angeles Policemen Acquitted in Taped Beating," *New York Times*, April 30, 1992.

15. Oakes and Rogers, *Learning Power*, 115.

16. Ibid., 123.

17. Ibid.

Chapter 19. Scaling Agitation Upward

1. A. Caputo-Pearl, "Coalition for Educational Justice: Antiracist Organizing and Teacher Education," in *Teacher Education with an Attitude: Preparing Teachers to Educate Working-Class Students in Their Collective Self-Interest*, ed. P. Finn and M. E. Finn (Albany NY: SUNY Press, 2007), 47–62.

2. J. Anyon, *Radical Possibilities: Public Policy, Urban Education, and a New Social Movement* (New York: Teachers College Press, 2005), 134.

3. A. Bernstein, "Can This Man Save Labor?" *Business Week*, September 13, 2004.

4. J. Oakes and J. Rogers, *Learning Power: Organizing for Education and Justice* (New York: Teachers College Press, 2006), 9.

5. J. Oakes, "*Williams v. The State of California*," special Issue, *Teachers College Record* 106, nos. 10–11 (2003).

6. Oakes and Rogers, *Learning Power*, 135–36.

7. Dewey public intelligence. Oakes and Rogers, *Learning Power*, 16.

8. A. Schwarzenegger, *The Capitol Morning Report* (Sacramento, CA: Office of the Governor, 2004), quoted in Oakes and Rogers, *Learning Power*, 152.

9. Oakes and Rogers, *Learning Power*, 153.

10. Oakes and Rogers, *Learning Power*, 152.

11. M. A. Rebell, "Court Ordered Reform of New York State School Aid," in *Urban Education with an Attitude*, ed. L. Johnson, M. E. Finn, and R. Lewis (Albany NY: SUNY Press, 2005), 33–40.

12. Rebell, *Court Ordered Reform*, 38

13. E. Gold, E. Simon, and C. Brown, *Strong Neighborhoods, Strong Schools: The Education Organizing Indicators Framework: A User's Guide* (Chicago: Cross City Campaign for Urban School Reform, 2002). The Cross City Campaign for Urban School Reform was a national network of school reform leaders from nine cities: Baltimore, Chicago, Denver, Houston, Los Angeles, New York, Oakland, Philadelphia, and Seattle. Cross City Campaign ceased operations in 2007.

14. Anyon, *Radical Possibilities*, 134.

15. J. M. R. Duncan-Andrade, "Urban Teacher Development that Changes Classrooms, Curriculum and Achievement," in P. J. Finn and M. E. Finn, *Teacher Education with an Attitude*, 173–90.

Chapter 20. Important Concepts and a Few Lines from *Les Miserables*

1. B. Moyers, "This Is the Fight of Our Lives" (keynote address, Inequality Matters Forum, New York University, June 3, 2004), http://www.commondreams.org.

2. J. Oakes and J. Rogers, with Martin Lipton, *Learning Power: Organizing for Education and Justice* (New York: Teachers College Press, 2006).

3. J. Anyon, *Radical Possibilities: Public Policy, Urban Education, and a New Social Movement* (New York: Teachers College Press, 2005); Oakes and Rogers, *Learning Power*.

4. http://www.metrolyrics.com/do-you-hear-the-people-sing-lyrics-les-miserables.html.

Bibliography

Adams, R. *Great Negroes: Past and Present*. Chicago: Afro-Am Publishing Company, 1969.

Alschuler, Alfred S. *School Discipline: A Socially Literate Solution*. New York: McGraw-Hill, 1980.

Altenbaugh, Richard J. *Education for Struggle: The American Labor College of the 1920s and 1930s*. Philadelphia: Temple University Press, 1990.

Annenberg Institute on Public Engagement for Public Education. *Reasons for Hope, Voices for Change: A Report of the Annenberg Institute on Public Engagement for Public Education*. Providence, R.I.: Annenberg Institute on Public Engagement for Public Education, Brown University, 1998. (http://www.aisr.brown.edu)

Anyon, Jean. *Radical Possibilities: Public Policy, Urban Education, and a New Social Movement*. New York: Routledge, 2005.

———. *Ghetto Schooling: A Political Economy of Urban Educational Reform*. New York: Teachers College Press, 1997.

———. "Social Class and School Knowledge." *Curriculum Inquiry* 11, 1 (1981).

———. "Social Class and the Hidden Curriculum of Work." *Journal of Education* 162, 2 (1980).

Apple, M. W. *Ideology and Curriculum*. Boston: Routledge and Kegan Paul, 1979.

Arnove, Robert F. "The Nicaraguan National Literacy Crusade of 1980." In *Perspectives on Literacy*, edited by Eugene R. Kintgen, Barry

M. Kroll, and Mike Rose. Carbondale: Southern Illinois University Press, 1988.

Aronowitz, Stanley, and H. Giroux. *Education Still Under Siege.* 2nd ed. Westport, CT: Bergin and Harvey, 1993.

Ask the Right Question Project, Inc. http://www.rightquestion.org (accessed December 26, 2008).

Atwell, N. *In the Middle: Reading, Writing, and Learning with Adolescents.* Portsmouth, N.H.: Heinemann, 1987.

Baltimore Catechism: A catechism of Christian doctrine, prepared and enjoined by order of the Third Plenary Council Baltimore; with explanations in the form of short notes and of sections in simple question and answer. Published by ecclesiastical authority. Chicago: The John P. Daleiden Company, 1918.

Barber, Benjamin. *Strong Democracy: Participatory Politics for a New Age.* Berkeley: University of California Press, 1984.

Barboza, David D. "China Drafts Law to Boost Unions and End Abuse." *New York Times,* October 13, 2006.

Bechtel, J. "Videotape Analysis of the Composing Process of Six Male College Freshman Writers." Paper presented at the Annual Meeting of the Midwest Regional Conference on English in the Two Year College. ERIC Document ED 177 558.

Bensman, David, and Roberta Lynch. *Rusted Dreams: Hard Times in a Steel Community.* New York: McGraw Hill, 1987.

Berman, Sheldon. "Introduction." In *Promising Practices in Teaching Social Responsibility.* Ed. S. Berman and P. LaFarge. Albany: State University of New York Press, 1993.

Bernstein, Aaron. "Can This Man Save Labor?" *Business Week,* September 13, 2004.

Bernstein, Basil. *Theoretical Studies Towards a Sociology of Education.* London: Routledge and Kegan Paul, 1971.

———. *Applied Studies Towards a Sociology of Education.* London: Routledge and Kegan Paul, 1973.

———. *Towards a Theory of Educational Transmission.* London: Routledge and Kegan Paul, 1973.

———. *The Structuring of Pedagogic Discourse.* London: Routledge and Kegan Paul, 1990.

Bigelow, W. "Inside the Classroom: Social Vision and Critical Pedagogy." In *Becoming Political: Readings and Writings in the Politics of Literacy Education*. Ed. P. Shannon. Portsmouth, N.H.: Heinemann, 1992.

Bloom, Lisa A., and Mary Jean Ronan Herzog. "The Democratic Process in Teacher Education: Two Case Studies." In *Democratic Teacher Education: Programs, Processes, Problems, and Prospects*. Ed. John M. Novak. Albany: State University of New York Press, 1994.

Bomer, Randy, Joel E. Dworin, L. May, and Peggy Semingson. "Miseducating Teachers about the Poor: A Critical Analysis of Ruby Payne's Claims About Poverty." *Teachers College Record*, in press.

Borowicz, Suzanne. "Embracing Lives through the Video Lens: An Exploration of Literacy Teaching and Learning with Digital Video Technology in an Urban Secondary English Classroom." PhD diss., University at Buffalo, State University of New York, 2005.

Bos, Johannes M., Aletha Huston, Robert Granger, Greg Duncan, Tom Brock, and Vonnie McLoyd. *New Hope for People with Low Incomes: Two-year Results of a Program to Reduce Poverty and Reform Welfare*. New York: Manpower Demonstration Research Corporation, 1999.

Bourdieu, P., and J. Passeron. *Reproduction in Education, Society, and Culture*. Beverly Hills: Sage, 1977.

Bowles, S., and H. Gintis. *Schooling in Capitalist America: Educational Reform and Contradictions of Economic Life*. New York: Basic Books, 1976.

Brown, Cynthia. *Literacy in 30 Hours: Paulo Freire's Process in North East Brazil*. London: Centre for Open Learning and Teaching, Writers and Readers Publishing Cooperative, 1975.

Buckhalt, J., R. Rutherford, and K. Goldberg. "Verbal and Nonverbal Interactions of Mothers and Their Down's Syndrome and Nonretarded Infants." *American Journal of Mental Deficiency* 82 (1978).

Caputo-Pearl, Alex. "Coalition for Educational Justice: Antiracist Organizing and Teacher Education." In Finn and Finn, *Teacher Education with an Attitude: Preparing Teachers to Educate Working-Class Students in Their Collective Self-Interest*. Albany NY: SUNY Press. 2007.

Carter, John Stewart. *Full Fathom Five*. Boston: Houghton Mifflin Co., 1965.

Chall, Jeanne, and Vicki Jacobs. "Writing and Reading in the Elementary Grades: Developmental Trends Among Low SES Children." In *Composing and Comprehending*. Ed. Julie M. Jensen. Urbana, Ill.: ERIC. Clearing House on Reading and Communication Skills, 1984.

Christensen, Linda. *Reading, Writing and Rising Up: Teaching about Social Justice and the Power of the Written Word*. Milwaukee, WI: Rethinking Schools, 2000.

Citizens for Tax Justice. "We're Paying Dearly for Bush's Tax Cuts." http://www.ctj.org (accessed September 23, 2003).

Coles, Robert. *The Spiritual Life of Children*. Boston: Houghton Mifflin, 1990.

———. *The Story of Ruby Bridges*. New York: Scholastic Press, 1995.

Collins, J. "Hegemonic Practices: Literacy and Standard Language in Public Education." In *Rewriting Literacy: Culture and the Discourse of the Other*. Ed. C. Mitchell and K. Weiler. New York: Bergin & Garvey, 1991.

Colquhoun, P. *A New and Appropriate System of Education for the Labouring People*. London: J. Hatchard, 1806.

Compton-Lilly, Catherine. *Reading Families: The Literate Lives of Urban Children*. New York: Teachers College Press, 2003.

Connolly, Megan Elizabeth. *Paper 1, LAI 563 Language, Society, and Language Arts Instruction*. Photocopied. Department of Learning and Instruction, State University of New York at Buffalo, 1998.

Costello, A. "Digital Video and Drama Production as Literacy Learning Tools in English Classrooms." PhD diss., University at Buffalo, State University of New York, 2006.

Costello, E. Jane, Scott N. Compton, Gordon Keeler, and Adrian Angold. "Relationships between Poverty and Psychopathology: A Natural Experiment." *Journal of the American Medical Association* 290, no. 15 (October 2003): 2023–29.

Craik, William W. (1964). *The Central Labour College, 1909–1929: A Chapter in the History of Adult Working-Class Education*. London: Lawrence & Wishart, 1964.

Cross, T. "Mothers' Speech Adjustment: The Contribution of Selected Child Listener Variables." In *Talking to Children: Language Input and Acquisition*. Ed. C. A. Snow and C. A. Ferguson. Cambridge: Cambridge University Press, 1977.

Cremin, Lawrence A. *The Transformation of the School*. New York: Random House, Inc., Vintage Books, 1964.

Cubberly, Ellwood P. *Public Education in the United States*. Boston: Houghton-Mifflin Company, 1919.

Dewey, John. "Labor Politics and Labor Education." *The New Republic*, January 9, 1929.

Donald, J. "How Illiteracy Became a Problem and Literacy Stopped Being One." In *Rewriting Literacy: Culture and the Discourse of the Other*. Ed. C. Mitchell and K. Weiler. New York: Bergin & Harvey, 1991.

Duncan-Andrade, Jeff. "Urban Teacher Development that Changes Classrooms, Curriculum and Achievement." In Finn and Finn, *Teacher Education with an Attitude*, 173–90.

Dworin, Joel E., and Randy Bomer. "What We All (Supposedly) Know about the Poor: A Critical Discourse Analysis of Ruby Payne's 'Framework.'" *English Education* 40 (2006): 101–21.

Edelsky, Carol, ed. *Making Justice Our Project: Teachers Working Toward Critical Whole Language Practice*. Urbana, IL: National Council of Teachers of English, 1999.

Educators for Social Responsibility. Good Works Job Listing. 1998. (http://www.tripod.com)

Fecho, Bob, and JoBeth Allen. "Teacher Inquiry into Literacy, Social Justice, and Power." In *Handbook of Research on Teaching the English Language Arts*, edited by J. Flood, D. Lapp, J. R. Squire, and J. M. Jensen, 232–46. Mahwah, NJ: Lawrence Erlbaum, 2003.

Finn, Mary E. "For Further Thought." In Finn and Finn, *Teacher Education with an Attitude*, 231–46.

Finn, Patrick J. *Literacy with an Attitude: Educating Working-Class Children in Their Own Self-Interest*. Albany, NY: SUNY Press, 1999.

Finn, Patrick J., Lauri Johnson, and Mary E. Finn. "Workshops with an Attitude." In *Urban Education with an Attitude*, 193–218.

Finn, Patrick J., and Mary E. Finn, eds. *Teacher Education with an Attitude: Preparing Teachers to Educate Working-Class Students in Their Collective Self-Interest*. Albany, NY: SUNY Press, 2007.

Fitzgerald, Jim. "Jury Hears Tapes in Texaco Case." Associated Press: April 29, 1998. http://www.blackvoices.com/news/98/04/29/story07 .html.

Fraser, Thomas W. *Reading, Writing, and Justice: School Reform as if Democracy Matters*. Albany: State University of New York Press, 1997.

Freeman, Ruth S. *Yesterday's Schools*. Watkin's Glen, N.Y.: Century House, 1962.

Freire. Paulo. *Cultural Action for Freedom*. Cambridge, MA: Harvard Education Review, 1970.

———. *Pedagogy of the Heart*. New York: Continuum, 1997.

———. *Pedagogy of the Oppressed*. New York: Seabury Press, 1970.

———. *Teachers as Cultural Workers: Letters to Those Who Dare to Teach*. Boulder, CO: Westview Press, 1998.

———. *Teachers as Cultural Workers: Letters to Those Who Dare to Teach*. Boulder, CO: Westview Press, 1998.

Friedman, Milton. "The Role of Government in Education." In *Economics and the Public Interest*, edited by Robert A. Solo, 1955. Reprinted by permission of Rutgers University Press. http://www .schoolchoices.org/roo/fried1.htm.

Gee, James. "What is literacy?" In *Rewriting literacy: Culture and the Discourse of the Other*, edited by C. Mitchell & K. Weiler, 3–11. New York: Bergin & Garvey, 1994.

———. "Orality and Literacy: From *The Savage Mind* to *Ways with Words*." In *Language and Literacy in Social Practice*. Ed. J. Mabin. Clevedon, England: Multilingual Matters Limited, The Open University, 1994.

Gilmore, Perry. "'Gimme Room': School Resistance, Attitude, and Access to Literacy." In *Rewriting Literacy: Culture and the Discourse of the Other*. Ed. Candice Mitchell and Kathleen Weiler. New York: Bergin & Garvey: 1991.

Givon, T. *On Understanding Grammar*. New York: Academic Press, 1979.

Glasser, W. *Control Theory*. New York: Harper Row, 1984.

———. *The Quality School*. New York: Harper Row, 1990.

Gold, Eva, Elaine Simon, and Chris Brown. *Strong Neighborhoods, Strong Schools: The Education Organizing Indicators Framework: A User's Guide*. Chicago: Cross City Campaign for Urban School Reform, 2002.

Gonzales, Norma, Luis Moll, and Cathy Amanti, eds. *Funds of Knowledge: Theorizing Practices in Households, Communities, and Classrooms*. Mahwah, NJ: Erlbaum, 2005.

Graves, D. *Writing: Teachers and Children at Work*. Portsmouth, N.H.: Heinemann, 1983.

Halliday, M. A. K. *Learning How to Mean: Explorations in the Study of Language*. London: Edward Arnold Publishers, 1975.

Hamilton, S. "The Social Side of Schooling." *Elementary School Journal* 83 (1983).

Havelock, E. A. *Preface to Plato*. Cambridge: Harvard University Press, 1963.

Harste, J. C., V. A. Woodward, and C. L. Burke. *Language Stories and Literacy Lessons*. Portsmouth, N.H.: Heinemann, 1984.

Hartfield, Ashley. "The Runaway Elephant." In Patrick J. Finn. *Helping Children Learn to Read*. New York: Longman, 1990.

Heath, Shirley Brice. "Separating 'Things of the Imagination' from Life: Learning to Read and Write." In *Emergent Literacy*. Ed. W. H. Teale and E. Sulzby, Norwood, N.J.: Ablex Publishing Corporation, 1986.

———. *Ways with Words*. Cambridge: Cambridge University Press, 1983.

Herbert, Bob. "In America: Workaday Racism." New York: The New York Times Company, 1996. http://www.dorsai.org/~jdadd/texaco3.html.

Hicks, Deborah D. *Reading Lives: Working-Class Children and Literacy Learning*. New York: Teachers College Press, 2002.

Hillkirk, Keith. "Teaching for Democracy: Preparing Teachers to Teach Democracy." In *Democratic Teacher Education: Programs, Processes, Problems, and Prospects*. Ed. John M. Novak. Albany: State University of New York Press, 1994.

Howell, D., and E. Wolff. "Trends in Growth and Distribution in the U. S. Workplace, 1960–1985." *Industrial and Labor Relations Review* 44, no. 3 (1991): 486–502.

Huston, Aletha C., Cynthia Miller, Lashawn Richburg-Hayes, Greg Duncan, Carolyn A. Eldred. Thomas S. Weisner, Edward D. Lowe, et al. *New Hope for Families and Children: Five-Year Results of a Program to Reduce Poverty and Reform Welfare*. New York: Manpower Development Research Corporation, 2003.

Johnson, Clifton. *The Country School in New England*. New York: D. Appleton and Company, 1893.

———. *Old Time Schools and School Books*. New York: The Macmillan Co., 1904.

Johnson, Lauri, Mary E. Finn, and Rebecca Lewis, eds. *Urban Education with an Attitude*. Albany, NY: SUNY Press, 2005.

Judd, D. R., and T. Swanstrom, *City Politics: Private Power and Public Policy*. New York: Harper Collins, 1994.

Katz, Michael B. *Improving Poor People: The Welfare State, the "Underclass," and Urban Schools as History*. Princeton, NJ: Princeton University Press, 1995.

Keller, B. "Payne's Pursuits." *Education Week*, May 3, 2006.

Kelly, Thomas E. "Democratic Empowerment and Secondary Teacher Education." In *Democratic Teacher Education: Programs, Processes, Problems, and Prospects*. Ed. John M. Novak. Albany: State University of New York Press, 1994.

King, M. "Speech to Writing: Children's Growth in Writing Potential." In *Reading and Writing Connections*. Ed. J. Mason Boston: Allyn and Bacon, 1989.

Kohl, Herbert. "The Politics of Children's Literature: What's Wrong with the Rosa Parks Myth." In *Rethinking Our Classrooms: Teaching for Equity and Justice*. Ed. B. Bigelow, L. Christensen, S. Karp, B. Miner, and B. Peterson. Milwaukee: Rethinking Schools, Ltd., 1994.

Kozol, Jonathan. *Savage Inequalities*. New York: Harper Perennial, 1992.

Labov, W., and C. Robbins. "A note on the Relation of Reading Failure to Peer-Group Status in Urban Ghettos." *The Record—Teacher's College* 70(1969).

Lafer, Gordon. *The Job Training Charade*. Ithaca, NY: Cornell University Press, 2002.

Lareau, Annette, and Erin M. Horvat. "Moments of Social Inclusion and Exclusion: Race, Class, and Cultural Capital in Family-School Relationships." *Sociology of Education 72* (1999): 37–53.

Lauricella, Ann Marie. *"Digital Video Production as a Tool for Learning: Exploring Multiple Text Documents in an Urban Social Studies Classroom."* PhD diss., University at Buffalo, State University of New York, 2006.

Leacock, E. *Teaching and Learning in City Schools.* New York: Basic Books 1969.

Lee, V., and D. Burkham. *Inequality at the Starting Gate: Social Background and Achievement at Kindergarten Entry.* Washington, DC: Educational Policy Institute, 2002.

Leichter, Hope, ed. *Families and Communities as Educators.* New York: Teachers College Press, 1978.

Les Miserables. "Do You Hear the People Sing?" http://www.metrolyrics.com/do-you-hear-the-people-sing-lyrics-les-miserables.html (accessed December 26, 2008).

Levitas, Maurice. *Perspectives in the Sociology of Education.* Boston: Routledge & Kegan Paul, 1974.

Macedo, Donaldo P. *Literacies of Power: What Americans Are Not Allowed to Know.* Boulder, CO: Westview Press, 1994.

MacLeod, Jay. *Aint No Makin' It.* Boulder, CO: Westview Press, 1995.

Marshall, Alfred. "The Future of the Working Class." In *Memorials of Alfred Marshall*, edited by A. C. Pigou. London: Macmillan, 1925. Cited in Marshall and Bottomore, *Citizenship and Social Class*, 3–8.

Marshall, T. H. "Citizenship and Social Class." In Marshall and Bottomore, *Citizenship and Social Class*, 1–54.

Marshall, T. H., and Tom Bottomore, eds. *Citizenship and Social Class.* London: Plutobooks, 1992.

Maydans, S, "The Police Verdict: Los Angeles Policemen Acquitted in Taped Beating." *New York Times*, April 30, 1992.

McCurdy, M. "Writing on Their Own: Kindergarten and First Grade." In *Classroom Experiences: The Writing Process in Action.* Ed. N. Gordon. Portsmouth, N.H.: Heinemann, 1984.

McDermott, J. Cynthia. "An Institute for Independence through Action, Process, and Theory." In *Democratic Teacher Education: Programs, Processes, Problems, and Prospects*. Ed. John M. Novak. Albany: State University of New York Press, 1994.

McEwan, Barbara. "Deliberately Developing Democratic Teachers in a Year." In *Democratic Teacher Education: Programs, Processes, Problems, and Prospects*. Ed. John M. Novak. Albany: State University of New York Press, 1994.

McLaren, Peter. *Life in Schools: An Introduction to Critical Pedagogy in the Foundations of Education*. White Plains, NY: Longman, 1989.

Michaels, S. "Hearing the Connections in Children's Oral and Written Discourse." In *Rewriting Literacy: Culture and the Discourse of the Other*. Ed. C. Mitchell and K. Weiler. New York: Bergin & Garvey, 1991.

———. "Narrative Presentations: An Oral Preparation for Literacy with First Graders." In *The Social Construction of Literacy*. Ed. J. Cook-Gumperz. Cambridge: Cambridge University Press, 1986.

Miller, Kerby, and Paul Wagner. *Out of Ireland: The Story of Irish Immigration to America*. Washington, D.C.: Elliott & Clark Publishers, 1994.

Miller, Suzanne M. "Teacher Learning for New Times: Repurposing New Multimodal Literacies and Digital-Video Composing for Schools." In *Handbook of Research on Teaching Literacy Through the Communicative and Visual Arts*, vol. 2, edited by J. Flood, S. B. Heath, and D. Lapp, 441–60. New York: Erlbaum, 2008.

Miller, Suzanne M., and Suzanne Borowicz. "City Voices, City Visions: Digital Video as Literacy/Learning Supertool in Urban Classrooms." In Johnson, Finn, and Lewis, *Urban Education with an Attitude*, 87–108.

———. "New Literacies with an Attitude: Transformative Teacher Education Through Digital Video Learning Tools." In Finn and Finn, *Teacher Education with an Attitude*, 111–26.

———. *Why Multimodal Literacies? Designing Digital Bridges to 21st Century Teaching and Learning*. Buffalo, NY: GSE Publications, 2006.

Mishel, Lawrence, and Ruby A. Teixeira. *The Myth of the Coming Labor Shortage: Jobs, Skills, and Incomes of America's Workforce 2000*. Washington, DC: Economic Policy Institute, 2001.

Moll, Luis, Cathy Amanti, D. Neff, and Norma Gonzalez. "Funds of Knowledge for Teaching: Using a Qualitative Approach to Connect Homes and Classrooms." *Theory Into Practice*, *31*, no. 2 (1992): 133–41.

Morrison, R. *We Build the Road as We Travel*. Philadelphia: New Society Publishers, 1991.

Morris, Pamela, Aletha C. Huston, Greg Duncan, Danielle Crosby, and Johannes Bos. *How Welfare and Work Policies Affect Children: A Synthesis of the Research*. Washington, DC: Manpower Development Research Corporation, 2001.

Moyers, Bill. "This Is the Fight of Our Lives." Keynote address, Inequality Matters Forum, New York University, June 3, 2004. http://www.commondreams.org/views04/0616-09.htm.

National Coalition of Education Activists. "Community Organizing: The Missing Piece in School Reform?" *Action for Better Schools: The Newsletter of the National Coalition of Education Activists 5, 3* (Fall/Winter 1997).

Natriello, Gary, Edward L. McDill, and Aaron M. Pallas. *Schooling Disadvantaged Children, Racing Against Catastrophe*. New York: Teachers College Press, 1990.

New London Group. "A Pedagogy of Multiliteracies: Designing Social Futures." *Harvard Educational Review* 66 (1996): 60–92.

Oakes, Jeannie. "*Williams v. The State of* California." *Teachers College Record* 106, nos. 10 and 11 (2003).

Oakes, Jeannie, and John Rogers. *Learning Power: Organizing for Education and Justice*. With Martin Lipton. New York: Teachers College Press, 2006.

O'Conner, A. "Rise in Income Improves Children's Behavior." *New York Times*, October 21, 2003.

Ogbu, John U. "Cultural Diversity and School Experience." In *Literacy as Praxis: Culture, Language, and Pedagogy*. Ed. Catherine E. Walsh. Norwood, N.J.: Ablex, Publishing Corporation, 1991.

Oller, John, and Kyle Perkins. "Intelligence and Language Proficiency as Sources of Variance in Self-Reported Affective Variables." *Language Learning* 28 (1978): 85–97.

Osterman, Paul. *Gathering Power: The Future of Progressive Politics in America*. Boston: Beacon Press, 2002.

Payne, Ruby. *A Framework for Understanding Poverty*. 4th rev. ed. Highlands, TX: aha! Process, Inc.,1996.

Peck, M. S. *The Different Drum: Community Making and Peace*. New York: Simon and Schuster, 1987.

Persky, J., E. Sklar, and W. Wiewel. *Does America Need Cities: An Urban Investment Strategy for National Prosperity*. Washington, D.C.: Economic Policy Institute and the National Conference of Mayors, 1992.

Peterson, R. E. "Teaching How to Read the World and Change It: Critical Pedagogy in the Intermediate Grades." In *Literacy as Praxis: Culture, Language, and Pedagogy*. Ed. C. E. Walsh. Norwood, N.J.: Ablex Publishing Corporation, 1991.

Pianco, S. H. "A Description of the Composing Process of College Freshmen Writers." *Research in College Teaching 13* (1979).

Rebell, Michael. "Court Ordered Reform of New York State School Aid." In Johnson, Finn, and Lewis, *Urban Education with an Attitude*, 33–40.

Reich, Robert B. *The Work of Nations: Preparing Ourselves for 21st Century Capitalism*. New York: Vintage Books, 1991.

Richardson, Gillian. "Structural Barriers and School Reform: The Perceptions of a Group of Working-Class Parents." In Johnson, Finn, and Lewis, *Urban Education with an Attitude*, 173–92.

Rothstein, Richard. *Class and Schools: Using Social, Economic, and Education Reform to Close the Black-White Achievement Gap*. New York: Teachers College Press, 2004.

Resnick, Daniel P. "Historical Perspectives on Literacy and Schooling." *Daedalus* 119, 2 (1990).

Salmore, B. G., and S. A. Salmore. *New Jersey Politics and Government: Suburban Politics Comes of Age*. Lincoln: University of Nebraska, 1993.

Sampson, Susan Marie. *Paper 1, LAI 563 Language, Society, and Language Arts Instruction*. Photocopied. Department of Learning and Instruction, State University of New York at Buffalo, 1998.

Schatzman, L., and A. Strauss. "Social class and communication." *American Journal of Sociology* 60(1955).

Scollon, R., and S. B. K. Scollon. *Narrative, Literacy, and Face in Inter-ethnic Communication*. Norwood, N.J.: Ablex Publishing Corporation, 1981.

Scott, Foresman Publishing Co. *Golden Streets*. Glenview, Ill., 1980.

Shannon, P. "Reading Instruction and Social Class." In *Becoming Political: Readings and Writings in the Politics of Literacy Education*. Ed. P. Shannon. Portsmouth, N.H.: Heinemann, 1992.

Sheehy, Gail. "The Accidental Candidate." *Vanity Fair*, October 2000.

Shor, Ira, and Caroline Pari. *Education Is Politics*: *Critical Teaching across Differences, K-12*. Portsmouth, NH: Boynton/Cook, 2000.

Sieber, R. T. "The Politics of Middle-Class Success in an Inner City Public School." *Journal of Education* 164 (1981).

Simon, Brian. *Studies in the History of Education*: *The Two Nations and the Educational Structure 1780–1870*. London: Lawrence & Wishart, 1960.

Skilton-Sylvester, Ellen. "Literate at Home but Not at School: A Cambodian Girl's Journey from Playwright to Struggling Writer." In *School's Out! Bridging Out-of-School Literacies with Classroom Practice*, edited by G. Hull and K. Schultz, 61–90. New York: Teachers College Press, 2002.

Smith, Hilton. "Foxfire Teachers' Networks (Viewed Through Maxine Greene's *The Dialectic of Freedom*)." In *Democratic Teacher Education: Programs, Processes, Problems, and Prospects*. Ed. John M. Novak. Albany: State University of New York Press, 1994.

Snow, C. E. "The Development of Conversation between Mothers and Babies." *Journal of Child Development* 4 (1977).

Sola, M., and A. Bennett. "The Struggle for Voice: Narrative, Literacy, and Consciousness in an East Harlem High School." In *Rewriting Literacy: Culture and the Discourse of the Other*. Ed. C. Mitchell and K. Weiler. New York: Bergin & Garvey, 1991.

Sowell, Thomas. "Three Black Histories." In *Essays and Data on American Ethnic Groups*. Ed. Thomas Sowell. Washington, D.C., Urban Institute: 1978.

Spufford, M. *Small Books and Pleasant Histories: Popular Fiction and Its Readership in Seventeenth-century England*. Cambridge: Cambridge University Press, 1981.

Stauffer, Russel G. *The First Grade Reading Studies: Findings of Individual Investigations*. Newark, DE: International Reading Association, 1967.

Swenson, Janet. "Transformative Teacher Networks, On-Line Professional D, and the Write for Your Life Project." *English Education 35, no.* 4 (1999): 263–321.

Swift, David W. *Ideology and Change in the Public Schools: Latent Functions of Progressive Education*. Columbus: Charles E. Merrill Publishing Company, 1971.

Symonds, William. "College Admissions: The Real Barrier Is Class." *Business Week*, April 14, 2003, 68–69.

Taylor, Denny, and Catherine Dorsey-Gaines. *Growing Up Literate: Learning from Inner-City Families*. Portsmouth, NH: Heinemann, 1988.

Thompson, E. P. *The Making of the English Working Class*. New York: Vintage Books, 1963.

Tough, Paul. "The Class-Consciousness Raiser." *The New York Times Magazine*, June 10, 2008, 52–58.

United for a Fair Economy. "CEO Pay/Worker Pay Ratio Reaches 301-to-1." Common Dreams Progressive News Service. http://www.commondreams.org (accessed April 14, 2004).

University of Wisconsin, Milwaukee, Center for Urban Community Development. "Designing Pathways to Parental Involvement in School to Work: A Template for Planning and Action," by Participants in a Milwaukee Public Schools' Action Learning Seminar, facilitated by P. Bangura, D. Folkman, and K. Rai.

U. S. Commissioner of Education. *Annual Report of the Commissioner of Education Made to the Secretary of the Interior for the Year 1870*. Washington, D.C.: 1875.

Varenne, Herve, and Ray P. McDermott. "'Why' Sheila Can Read: Structure and Indeterminacy in the Reproduction of Familial Literacy." In *The Acquisition of Literacy: Ethnographic Perspectives, edited by* B. Schieffelin and P. Gilmore, 188–210. Norwood, NJ: Ablex, 1986.

Weis, Lois. *Working Class without Work: High School Students in a Deindustrializing Economy*. New York: Routledge, 1990.

Wells, Gordon. "Apprenticeship in Literacy." In *Language as Praxis: Culture, Language, and Pedagogy*. Ed. C. E. Walsh. Norwood, N.J.: Ablex Publishing Corporation, 1991.

———. "Language as Interaction." In *Language through Interaction*. Ed. Gordon Wells. Cambridge: Cambridge University Press, 1981.

Wigginton, E. *The Foxfire book: hog dressing; log cabin building; mountain crafts and foods; planting by the signs; snake lore, hunting tales, faith healing; moonshining; and other affairs of plain living*. Garden City, N.Y.: Doubleday, 1972.

———. *Foxfire 2: ghost stories, spring wild plant foods, spinning and weaving, midwifing, burial customs, corn shuckin's wagon making and more affairs of plain living*. Garden City, N.Y.: Anchor Press, 1973.

———. *Foxfire 3: Animal Care, Banjos and Dulcimers, Wild Plant Foods, Butter Churns, Ginseng, and Still More Affairs of Plain Living*. Garden City, N.Y.: Doubleday, 1975.

———. *Foxfire 4: fiddle making, springhouses, horse trading, sassafras tea, berry buckets, gardening, and further affairs of plain living*. Garden City, N.Y.: Anchor Press/Doubleday, 1977.

———. *Foxfire 5: ironmaking, blacksmithing, flintlock rifles, bear hunting, and other affairs of plain living*. Garden City, N.Y.: Anchor Press/Doubleday, 1979.

———. *Foxfire 6: shoemaking, gourd banjos, and songbows, one hundred toys and games, wooden locks, a water powered sawmill, and other affairs of just plain living*. Garden City, N.Y.: Anchor Press/ Doubleday, 1980.

Willinsky, John. *The New Literacy: Redefining Reading and Writing in the Schools*. New York: Routledge, Chapman and Hall, Inc., 1990.

———, and J. O. Hunniford. "Reading the Romance Younger: The Mirrors and Fears of a Preparatory Literature." *Reading-Canada-Lecture* 4, 1 (1986).

Wood, George. "The Institute for Democracy in Education: Supporting Democratic Teachers." In *Democratic Teacher Education: Programs, Processes, Problems, and Prospects*. Ed. John M. Novak. Albany: State University of New York Press, 1994.

Willis, Paul E. *Learning to Labor: How Working Class Kids Get Working Class Jobs*. Westmead, England: Saxon House, 1977.

Yagelski, Robert. *Literacy Matters: Writing and Reading the Social Self.* New York: Teachers College Press, 2000.

Young, Michael. *The Rise of the Meritocracy.* London: Thames & Hudson, 1958.

Zinn, H. "Why Students Should Study History: An Interview with Howard Zinn." In *Rethinking Our Classrooms: Teaching for Equity and Justice.* Ed. B. Bigelow, L. Christensen, S. Karp, B. Miner, and B. Peterson. Milwaukee: Rethinking Schools, Ltd., 1994.

Index